G000054498

Redefining the French Republic

MANCHESTER
1824

Manchester University Press

Redefining the French Republic

edited by
Alistair Cole
and
Gino Raymond

Manchester University Press
Manchester and New York

distributed exclusively in the USA by St. Martin's Press

Published by Manchester University Press
Oxford Road, Manchester M13 9NR, UK
and Room 400, 175 Fifth Avenue, New York, NY 10010, USA
www.manchesteruniversitypress.co.uk

Distributed exclusively in the USA by
Palgrave, 175 Fifth Avenue, New York NY 10010, USA

Distributed exclusively in Canada by
UBC Press, University of British Columbia, 2029 West Mall,
Vancouver, BC, Canada V6T 1Z2

British Library Cataloguing-in-Publication Data
A catalogue record for this book is available from the British Library

Library of Congress Cataloging-in-Publication Data
A catalog record for this book is available from the Library of Congress

ISBN-10: 0 7190 7151 8

ISBN-13: 978 0 7190 7151 5

First edition published 2006 by Manchester University Press

First digital, on-demand edition produced by Lightning Source 2010

Contents

Tables

Contributors

Alistair Cole is Professor of European Studies at the University of Cardiff. His research interests lie in the sphere of contemporary and comparative European politics and policy, with special reference to France and Franco-British comparisons. He has published widely and his books include *François Mitterrand: A Study in Political Leadership* (1997), *La Gouvernance locale du changement éducatif en Angleterre et en France* (with Michèle Breuillard, 2003) and *French Politics and Society* (second edition 2005).

Gordon Cumming is a Lecturer in French Studies at the University of Cardiff. His field of research encompasses French and British foreign policies and policy-making processes, especially French and UK policies towards sub-Saharan Africa. His recent publications include *Aid to Africa: French and British Aid from the Cold War to the New World Order* (2001) and 'Towards a new era in French African aid relations' (*Modern and Contemporary France*, 2000).

David Hanley is Professor of European Studies at the University of Cardiff. His research has spanned French politics and comparative European politics, with particular focus on political processes and institutions such as parties. His publications include *Christian Democracy: A Comparative Perspective* (1994) and *Party, Society, Government: Republican Democracy in France* (2002).

Nadia Kiwan is a research fellow in the EU-funded Changing City Spaces project at the University of Southampton. She possesses both a French doctorate and a PhD; her thesis 'The Construction of Identity among Young People of North African Origin in France' has been accepted for publication in 2005.

Mairi Maclean is Professor of European Studies at the University of the West of England. Her research is fundamentally interdisciplinary, informed by business history and political science. Her recent major publications include *The Mitterrand Years: Legacy and Evaluation* (1998), *France, Germany and Britain: Partners in a Changing World* (ed. with J-M. Trouille, 2001) and *Economic Management and the Modernisation of French Business* (2002).

Susan Milner is Reader in French and European Studies at the University of Bath. Her research interests cover working patterns and employment practices in the European Union, social aspects of European integration, social capital and 'associationism' in France. She is the author of *Dilemmas in Internationalism: Syndicalism and the International Trade Union Movement* (1990) and co-editor of *Reinventing France: State and Society in the Twenty-first Century* (2003).

Gino Raymond is a Reader in French Studies at the University of Bristol. He researches into the emanations of France's political culture in all its aspects, from literary production to the language of contemporary politics. His books include *France during the Socialist Years* (ed., 1994), *André Malraux: Politics and the Temptation of Myth* (1995) and *Structures of Power in Modern France* (ed., 1999). He is also the translator of some of Pierre Bourdieu's seminal writings in *Language and Symbolic Power* (1991).

Jean-Paul Révauger is *Professeur des Universités* at Bordeaux. His research is focused on the comparative study of French and British societies and social policies, as well as French and English-speaking Caribbean societies. His recent publications include 'Les politiques de retour à l'emploi en Grande Bretagne et en France' (*Revue française de civilisation britannique*, 2003) and 'Stuart Hall et les Cultural studies : un intellectuel de la diaspora antillaise observe la société britannique' (*Etudes Caraïbes*, 2005).

Steve Wharton is a Senior Lecturer in French and European Studies at the University of Bath. His principal research interests are homosexuality, identity and activism in Britain and France. His recent publications include 'Progress, what progress? Gay and lesbian liberation in the Fifth Republic', in M. Allison and O. Heathcote (eds), *Forty Years of the Fifth French Republic* (1999); 'Pédés, PACS et pognon: establishing a community of lesbian and gay citizens?', in L. Cairns (ed.), *Lesbian and Gay Cultures in France* (2003); 'Bars to understanding? Depictions of the "gay bar" in film', in R. Griffiths (ed.), *European Queer Cinema* (2005).

Acknowledgements

This volume was inspired by a series of conferences at the Universities of Cardiff and Bristol on a range of issues affecting contemporary France, and has drawn great benefit from the original fieldwork conducted by a number of contributors among social, political and economic actors engaged in driving the processes of change in France. A considerable debt of gratitude is therefore owed to the francophone interviewees whose opinions are reproduced in it. Their words have been translated but full indications are given as to where the original transcripts, in length and language, of their interviews can be accessed. Among the institutional sponsors whose support made the academic activities leading to the appearance of this volume possible, the editors wish to express particular thanks to the British Academy, the ESRC, L'Institut Français, the Leverhulme Trust, the University of Cardiff, the Bristol Institute for Research in the Humanities and Arts (BIRTHA) and, on a personal note, to Christina Hollow, whose keen eye and conscientious work were invaluable in the preparation of the manuscript.

Abbreviations

AC!	Agir ensemble contre le chômage
ARB	Armée révolutionnaire bretonne
ATTAC	Association for the Taxation of Financial Transactions for the Aid of Citizens
C2D	Contrats de désendettement
CAP	Common Agricultural Policy
CCB	Commission communale des bâtiments
CCC	Conseil communal de concertation
CCFD	Comité Catholique contre la faim et pour le développement
CEEP	Centre européen des entreprises à participation publique
CELIB	Comité de d'étude et de liaison des intérêts Bretons
CERES	Centre de recherches et d'etudes socialistes
Cevipof	Centre de recherché politique de Sciences Po
CFA	Communauté financière africaine
CFCM	Conseil français du culte musulman
CFTC	Confédération française des travailleurs chrétiens
CGT	Confédération générale du travail
CNPF	Conseil national du patronat français
CRAPS	Centre de recherches administratives, politiques et sociales
CSG	Contribution sociale généralisée
CUC	Contrat d'union civile
CUDL	Communauté urbaine de Lille
CURAPP	Centre universitaire de recherches administratives et politiques de Picardie
DAC	Development Assistance Committee
DOM-TOM	Départements d'Outre Mer et Territoires d'Outre Mer
EADS	European Aeronautic Defence & Space Company
EC	European Community
ECB	European Central Bank
ECJ	European Court of Justice

EdF	Electricité de France
EFB	Entente fédéraliste Breizh
EMS	European Monetary System
EMU	European Monetary Union
ENA	Ecole nationale d'administration
EPCI	Établissements publics de co-opération intercommunale
EPIC	Etablissement public à caractère industriel et commercial
ETA	Euskadi ta Askatasuna ('Basque Fatherland and Liberty')
EU	European Union
FHAR	Front homosexuel d'action révolutionnaire
FLB	Front de la libération de la Bretagne
FN	Front national
FNLC	Front national pour la libération de la Corse
FNSEA	Fédération nationale des syndicats des exploitants agricoles
FO	Force ouvrière
GATT	General Agreement on Tariffs and Trade
GdF	Gaz de France
GIP	Groupment d'intérêt public
HCCI	Haut conseil de la coopération internationale
ICB	Institut culturel de Bretagne
IMF	International Monetary Fund
INSEE	Institut national de la statistique et des études économiques
IRA	Irish Republican Army
JAC	Jeunesse agricole chrétienne
JEC	Jeunesse étudiante chrétienne
JOC	Jeunesse ouvrière chrétienne
LCR	Ligue communiste révolutionnaire
MEDEF	Mouvement des entreprises de France
MIRE	Maîtrise ingénierie réalisation échafaudage
MJD	Mouvement de justice et la dignité
MOB	Mouvement d'organisation de la Bretagne
MRB	Mouvement régionaliste de Bretagne
MRP	Mouvement républicain populaire
NATO	North Atlantic Treaty Organisation
NGO	Non-governmental organisations
OECD	Organisation for Economic Co-operation and Development
OIP	Office of International Programs
PAB	Parti autonomiste Breton
PACS	Pacte civil de solidarité
PCF	Parti communiste français
PNB	Parti national de Bretagne
POBL	Parti pour l'organisation d'une Bretagne libre
PS	Parti socialiste
PSU	Parti socialiste unifié

RIC	*Réseau initiatives et citoyenneté*
RMI	Revenu minimum d'insertion
RPR	Rassemblement pour la République
SFIO	Section française de l'Internationale ouvrière
SNCF	Société nationale des chemins de fer
SNECMA	Société nationale d'étude et de construction de moteurs d'aviation
SOFRES	Société française des enquêtes par sondage
SOSR	SOS Racisme
UDB	Union démocratique bretonne
UMP	Union pour une majorité populaire
URB	Union régionaliste breton
WTO	World Trade Organisation
ZEP	Zones d'éducation prioritaires

Introduction

Alistair Cole and Gino Raymond

The themes of continuity and change constitute a binary opposition that is often used to characterise the evolution of modern France. There is, on the one hand, the undeniably enduring legacy of the abrupt and sometimes violent transition to the Modern Age effected by the advent of the Revolution of 1789 and, on the other, the fact that, in spite of this formidable blueprint for the construction of a national community, its emergence has been punctuated by profound challenges to the revolutionary legacy, thereby leading to a kind of characteristically Gallic dialectic of progress through rupture in which, as de Gaulle observed, nothing really changes in the Republic until the people take to the streets. Implicit in de Gaulle's observation on this rappel à l'ordre, or call to order, of the governing elite by the people is the assumption that, notwithstanding the wrong turns that may be taken by those delegated with the responsibility of managing its destiny, the Republic has a vocation that defines it, guides it and embodies its specificity. This volume examines the performance of the Republic along a variety of interconnecting axes, in order to go beyond the familiar question of whether the Republic is acting in accordance with its vocation, but also to ask whether that vocation is still viable and, by implication therefore, whether there remains a specificity that sets the French polity fundamentally apart from any other of model of modern liberal democracy. Drawing on contributions that reflect a variety of methodological approaches, ranging from theoretical speculations and modelling to the interpretation of fieldwork data, the study examines the dynamics of the relationship between the Republic and its constituencies, in the fields of political relations, territorial identities, social movements, public policy and foreign policy, and in each context juxtaposing what is perceived as the model for that relationship with the current reality.

In Chapter 1 Raymond opens with a critical perspective on the process of political socialisation in France and the culture of participation in the public space that underpins the universalist values of the Republic. Observing that in France, as in English-speaking liberal democracies, the tide of participation has receded markedly, Raymond investigates the way this has been theorised, on the one hand, by those who see it as the demise of the blueprint for modernity that was the legacy of the Revolution and, on the other, by those who regard it as an opportunity for the Republic to break out of the straitjacket of an ideology that is essentially Jacobin and to reconcile itself to a society that is infinitely more diverse than could have been imagined by the Jacobins as they embarked on their homogenising project of social constructivism. This is followed by Cole and Hanley's rigorous appraisal in Chapter 2 of what constitutes the orthodox French model of politics and policy making. The institutional norms which guide the ship of state are first to be analysed, followed by an overview of the pressures exerted on those norms by the vectors for change that occur both domestically and internationally, before the chapter concludes with an elucidation of the nature of the profound complex of democratic institutions, interests and ideas that make the French model far more cohesive and enduring than many of its critics appreciate.

Chapters 3 and 4 enable us to juxtapose the traditional understanding of the Republic's mission to centralise and standardise with the practices that reveal a much more differentiated and even customised reality at regional and local level. Cole begins with an assessment of the French model of the unitary state, offering an overview of how this archetype emerged. He then provides an original case study of Brittany, based on extensive fieldwork, that illustrates how a region that was typically known for its problematic relationship with the centralising French state has transformed its traditional social and political culture in order to capitalise on opportunities such as the state policy of decentralisation and create a consensus that successfully defends Breton interests at the highest level. In Chapter 4 Milner focuses on grass-roots democracy in France, drawing on research among actors at the municipal level in Lille. While we may be familiar with the top-down mode of hierarchical obligations that is the classic formula for 'territorial administration', i.e. central–local relations in France, we sometimes overlook the fact that such was never uniformly the case. As the case of Lille illustrates, the decentralisation of the 1980s and subsequent legislative changes in the 1990s have provided the scope for impressive bottom-up initiatives in the field of local democracy that could be seen as pulling the French state on to the same path of urban governance as other Western democracies.

In Chapter 5 Wharton broaches the complex issue of le droit à la différence, the right to individual specificity as citizens, in a Republic whose own specificity is dependent on the crucial belief that what liberates its citizens is the universalism of the rights that they enjoy equally. Taking up the case of France's gay citizens, Wharton illustrates the way in which the abstract notion of equality is nonetheless mediated by normative social values that operate to the detriment of sexualities other than heterosexuality. Articulating a nuanced view of the legislative changes that have attempted to accommodate the differences embodied by those whose relationships fall outside of society's norms, he acknowledges the progress that has been made but underlines the road that still needs to be travelled if the Republic is to be seen as capable of offering its individual citizens concrete, as well as abstract, rights. It is the very understanding of what is meant by citizenship, its construction and interpretation, which lies at the heart of Chapter 6 by Kiwan. Joining theory with the practice of fieldwork among the urban young of the Parisian periphery, she uncovers the mismatch between the totalising abstraction of citizenship rights in the Republic and the clear deficiencies in the enjoyment of those rights among the youth of North African origin. Employing the critical tools provided by the sociology of the Subject, Kiwan adumbrates the process of constant negotiation between the obligations of citizenship and the communitarian identification that may enable the young people in question to construct a new and positive sense of self in the Republic.

Chapters 7 and 8 elucidate what is perceived as the traditional role of the Republican state as a social and economic actor. While France may draw envious comparisons from social democrats in other countries for what is reputedly the best health service in the world and a broad set of fiscal policies aimed at alleviating the consequences of economic deprivation among its citizens, Révauger depicts a reality that is somewhat different. In particular, he charts the emergence of a system of social provision that is much less uniform and comprehensively conceived than is commonly assumed, and argues cogently that the French 'model' in fact possesses a considerable degree of hybridity, sharing features with systems that are supposedly antithetical. As Maclean illustrates from the outset in Chapter 8, the tradition of proactive public intervention in the economy is a formidable one in France. The emergence of new obligations, however, on both a global and a European level, have reduced the margin in which the Republic can manoeuvre to lend state support to national champions. But, as Maclean concludes, the asymmetry in markets, such as that for energy, is testament to the deftness of the Republic in negotiating supranational obstacles to the partisan pursuit of economic interests that are national.

In the final chapter Cumming looks at the most contentious aspect of French republican ideology, its 'civilising mission', and the way it has been translated into French foreign policy, notably in relations with the former colonies in Africa. Peeling away the rhetoric, Cumming reveals practice that has more in common with pragmatic self-interest than universalist principles. However, domestic, European and global pressures have forced the governing elite in France to rethink the Republic's African vocation and notably the Jacobin obsession with state-centred solutions, resulting in more co-operation with international organisations and indigenous sub-state actors in tackling the problems of its former colonies. But the belief in the universalism of the French republican model and the rayonnement or dissemination of its values is far from destined to disappear, and Cumming concludes with the suggestion that it may find new form in the construction of the European Union's global mission.

It is unquestionably the case that the French Republic of the twenty-first century is facing challenges –such as those to French economic and political sovereignty – that could not have been imagined a generation ago, even by those who led the process of change resulting in the 'big bang' in the country's financial markets and the advocates of greater political union in Europe. The test for the Republic is whether it will endure the redefinition imposed by internal contestation and those supranational or even global forces that now shape its environment, or whether it will find a way of adapting to these pressures while preserving a part of the vocation and ambition that make it characteristically French.

1

The republican ideal and the reality of the Republic

Gino Raymond

France, France, without you the world would be alone. (Victor Hugo)

As Régis Debray explains in his essay *La République expliquée à ma fille*, 'The Republic and France are so closely identified in people's minds that even the Republic's adversaries no longer dare question its existence.'[1] Debray's confident assertion harks back to the idealism that found concrete form at last in the early days of the Third Republic, when, after almost a century of upheaval, a permanent constitutional settlement established the triumph of the republican principles that had first been proclaimed by the authors of the Revolution of 1789. The constitutional foundations for the Republic that were finally laid by the Assembly with the vote that was passed in 1875 would give France a political regime that would elevate the aspirations of the Declaration of the Rights of Man and the Citizen; inalienable and individual rights, served by accountable government, held together by an impartial justice that embodied the sovereignty of the people, operating in a public space where the individual defined himself by assuming the right and responsibility to act, all contained within a polity that would be the Republic one and indivisible.

After enduring two failed monarchical regimes, the short-lived hopes of the Second Republic and the vain aspirations of a Second Empire that collapsed so ignominiously in the debacle of the Franco-Prussian War, it is not difficult to understand the investment – intellectual, cultural, social and political – made by the founding figures of the Third Republic in the ideals established by the Revolution of 1789, and the co-identity they established between the Republic and France. It was the faith in this co-identity that brought the Third Republic through the Dreyfus Affair and that was so passionately defended by Emile Zola when, in *J'accuse*, he condemned the antisemitism of the anti-Dreyfusards as threatening the existence of 'la grande France libérale des droits de l'homme'.[2] The pedagogical assumptions motivating Debray at the end of the twentieth century would have been recognisable to Jules Ferry and his associates at the end of the nineteenth century as they embarked on their project of establishing the modern state school system. As Ferry argued in the *Revue pédagogique* of 1882, the universal, secular and free school system of the Third Republic would train the innumerable reserves who would defend republican democracy.

Whether Debray's lesson on the virtues of the Republic is an expression of confidence in the strength of its roots in French society is, however, a matter of interpretation. A plethora of books appeared in France as the twentieth century was drawing to a close, aimed at reasserting the centrality of the Republic, and the exercise of the civic values it represents, as the means of successfully confronting some of the more testing challenges to the cohesion of French society. Aimed particularly at the young, and couched in a language they would understand, these books were in effect a resort to old-fashioned *manuels* packaged with the latest pedagogical techniques, all pointing to the need to refer back to collective core beliefs in order successfully to balance individual or communal self-realisation with collective needs. While some dealt directly with the means of advancing the values of what Zola called the France of freedom and the rights of man, others looked at the challenges raised by immigration from outside Christian Europe such as racism and communitarianism, but all pointed to the Republic as the touchstone of values that would allow a successful response to these challenges to be defined.[3] As the debate surrounding the bicentenary of the French Revolution illustrated, the postmodern revisionist tendency to see all losers as victims meant that there was no blanket unanimity as to the significance of the Revolution, and the need to manage the sensibilities of formerly counter-revolutionary regions such as Brittany and the Vendée militated against recourse to traditional republican triumphalism. The subliminal anxiety in certain circles about what was understood by the Revolution was exacerbated by the surveys of the time, which showed that the knowledge of many French citizens about the Revolution contained some surprising and elementary gaps.[4]

One can justifiably argue, therefore, that the conscious attempt among commentators, intellectuals and members of the political elite to reaffirm the mediating function of the Republic as the key guarantor of unity and equity is motivated, at the very least, by an apprehension that the vocation of the Republic is either not understood by a growing body of citizens or even mistrusted. This chapter will therefore survey first of all some of the essentially conservative arguments suggesting that the revolutionary impetus, and the political culture it engendered, has come to an end in France. It will then examine the view that, rather than marking a dangerous form of *anomie*, the decline of the old republican paradigm has in fact released new forces and provided a platform for a new politics. And in the final section a synthesis will be offered which suggests that the Republic retains a vocation, albeit a more modest and accommodating one.

The retreat of the Republic and the end of politics

Observations and anxiety about the failure of a growing number of citizens to take an active part in political life through the processes of representative democracy are not new and certainly not unique to France. Empirical surveys carried out, notably in the United States in the 1950s and 1960s, illustrated the considerable gulf that existed between the active citizens envisaged by the fathers of the American Revolution or the *citoyen actif* conceptualised by the authors of the French Revolution, and their modern twentieth-century counterpart.[5] What emerged was the image of a citizen who was poorly informed politically, undynamic and lacking in self-motivation with regard to participation in the life of the body politic. Subsequent surveys in Britain and France during the two following decades suggested that democracies that had enjoyed generations or even centuries of stability had developed a complaisant coexistence with the apathy of many of their citizens. The sociological interpretation of this that emerged especially from the research of figures like Pierre Bourdieu in France shed a particular light on the classic notion of the active citizen by asking whether it was ever only an illusion. The nineteenth-century barriers to participation posed by property qualification had gone, but, according to Bourdieu, the right to influence decision making remains illusory owing to the cultural capital that is shared by modern political elites in a market from which the ordinary citizen is excluded. And Bourdieu's ideas were fed back into the debates occurring in English-speaking countries about the cultural underpinning of political representation.[6]

But one could argue that, notwithstanding the parallels with other modern liberal democracies, the specificity of France's political culture made the sense of anxiety engendered by the crisis of representation more acute there than elsewhere. As Jürgen Habermas has observed, the eighteenth century marked a watershed in the context framing the relationship between the governing and the governed in Europe by offering the individual the principle of public deliberation as a means of legitimate control over political authority.[7] The relationship between those exercising power and the people was expressed by the emergence of a public space or dimension that conditioned new forms of sociability, defining the individual through his commitment to action in that space. The ambition to create a *res publica* or public entity that emerged from the Revolution of 1789 can be seen as setting a new template and temporal framework for modernity, and the depth of that conviction is evoked by George Steiner when he writes:

> The barest enumeration of some of the principal consequences of 1789 enforces the realization that the world as we know it today is the composite of reflexes, political assumptions and structures . . . bred by the French Revolution . . . the French Revolution is the pivotal historical-social date after that of the foundation of Christianity . . . Time itself, the cycle of lived history, was deemed to have begun a second time.[8]

The lyricism, or even, in some eyes, the hyperbole with which Steiner evokes the scale of the ambition embodied by 1789 provides an implicit link with the metaphysical understanding of citizenship that characterises the French approach in contrast to the empiricism of the Anglo-American one, and points to the inevitable sense of anxiety that must surface when the republican ideal collides with the reality. Almost from the beginning of that new dawn in history, as Steiner would have it, there has been tension between the prerogatives afforded to the citizen according to the republican ideal and the way it was translated in terms of political practice. Entry and action in the public space did not conform to the idealised image of the active citizen. It is noteworthy that when, on 29 October 1789, the National Assembly passed the decree introducing the category of 'active citizens' what the term implied in practice was challenged from the outset. The right to vote accorded to active citizens was hedged about with conditions that were quite at odds with the principles of civil equality that had been proclaimed on 26 August 1789 in the Declaration of the Rights of Man and the Citizen. Although in 1790 the franchise was extended to those approximately 4,300,000 active citizens who were male, and who paid the equivalent of three days' unskilled labour in taxes, the obstacles to genuine participation were in fact greater than they had been for the elections to the Estates General under the *ancien régime*. Although the Deputies of the National Assembly in 1789 were glad of the mass support that had brought them to power, they had no wish to be controlled by it. When Camille Desmoulins commented bitterly, 'But what is this much repeated word active citizen supposed to mean? The active citizens are the ones who took the Bastille',[9] it expressed frustration at a form of participation offered to the citizenry that was more theoretical than real.

In the years that followed, French interpretations of the significance of the Revolution showed a variety of emphases but expressed a common assumption that the Revolution had offered the individual a defining role as an actor in the public space, and concomitant anxiety that the reality of life in the French polity post-1789 had fallen short of this ideal. Thus, for Alexis de Tocqueville, revolutionary radicalism ultimately proved to be the atavistic reflex of the absolute state: the despotism of the *ancien régime* was replaced by the despotism of the omnipresent and intrusive state which, although it had broken the ties which once yoked men unequally, proceeded to make them equally unfree as dependent and servile subjects. For Edgar Quinet, the civil equality that followed 1789 was transient, failed to materialise in institutional terms and was ended by what Quinet judged to be the restoration of a traditional form of absolute power by the Jacobins. By way of contrast, for Michelet, writing his narrative of the Revolution in the aftermath of 1848, the aspirations of 1789 marked the advent of a secular faith in equality and fraternity but that the exercise of the corresponding individual prerogatives would have to wait for another era in which to triumph.

Those who, in the nineteenth century, theorised the way the role offered to the citizen by the Revolution had not been realised in terms of political practice would have recognised the 'democracy minus the people' identified by Duverger in the early life of the Fifth Republic, when the operation of the public space was incomparably more transparent and the processes of representation more established. As Duverger argued, the fundamental mediating role that should be played by political parties in translating the preferences of civil society into the choices of the state is weaker in France than in other comparable democracies such as Britain or Germany. Whereas the mass party memberships in those democracies provided a form of leverage that allowed considerable direct pressure to be brought on the leaderships in question, the weak membership bases of mainstream French political parties (with the historical exception of the French Communist Party), and the reliance on tendencies and factions as the conduit of changes in party policy, have resulted in what has been perceived as the rise of a class of party notables who have come to dominate public life. Furthermore, by operating through a form of *centrisme* that perpetuates itself precisely by occluding the fundamental oppositions that should separate the adversaries, the parties deprive the voters of a genuine choice and preside over a system that could be termed *la démocratie sans le peuple*, or democracy minus the people. [10]

The frustration identified underlined the enduring challenge of reuniting the citizen with the vocation defined by the Revolution, and, whether it was Duverger or other figures exercising a seminal intellectual influence, [11] the guiding assumption was that the citizen should fulfil him or herself without engaging actively in the life of the Republic. But as the Fifth Republic approached the close of the twentieth century the focus of anxiety moved from those obstacles to participation to the fundamental relationship between the individual citizen and politics in the Republic. The interaction between the citizen and those mediating institutions identified by Duverger and others was conceived, originally, in a way that buttressed the specificity of the French Republic. The ethical voluntarism that characterised the Revolution posited the notion of a citizen emancipated from the claims of heredity and whose judgement was founded on the exercise of reason alone. In terms of political fidelity, the claims of genealogy had to give way to the choices constructed within a broad set of values defined by the collectivity, the nation. The inevitable corollary of Jacobin ideology was that the children of the Revolution were 'constitutionally innocent', [12] because any kind of social determinism passed from one generation to the next would militate against the democratic structuring of political choices that individuals would make as free and equal citizens.

Political theorists from other democratic cultures could be tempted to establish a causal link between the political convictions of parents and the partisan preferences of their children, even to the point of extrapolating from this a fundamental factor responsible for the stability of a mature democracy like that of the United States. France, from the same perspective, remained an idealised counter-model where, it has been argued, the weakness of family-based factors in the formation and transmission of political loyalties is a determining factor in the turbulence that sometimes characterises political life, and especially the susceptibility to the sudden emergence of new movements.[13] The French reaction to the notion that a correlation could be drawn between the state of the polity and the state of the family was, understandably, to query the criterion chosen as the basis for such a model. The indicator of continuity in terms of political commitment could lie within a broad ideological tradition that in a country like France was perpetuated by classic divisions such as those between left and right, and constituted non-family factors of political socialisation that were just as influential and self-perpetuating as family factors were perceived to be elsewhere.[14]

A difficulty arises when defending the vigour of political socialisation in France, if those non-family factors that had characterised the strength of the Republic are perceived to have faded. It can justifiably be argued that the very notions of left and right and the ideological antitheses they imply were universalised from the French revolutionary tradition. The ensuing narrative of social transformation perpetuated allegiances and galvanised constituencies as it was defined through struggles like anticlericalism in the inextricably linked pursuit of freedom and secularism and the attempt to give concrete social form to the ideal of equality in the face of the inequalities generated by the amoral forces of money and markets. But as some commentators observed, as the French Republic reached the threshold of the new millennium, that concept of liberty as a project building on the visions of the kind of new society described by figures like Rousseau and Saint-Just was in retreat faced with the rise of a 'parasitic' notion of liberty, that is, liberty as a niche or individual space to be hollowed out of the body politic – a process accelerated by what was regarded by an increasing number of French citizens as the redundancy of the political cleavages and causes emanating from 1789.[15] This desertion of *l'espace public*, the public space that is supposed to be the privileged platform for the actions of the citizen as a political animal, was the consequence of what had been identified elsewhere as the distancing of the individual from both normative systems of belief like ideology and a sense of their social origins, resulting in an imperative of fulfilment that had become powerfully and personally differentiated in a kind of vacuum.[16]

Empirical studies, as opposed to theoretical speculations, suggested that although it was premature to conclude that old cleavages like left and right no longer conditioned political commitment, it could certainly be asserted that they were far from sufficient in operating as coherent global indicators of the way political identities were formed in individuals. The analysis of attitudes among the electorate suggested rather that their fidelities and choices were subject to a process of *déstructuration* or dismantling with the fading of former patterns of allegiance.[17] In an implicit admission of the diminishing ability of mediating institutions to socialise and motivate the participation of the individual citizen in the life of the polity, surveys carried out in France as the 1990s drew to a close appeared to acknowledge that the very existence of a pre-existing parental template of political preferences could play a significant part in anchoring the individual citizen in his or her role as a political actor. In an analysis of the post-electoral Cevipof survey of 1995 it was argued that the transmission of political convictions from one generation to the next in a family context could operate as a conditioning factor, and moreover a positive one, since those citizens without it could find themselves less able to make clear choices as voters and therefore be relegated to the sidelines as *hors jeu politiques* instead. In the wider context of the functioning of the political system itself, the rise in the number of individual citizens without a parental legacy of political commitment might lead to a worst-case scenario where they would be the constituency most vulnerable to expressions of political extremism.[18]

Such an implication, however qualified by the usual caveats that accompany empirical research, would suggest an undermining of the vocation of the French Republic on two related fronts: on the first front, the *déstructuration* diminishing the range of binary oppositions that once defined the variety of options to which the individual could commit as a active citizen; on the second front, the 'metaphysical' conception of the citizen that had given the Republic its specificity might in fact be inadequate faced with the new realities of French society, and that the yardstick of stability used by Anglo-American commentators might not be entirely inappropriate for France after all. In short, the *déstructuration* of political choice at home and the convergence with other liberal democracies abroad might represent a fatal blow to the singular and very specific ideal of the French Republic.

At the most pessimistic end of the scale, one kind of reaction to the decline of the ideal of the Republic has been to declare its veritable demise as a mobilising concept for the active citizen. The notion of *filiation politique* or inherited political conviction, whether attributable to familial factors or the broader context of ideological ones, could not withstand the kind of *idolâtrie démocratique* that has pushed the individuality of choice to an extreme that is neither sustainable nor desirable. It is the fruit of an unhealthy adulation of the individual that has cut him or her from the ties that provide a framework of orientation.[19] This is an evolution that in some eyes constitutes a reversal of the modernising thrust of the Revolution. With the unravelling of the nexus provided by a political culture that once bound the citizen to the Republic comes a situation where the boundaries determined by its institutions are occluded by 'grey zones' no longer susceptible to the authority of those institutions, thereby undoing the integrating impetus of 1789 and in so doing drawing France into a kind of new 'Middle Ages'.[20]

Conversely, there is a much more sanguine reading of the *déstructuration* of the range of political options to which the active citizen can commit. Rather than the retreat of the Republic being seen as the abandonment of *l'espace public* to its inevitable transformation into a wilderness, it has also been interpreted as a new horizon of possibility in which the notion of commitment and the sphere of politics can be fundamentally rethought.

The retreat of the Republic and the new politics

As has already been implied, the perception of the Republic and its vocation is inextricably woven into the great narrative of modernisation. The inculcation of the Republic's values was crucial to the political socialisation of its citizens and its institutions were the key to their integration. But the viability of that narrative and therefore the credibility of the Republic's mission rested on the claim to universality, that translated practically into a monopoly of the forms of engagement in the public space by which the citizen could define him or herself. The desire to step outside the *offre politique* provided by its mediating institutions would inevitably be perceived as a crisis for the concept of 'the community of citizens',[21] whose fulfilment is meant to be defined and underwritten by the universalism of the Republic's values. As has been cogently argued elsewhere, that claim to embody the values that would elevate and gratify the fundamental aspirations of all citizens was sustained by the corresponding resort to a process of 'othering'.[22] The ambitions of the Republic were historically underpinned by the systematically negative construction placed on what was portrayed as the embodiment of antithetical values, whether it was the caricatural contrasting of ethno-cultural concepts of citizenship with France's universalist one[23] or the depiction of those (such as in the colonies) who could not be elevated to the metaphysical citizenship offered by the Republic and were therefore categorised as subjects to be administered, as opposed to citizens empowered to act by rights.

This projection of particularism, corporality and difference on others outside the Republic could sustain the contract with the active citizen operating in the public space as long as the republican state could maintain the credibility of its modernising mission of securing economic progress, cultural unification and the formulation of political responses to social demands. But the increasing difficulty of responding successfully to those challenges is what can be characterised as the crisis of modernity for Western countries,[24] and, one could argue, especially for France, where it constituted the essential trade-off between the concrete particularisms defining the individual and the disembodied universalist rights empowering him or her as a citizen. Implicit in the complaint 'Nobody knows today what it is to be a citizen'[25] is the fear that if the Republic loses the monopoly of defining the nature of citizenship then the cohesion of the collectivity it embodies is seriously threatened. Conversely, the argument can be turned on its head with the proposition that it is the opening up of the public space to the clash of particularisms that now drives the definition of citizenship,[26] and by extension should redefine the role of the Republic. The cohesion of the collectivity may be better served by accommodating the new reality in which the prerogatives of citizenship have been wrested from the realm of metaphysical universalism and integrated in the identity of the individual subject. The consequence for his or her legitimate field of action in the public space is to open it up to characterisation precisely according to those parochialisms and cultural, social and economic particularisms that collide with the idealised vocation of the Republic. And arguably the most potent example of this after France entered the new millennium was the right claimed by some female members of the national community to assert their co-identity as Muslims and active citizens of the Republic by wearing the veil to school and in public sector occupations.

In an interesting variation on Duverger's criticism of the political class for their *centrisme* in ideological and policy terms, much more recently criticism has been levelled at this elite for a kind of discursive *centrisme* that has failed to persuade citizens of the options available to them through the political institutions of the Republic. The loss of confidence among the political class itself of its ability to appeal to citizens according to traditional oppositions such as left and right has led it to give ground to a libertarian individualism that does not allow it to assume a leading responsibility for determining the evolution of collective values, since underlying these are moral choices that are increasingly perceived as belonging to the individual alone. Consequently, the political elite finds refuge in a quasi-managerial discourse focused on rational organisation and efficiency gains, comforted in its abdication of responsibility by what have been described as *libérale-libertaire* assumptions that function as a default ideology.[27]

But the assumption motivating such an argument remains that the Republic should retain the monopoly in determining the active form of citizenship, and that through the elites that maintain its mediating institutions it should set the parameters for the public space in which that active form of citizenship is pursued. Empirical evidence suggests, however, that the monopoly in question is being increasingly challenged by bottom-up pressures in French society. On the one hand, the political life of the Republic over the last three decades has been marked by the ever rising watermark of abstention among its citizens from the rationalist and universalist activity that evokes Ernest Renan's nineteenth-century description of the nation as a 'daily plebiscite': in the definition offered to a representative cross-section of the electorate of what constituted a good citizen, the characteristic of being a 'regular voter' had, in 1976, been cited by 51 per cent of the respondents; in 1983 this figure had dropped to 43 per cent and by 1989 it was down to 38 per cent,[28] and in the referendum that marked the opening of the new millennium the disinclination to engage was starkly illustrated by the 69.2 per cent of citizens who abstained from voting on the reform of the presidential mandate.[29] On the other hand, however, recent surveys of French society reveal a remarkable willingness on the part of its citizens to commit themselves to a multiplicity of projects that challenge and impact on the life of the collectivity.[30] Although individuals are unquestionably less willing than in previous generations to subscribe and effectively fold their individuality into organisations with programmes that operate in the public space, many from varied backgrounds and generations are now prepared to invest in a project that is limited in time and space while preserving the distance that safeguards their individuality, an *engagement distancié*.[31] The investment in parochial concerns and punctual objectives has seen a remarkable flourishing of *la France associative*. Up to 1970 the number of new associations created annually was less than 20,000, but by the 1990s the figure was nudging up to 70,000. While in an obvious respect comprised of individuals committed to interacting collectively, the typical *association* is nonetheless task-driven rather than ideologically driven, whether responding to changing social needs, humanitarian or cultural imperatives, eschewing the assumptions that would characterise an enveloping political project. Such has been the rise in the popularity of these vehicles for action that, by some estimates, France entered the new millennium with up to 800,000 officially registered *associations*.[32]

More pertinently for the mission of the Republic is the way mobilisations have occurred in recent years challenging the institutions that mediate its role in formulating responses to social needs A salient example is the emergence in the 1990s of varied and widespread expressions of militancy by a social group that up to then had been envisaged in the kind of passive terms that reflected their economic inactivity. The marches of the unemployed launched by Agir ensemble contre le chômage (AC!) in 1994 encouraged a growing determination that a once virtually invisible section of society should deploy its demands in the public space, but do so on its own terms. The wave of protest that reached a climax in the winter of 1997–98 was vigorously independent of any kind of *récupération politique* or instrumentalisation by established parties or organisations like trade unions. For some, this dramatic affirmation of their needs was a new and subversive idea that rescued unemployed citizens from a state of non-existence, underlining the need for concrete, effective rights as opposed to abstract ones. As the leading lights of AC! argued, the trade union confederations did not possess the legitimacy to lead the mobilisation against unemployment. What AC! had created was a new type of social entity that was neither a trade union nor an *association*. It was an attempt to create an open forum where different social actors could exchange views and strategies, operating through a loose confederal network of local collectives characterised by the absence of dominant tendencies, official leaders and formal structures.[33]

As for the Republic's vocation of cultural integration, the mobilisation against racism that took shape in France during the 1990s provides a rich example of how the traditional expectations regarding the political mediation of social change are challenged by the multiplicity of ways that social change is ramified culturally. In many ways, SOS Racisme (SOSR), formed in 1984, became an archetype of the 'mediatised' social movement, with all the short-term advantages and medium-term disadvantages that entails. In the short term, the accomplished performances in the media of their charismatic first leader, Harlem Désir, set a benchmark with regard to the ability to communicate a message to a mass audience, since the television appearances provided the profile for an orchestrated campaign using the tools of regular press conferences, the co-opting of various celebrities to support the cause, which in turn provided more fodder for television exposure. That the movement succeeded in alerting the nation to the dangers posed by the rise of racism in 1980s France, especially the rise of the Front national (FN), is generally uncontested. The most optimistic interpretations of the significance of the movement credited it with being no less than the only force to have understood and subsequently mobilised the 'moral generation'.[34] But the immediate advantages of media exposure and instantly recognisable personalities also become disadvantages in the medium term, given the short shelf life the over-familiarity and the focus on the superficial that this kind of exposure brings. As results failed to match the initial explosion of expectations, some commentators were severe in taking anti-racism movements to task for their failure to cohere and to provide a properly organised and unified counterweight to the far right. For others, the root of the failure was deeper and lay in inability to think through what the ends of counter-racism should be. All that movements like SOSR had to offer in opposition to the dangers posed by the evolving and plural nature of racism was a media-driven discourse that was based on nothing more than fine moral sentiments advancing a shallow utopian consensus around the values of equality, solidarity and freedom. Moreover, this was made all the easier given the vacuum created by the collapse of left-wing utopian ideology.[35]

It could be countered, however, that these intellectual strictures reflect a cultural predilection for method and system that militates against a disposition to interpret social change in a broader, even if less intellectually rigorous, sense. The attempt to evaluate a social movement according to the measurable features of the collective actions it proposes, or even to conceptualise its *raison d'être* according to clearly identifiable intellectual ends, still assumes a homology between the pursuit of change and the public space offered as the framework for it by the Republic. But it is in the nature of social movements to stand outside the dominant system and offer alternative codes and symbols by which the individual can constitute meaning. More specifically, the success of social movements could be measured by their ability to challenge dominant models that aspire to uniqueness in the symbolic constitution of politics and culture,[36] and by extension the construction of individual identity within that symbolic structure. The anti-racism movements may not have obtained the measurable institutional impact commensurate with the initial enthusiasm they generated, but the impact on the consciousness of individuals and the processes of self-understanding, though less quantifiable, was nonetheless very significant. Many individuals who by their ethnic and or cultural origin had lived with the implicit pressure to conform to an abstract republican identity that denied them the positive display of those defining characteristics as citizens began to assume those particularist attributes, but in a way that circumvented the traditional political practices of the public space. Turning instead to the concretely parochial and the everyday, fieldwork among the urban young of North African origin has shown a high level of commitment to action in pursuit of a better quality of life for their local community and the promotion of the cultures represented locally.[37] In short, the anti-racism movements fed the determination among those communities in whose defence it had mobilised and their supporters that the assumption of national cultural homogeneity underlying the concept of citizenship could no longer pass unchallenged, thereby loosening the vertical integration of the concepts of nationhood, citizenship and culture traditionally embodied in the Republic.

What these movements appeared to challenge in practice was what others had articulated in theory, namely that a universalist concept of citizenship predicated on the value of equality can in fact veil hegemonic processes that can be experienced as controlling, oppressive and in effect inegalitarian. The greater the tension this creates in society the more the need emerges for an understanding of citizenship that gives individuals the opportunity to participate in a democracy that is radical and plural.[38] This would translate into an opening up of the public space to citizens as social actors where the interaction of plural identities would, by definition, work through antagonistic processes that are nonetheless positive rather than the unsustainable assumption of an abstract consensus. This concern with concrete rights and the prerogatives that citizens ought to possess in order to constitute the public space from below, as opposed to it being something imposed from above, has led some to argue for a fracturing of the traditional integration between the concepts of citizen and state in the Republic.[39] If the evolution of society has transformed France into what is in reality a 'multiple and moving border',[40] then the understanding of citizenship should reflect that evolution. This would imply the transformation of the concept from a national to a transnational one. For its most enthusiastic advocates, recasting citizenship in a European mould may be the only way to preserve the relationship between the individual citizen and his or her role as a political actor by preventing the triumph of those global liberal economic forces that provoke a kind of fatalism that disempowers and depoliticises the individual citizen.[41]

However attractive these transnational reconceptualisations may be with regard to breaking the homology between the citizen and the nation as represented by the Republic, these are evocations of a society that may or, depending on the evolution of the European Union (EU), may not be *en devenir*, i.e. in the process of being fulfilled. However great the potential may be for a European notion of citizenship to transcend the limitations of a national one, and thereby establish the virtues of commitment to the public space at the same time as the values of cultural pluralism, the absence of factors like the shared cultural symbols that are constitutive of a common identity mean that so far European citizenship has defined itself through the elaboration of regulations and the imposition of administrative barriers and controls. Moreover, the fact that the extension of membership to former Eastern Bloc countries has been accompanied by a stricter policing of the European Union's southern borders has revived the spectre of self-definition through the exclusion of the 'other'.[42] The reality for the Republic of today is that the established conceptualisation of the public space is still operational and may possess a greater potential for adaptation than its critics are prepared to admit.

The coexistence of old and new paradigms

The pessimism that Maurice Duverger expressed, barely a decade after the inception of the Fifth Republic, regarding the ability of a fundamental mediating institution like the party system to assume an effective role in the operation of representative democracy in France may be regarded as inevitable, given the shadow cast at the time by the figure of de Gaulle. On the other hand, by the end of the twentieth century, with de Gaulle a distant memory, the perception of the political class as a stratum of notables disconnected from the democratic grass-roots was widespread. For example, the debate over the enduringly thorny issue of the *cumul des mandats*, that is, the possibility for politicians to accumulate representative functions at local, regional and national levels, highlighted the anxiety that a systemic failure was allowing those individuals, irrespective of the professed ideological orientation of their parties, to operate according to an agenda that was essentially self-interested. Moreover, it was a telling paradox that the two presidential figures who steered the French Republic's transition from the twentieth to the twenty-first century were archetypal career politicians. Adolphe Thiers, the politician whose career straddled most of the regime changes and political turmoil of the nineteenth century, might have recognised a kindred spirit in François Mitterrand, who by the time he left presidential office in 1995 had had a career spanning six decades. By the time Mitterrand's successor, Jacques Chirac, was elected to his second mandate as President of the Republic in 2002, his career had spanned five decades. At the opposite end of the political system, the validity of Duverger's judgements about the failure of French parties to recruit members relative to their counterparts in other liberal democracies is borne out by recent surveys showing France to have the lowest levels of party membership in comparison with European neighbours such as Britain, Denmark, Germany, Netherlands, Sweden and Norway.[43]

The presidential elections of 2002, and more precisely the shock result of the first round when the Socialist, Lionel Jospin, was beaten to the second place spot by the FN's Jean-Marie Le Pen, focused a profound and wide-ranging debate about the relationship between the citizen and the Republic and the consequences for its mediating institutions. One of the paradoxes observed was, at one end of the spectrum, the unchanging nature of the *offre politique* or the options in terms of the prospective leaders entering the race. Unlike other systems where a losing candidate normally gives up the leadership of his or her party and retires to the political margins, the system in France repeatedly throws up the same faces. Lionel Jospin and Robert Hue were entering the contest for the second time, Jacques Chirac and Jean-Marie Le Pen for the fourth time, and Arlette Laguilller for a remarkable fifth time. This familiarity, or over-familiarity, it has been argued, bore a causal relationship with the explosion of options at the other end of the spectrum among those candidates with little established profile. With a total of sixteen candidates entering the first round, on the surface of things there appeared to be a balanced political choice, with eight candidates coming from the left or extreme left, and eight coming from the centre-right, the right and the extreme right. But in reality the results of the first round testified to the *émiettement*, or break-up, of the vote that had little to do with left–right allegiances: fifteen of the sixteen candidates each gathered more than 1 per cent of the votes cast and none of them crossed the threshold of 20 per cent. Moreover, for the first time in the life of the Fifth Republic there were four women candidates standing for the supreme office and a youth (in political terms) of twenty-seven, Olivier Besancenot, standing as the candidate of Ligue communiste révolutionnaire (LCR), who, according to the Louis Harris poll of 21 April 2002, attracted 14 per cent of the votes cast by eighteen to twenty-four-year-olds.[44] There were, therefore, on the one hand, a striking number of voters who were prepared to step outside the mainstream in their choice of candidates and, on the other, with a first-round rate of abstentions and spoilt ballots touching 30.05 per cent, no shortage of commentators to remark on the reluctance of citizens to exercise their rights actively in the public space.

Well before the events of 21 April 2002, however, there had been interpretations of the abstentionist phenomenon that did not see it as an inevitable, and cataclysmic indicator of disengagement. A rising level of abstentionism may be read as signalling political engagement by another means. Studies have shown that there are very few permanent abstentionists in France, and that they are difficult to categorise in fixed terms demographically and socio-economically. The refusal to vote among erstwhile supporters of mainstream parties can express a desire not to 'betray' the party with which they are most closely aligned, but which they also reproach for not fulfilling their expectations. On a broader and related level, abstentionism can be a deliberate choice in response to what is perceived as the absence of genuine alternatives. The voter may therefore opt to abstain, but it is not a blanket response, being instead one that is modulated according to a possible host of variables, resulting in multiple modes of behaviour, and constituting an eloquent reflection on what is on offer politically.[45] It may be that the voter may temper his or her incursion in the public space in a way that balances his or her sensibilities as an individual subject and as a citizen. Thus the *sujet-citoyen* intervenes when there is a *correspondance* or alignment of personal and collective convictions and withdraws when they can safely diverge, leaving the public space to be filled by a second-order partisan discourse. Less interest in party politics does not mean that there is less interest in democracy, as the massive mobilisation behind Jacques Chirac in the second round of the presidential election illustrated, allowing him to be elected on 5 May 2002 with 81.75 per cent of the vote and crushing his far-right rival Le Pen. This result, followed by the solid presidential majority acquired as a result of the legislative elections of the following month, can be translated as a return to the sources of the Fifth Republic[46] and viewed as a clear contradiction of the argument advanced by some commentators that France was on a path of convergence with other parliamentary regimes in Europe where the head of state is an arbiter but where the *enjeu décisif* or key consideration is who heads the government and therefore exercises real executive power,[47] given, notably, the way *cohabitation* had clipped the wings of the presidency. However, the resurgent abstentionism in the first round of the legislative elections of June, at 35.20 per cent, allows a more nuanced interpretation, certainly of the behaviour of the *sujet-citoyen*. The mobilisation behind Chirac in May 2002 could be read as evidence of a new *engagement légitimiste*, or legitimism that asserted a conviction, beyond partisan politics, in the enduring value of French democratic ideals and institutions and the need to defend them. By the same token, it is not the kind of engagement that is drawn by the ritualised conflict of party politics. Instead, it is an engagement that mobilises around themes, such as the right to work, education or residence when that coincides with the defence of fundamental democratic rights or the demand that those rights should be actualised.[48] It is a kind of engagement that requires a rethinking of *l'espace public*, possibly along the lines of an *espace commun* or common space, opening up and grounding the understanding of citizenship to accommodate the needs of subjectivation, and freeing the ends of action from the pressure for uniformity expressing itself as consensus, thereby removing the obstacles to active participation in the shaping of the Republic by the *sujet-citoyen* previously held back by the conflicting and identifying particularisms of his of her subjectivity. As Kiwan implies in Chapter 6, the concept of *filiation politique* or transmission of political engagement among the younger and culturally heterogeneous members of French society will not be determined by neat categories such as family and non-family factors, but may well combine a variety of concerns that fall between the interstices of contradictory factors and in a manner that is far from fixed. This process would thus space relations to the public space that are *ad hominem*, attempting to reconcile the person to the plenitude of his or her existence as an individual subject and as a citizen who is part of a greater whole.

If, as the notion of *l'engagement légitimiste* suggests, the appetite exists for a reaffirmation of the legitimacy of the French Republic's democratic ideals, then the onus is thrown back on its mediating institutions to frame the political options in a way that is capable of drawing that engagement. As Cole and Hanley argue, France is characterised by democratic structures that are deeply rooted, and in a sense the Republic has always been running to catch up with its citizens. Those movements whose relation to the polity falls outside the established modes of action in the public space may represent, today, what the battle for the Third Estate was two centuries ago, but focusing instead on the new divisions such as that between those with homes and the homeless,[49] and engaging above all with everyday social realities instead of abstract projects. While in some aspects of its foreign relations (see Cumming, Chapter 9) and in its economic policy (see Maclean, Chapter 8), the atavistic reflexes of the Republic, especially the propensity to 'othering', can be identified, in other areas the flexibility needed to adapt the abstract rights of citizenship to the concrete needs of individuals has been shown, whether in the acknowledgement of regional identities (see Cole, Chapter 3) or the accommodation of social and sexual preferences (see Wharton, Chapter 5), even if that has sometimes appeared somewhat grudgingly. The Republic has given evidence of its ability to adapt to the changing and individualised needs of its citizens, and furthermore of adapting to ideas from outside, in areas of social policy that were once considered peculiarly French (see Révauger, Chapter 7).

Conclusion

The suggestion by some commentators that the Revolution is not only over but that the foundation of the Republic has somehow been overturned with the defeat of its integrating and modernising mission by the excesses of individualism is surely exaggerated and overlooks the fact that, if there is one thing that embodies the leap forward it represents, it is the way the rights of the individual came to constitute the beating heart of the republican project.[50] Conversely, the suggestion that 'citizens doing it for themselves' by wresting universal rights out of the abstract and giving them individual and embodied particularities is the best way of revitalising the Republic overlooks the prospect that, even with a much broader concept of the public space which accepts as normal the perpetual collision of actors in pursuit of individual and communal difference, the need for a *modus vivendi* to be defined remains, and that the best embodiment of that consensus is the Republic. Even those commentators who have been most lucid in their elaboration of the claims of subjectivity and the light it has cast on the limited nature of the traditional *offre politique* to the citizen, implicitly concede that the Republic must have a role to play in mediating the needs of what we have called the *sujet-citoyen* confronted with the forces of globalisation.[51] It will be a Republic less inclined to resort to the 'othering' that is now the unacceptable and historic face of building a unitary national identity, but it will remain the Republic that through the many paroxysms that have characterised its existence has been the only option for the citizens of France in pursuit of collective renewal.

Notes

1 R. Debray, *La République expliquée à ma fille* (Paris: Seuil, 1998), p. 19. My translation. The original reads: 'La République et la France sont tellement identifiées dans la tête des gens que même ses adversaires n'osent plus la remettre en question.'

2 E. Zola, *J'Accuse . . . ! La Vérité en marche* (Brussels: Editions Complexe, 1988), p. 110.

3 See, for example, H. Festis and P. Seigneur, *Dictionnaire du citoyen* (Paris: Livre de poche/Hachette jeunesse, 1997); M. Gallo, *L'Amour de la France expliqué à mon fils* (Paris: Le Seuil, 1999); S. Naïr, *L'Immigration expliquée à ma fille* (Paris: Le Seuil, 1999); F. Dutheil and H. Fellner, *Le Petit Livre pour dire non à l'intolérance et au racisme* (Paris: Bayard Poche, 1998).

4 In a series of polls carried out by SOFRES testing the knowledge of ordinary French citizens at the time of the bicentenary celebrations, it emerged that one-third of

those interviewed did not know the nationality of Marie-Antoinette and almost half did not know how Danton died, the role played by Saint-Just in the Revolution and whether Robespierre was Montagnard or Girondin. The findings of these polls are summarised by O. Duhamel, 'La revolution française est terminée', *Pouvoirs*, 50 (1989), 121–5.

5 For example, B. Berelson, P. Lazarsfeld and W. MacPhee, *Voting* (Chicago IL: Chicago University Press, 1966); A. Campbell *et al.*, *The American Voter* (Ann Arbor MI: University of Michigan Press, 1969); G. Almond and S. Verba, *The Civic Culture* (London: Sage, 1989).

6 See P. Bourdieu, *Language and Symbolic Power*, trans. G. Raymond and M. Adamson (Cambridge: Polity Press, 1991).

7 See J. Habermas, *L'Espace public* (Paris: Payot, 1993).

8 G. Steiner, 'Aspects of counter-revolution', in G. Best (ed.), *The Permanent Revolution* (London: Fontana Press, 1988), pp. 129–53, p. 151.

9 Quoted in L. G. Wickham Legg, *Select Documents illustrative of the History of the French Revolution: The Constituent Assembly*, 2 vols (Oxford: Clarendon Press, 1905), I, pp. 173–4.

10 See M. Duverger, *La Démocratie sans le people* (Paris: Seuil, 1967).

11 The observations of a variety of commentators and theorists such as Georges Burdeau, François Bloch-Lainé, Jacques Juillard and Carlos Castoriadis on the Republic are predicated on the belief that the citizen is a political animal and that no democracy can claim authentically to be so without the generalised and enduring commitment of its citizens to the political process.

12 J. Borie, *Mythologies de l'hérédité au XIXe siècle* (Paris: Galilée, 1981), p. 215.

13 See Philip E. Converse and G. Dupeux, 'Politicisation of the electorate in France and the United States', *Public Opinion Quarterly*, 26 (1962), p. 23.

14 A. Percheron and M. K. Jennings, 'Le mythe de l'exceptionalité française', in N. Mayer and A. Muxel (eds), *La Socialisation politique* (Paris: Armand Colin, 1993), pp. 119–29.

15 N. Tenzer, *La Société dépolitisée* (Paris: Presses Universitaires de France, 1990), p. 216.

16 G. Lipovetsky, *L'Ère du vide : essais sur l'individualisme contemporain* (Paris: Gallimard, 1983), p. 14.

17 See E. Schweisguth, 'L'affaiblissement du clivage gauche–droite', in P. Perrineau (ed.), *L'Engagement politique : déclin ou mutation ?* (Paris: Presses de Sciences Po, 1994), pp. 215–37.

18 J. Jaffré and A. Muxel, 'Les repères politiques', in D. Boy and N. Mayer (eds), *L'Électeur a ses raisons* (Paris: Presses de Sciences Po, 1997), pp. 67–100, p. 85.

19 See A. Finkielkraut, *Ingratitude* (Paris: Gallimard, 1999).

20 See A. Minc, *Le Nouveau Moyen Âge* (Paris: Gallimard, 1993).

21 See D. Schnapper, *La Communauté des citoyens : sur l'idée moderne de la nation* (Paris: Gallimard, 1994).

22 The useful neologism proposed by M. Silverman, *Contemporary French Thought on Culture and Society* (London: Routledge, 1999), p. 133.

23 This, Brubaker argues, was the case in comparing French with German notions of citizenship. In R. Brubaker, *Citizenship and Nationhood in France and Germany* (Cambridge MA: Harvard University Press, 1992), p. 2.

24 F. Dubet and M. Wieviorka (eds), *Penser le sujet : autour d'Alain Touraine* (Paris: Fayard, 1995), pp. 13–4.

25 C. Castoriadis, *La Montée de l'insignifiance : les carrefours du labyrinthe IV* (Paris: Seuil, 1996), p. 92.

26 S. Naïr, *Le Regard des vainqueurs : les enjeux français de l'immigration* (Paris: Grasset, 1992), pp. 44–5.

27 N. Tenzer and R. Delacroix, *Les Élites et la fin de la démocratie française* (Paris: Presses Universitaires de France, 1992), p. 140.

28 In J. Jaffré, 'Après les municipales et les européennes : le nouveau décor électoral', *Pouvoirs*, 55 (1990), 147–62.

29 Evidence collated illustrates a steady rise in the proportion of abstentions and spoilt ballot papers in elections and referenda during the life of the Fifth Republic: 25.73 per cent during the sixteen that occurred from 1958 to 1969; 29.89 per cent during the eleven from 1970 to 1979; 33.08 per cent during the fourteen from 1981 to 1989; and 37.86 during the thirteen from 1992 to 2000. In R. Ponceyri, 'La fin de la République gaullienne', *Revue politique et parlementaire* (September–October 2000), 9–34, p. 14.

30 See, for example, X. Crettiez and I. Sommier, *La France rebelle : tous les foyers, mouvements et acteurs de la contestation* (Paris: Michalon, 2002).

31 J. Ion, *La Fin des militants ?* (Paris: Editions de l'Atelier, 1997), p. 88.

32 S. Waters, *Social Movements in France: Towards a New Citizenship* (Basingstoke: Palgrave Macmillan, 2003), pp. 22–3.

33 *Ibid.*, p. 117.

34 L. Joffrin, *Un coup de jeune : portrait d'une génération morale* (Paris: Arléa, 1987), p. 13.

35 See P. A. Taguieff, *Les Fins de l'antiracisme* (Paris: Michalon, 1995).

36 A. Melucci, *Challenging Codes: Collective Action in the Information Age* (Cambridge: Cambridge University Press, 1996), p. 357.

37 In a survey among a representative cross-section of young people of North African origin in Aubervilliers, on the outskirts of Paris, although only 40 per cent of those eligible to vote in elections did so, 85 per cent of the young women and 80 per cent of the young men were active or had been so in local *associations*. In N. Kiwan, 'The Construction of Identity amongst Young People of North African Origin in France: Discourses and Experiences', unpublished PhD thesis (University of Bristol, 2003), pp. 162 and 295.

38 See C. Mouffe (ed.), *Dimensions of Radical Democracy: Pluralism, Citizenship, Community* (London: Verso, 1992).

39 See, for example, E. Balibar, *Droit de cité : culture et politique en démocratie* (Paris: Editions de l'Aube, 1998), p. 54.

40 *Ibid.*, p. 6.

41 P. Bourdieu, *Contre-feux : propos pour servir à la résistance contre l'invasion néo-libérale* (Paris: Liber-Raisons d'Agir, 1998), p. 74.

42 See C. Withol de Wenden, *La Citoyenneté européenne* (Paris: Presses de Sciences Po, 1997).

43 See L. Billordo, 'Party membership in France: measures and data collection', *French Politics*, 1:1 (2003), 137–51. Billordo also identifies the peculiar distortions that occur in the management and representation of party membership figures in France: the lack of a legal obligation to report accurate membership figures, which encourages the parties to exaggerate them in order to bolster their image; the historically occult nature of party financing, which meant that inflated reported mem-

bership figures made for more plausible explanations concerning the provenance of party funds. *Ibid.*, p. 138.

44 A. Gattolin, 'Aux origines : une offre politique déstructurée, un scrutin dévalué', in A. Gattolin and F. Miquet-Marty, *La France blessée* (Paris: Denoel, 2003), pp. 25–50, p. 28.
45 F. Subileau and M-F. Toinet, *Les Chemins de l'abstention* (Paris: La Découverte, 1993), pp. 193–97. When considering the body of abstentionist voters, Jaffré and Muxel have suggested dividing them into categories of *dans le jeu* and *hors jeu*. Those who are *dans le jeu*, or in the game, use abstention as a means of criticising the range of options offered to them by the mainstream parties, while those who are *hors jeu*, or out of the game, are not nonetheless apolitical but instead hostile to a system they believe has thrown up unacceptably partisan choices. In J. Jaffré and A. Muxel, 'S'abstenir : hors du jeu ou dans le jeu politique?', in P. Bréchon, A. Laurent and P. Perrineau (eds), *Les Cultures politiques des Français* (Paris: Presses de Sciences Po, 2000), pp. 21–50.
46 A. Cole, *French Politics and Society* (London: Pearson Longman, 2005), p. 43.
47 P. Avril, 'Les conséquences des élections sur la nature du régime : l'improbable phénix', in P. Perrineau and C. Ysmal (eds), *Le Vote de tous les refus* (Paris: Presses de Sciences Po, 2003), pp. 363–78, p. 368.
48 M-O. Padis, 'Les nouveaux rapports à la citoyenneté', in Gattolin and Miquet-Marty, *La France blessée*, pp. 243–58, p. 246.
49 J. Guilhaumou, *La Parole des sans : les mouvements actuels à l'épreuve de la Révolution française* (Paris: ENS Edition, 1998), p. 32.
50 Alain Minc himself tries to end his essay *Le Nouveau Moyen Âge* on an upbeat note by resorting to the nebulous concept of *la grâce française*, by proposing a renewal of faith in the success that the unity and cohesion of the French republican state could bring, but now on the European stage as the anchor of the new Union, given the fragmented nature of German identity and the separatism that he believes characterises the United Kingdom. *Ibid.* p. 231. This could, however, be construed by others as another example of the process of 'othering'.
51 See the conclusion in A. Touraine, *Critique de la modernité* (Paris: Fayard, 1992).

Select bibliography

G. Almond and S. Verba, *The Civic Culture* (London: Sage, 1989).
E. Balibar, *Droit de cité : culture et politique en démocratie* (Paris: Editions de l'Aube, 1998).
B. Berelson, P. Lazarsfeld and W. MacPhee, *Voting* (Chicago IL: University of Chicago Press, 1966).
G. Best (ed.), *The Permanent Revolution* (London: Fontana Press, 1988).
J. Borie, *Mythologies de l'hérédité au XIXe siècle* (Paris: Galilée, 1981).
P. Bourdieu, *Language and Symbolic Power*, trans. G. Raymond and M. Adamson (Cambridge: Polity Press, 1991).
P. Bourdieu, *Contre-feux : propos pour servir à la résistance contre l'invasion néo-libérale* (Paris: Liber-Raisons d'Agir, 1998).
D. Boy and N. Mayer (eds), *L'Electeur a ses raisons* (Paris: Presses de Sciences Po, 1997).
P. Bréchon, A. Laurent and P. Perrineau (eds), *Les Cultures politiques des Français* (Paris: Presses de Sciences Po, 2000).
A. Campbell, P. Converse, W. Miller and D. Stokes, *The American Voter* (Ann Arbor MI: University of Michigan Press, 1969).

C. Castoriadis, *La Montée de l'insignifiance : les carrefours du labyrinthe IV* (Paris: Seuil, 1996).

A. Cole, *French Politics and Society* (London: Pearson Longman, 2005).

P. E. Converse and G. Dupeux., 'Politicization of the electorate in France and the United States', *Public Opinion Quarterly*, 26 (1962).

X. Crettiez and I. Sommier, *La France rebelle : tous les foyers, mouvements et acteurs de la contestation* (Paris: Michalon, 2002).

R. Debray, *La République expliquée à ma fille* (Paris: Seuil 1998).

F. Dubet and M. Wieviorka (eds), *Penser le sujet : autour d'Alain Touraine* (Paris: Fayard, 1995).

M. Duverger, *La Démocratie sans le peuple* (Seuil: Paris, 1967).

A. Finkielkraut, *Ingratitude* (Paris: Gallimard, 1999).

A. Gattolin and F. Miquet-Marty (eds), *La France blessée* (Paris: Denoel, 2003).

J. Guilhaumou, *La Parole des sans : les mouvements actuels à l'épreuve de la Révolution française* (Paris: ENS Edition, 1998).

J. Habermas, *L'Espace public* (Paris: Payot, 1993).

J. Ion, *La Fin des militants?* (Paris: Editions de l'Atelier, 1997).

N. Kiwan, 'The Construction of Identity amongst Young People of North African Origin in France: Discourses and Experiences', unpublished PhD thesis (University of Bristol, 2003).

G. Lipovetsky, *L'Ere du vide : essais sur l'individualisme contemporain* (Paris: Gallimard, 1983).

N. Mayer and A. Muxel (eds), *La Socialisation politique* (Paris: Armand Colin, 1993).

A. Melucci, *Challenging Codes: Collective Action in the Information Age* (Cambridge: Cambridge University Press, 1996).

A. Minc, *Le Nouveau Moyen Âge* (Paris: Gallimard, 1993).

C. Mouffe (ed.), *Dimensions of Radical Democracy: Pluralism, Citizenship, Community* (London: Verso, 1992).

S. Naïr, *Le Regard des vainqueurs : les enjeux français de l'immigration* (Paris: Grasset, 1992).

P. Perrineau (ed.), *L'Engagement politique : déclin ou mutation ?* (Paris: Presses de Scences Po, 1994).

P. Perrineau and C. Ysmal (eds), *Le Vote de tous les refus* (Paris: Presses de Sciences Po, 2003).

D. Schnapper, *La Communauté des citoyens : sur l'idée moderne de la nation* (Paris: Gallimard, 1994).

M. Silverman, *Contemporary French Thought on Culture and Society* (London: Routledge, 1999).

F. Subileau and M-F. Toinet, *Les Chemins de l'abstention* (Paris: La Découverte, 1993).

P. A. Taguieff, *Les Fins de l'antiracisme* (Paris: Michalon, 1995).

N. Tenzer, *La Société dépolitisée* (Paris: Presses Universitaires de France, 1990).

N. Tenzer and R. Delacroix, *Les Elites et la fin de la démocratie française* (Paris: Presses Universitaires de France, 1992).

A. Touraine, *Critique de la modernité* (Paris: Fayard, 1992).

S. Waters, *Social Movements in France: Towards a New Citizenship* (Basingstoke: Palgrave Macmillan, 2003).

L. G. Wickham Legg, *Select Documents illustrative of the History of the French Revolution: The Constituent Assembly*, 2 vols (Oxford: Clarendon Press, 1905).

C. Withol de Wenden, *La Citoyenneté européenne* (Paris: Presses de Sciences Po, 1997).

2

French politics in the twenty-first century

Alistair Cole and David Hanley

What is the state of French politics in the early twenty-first century? Our principal objective in this chapter is to provide an overview of the some of the main features of the changing French political system at the start of the new millennium. We begin by defining an 'orthodox model' of French politics and policy making. We then consider various challenges to this model. We conclude by addressing the theme of change and resistance to change in contemporary France.

The orthodox French model of politics and policies

Table 2.1 presents several core features of the post-war French model of politics and policies. There are undoubtedly others, but the selected themes provide a succinct checklist. These are a combination of institutions, interests and ideas. They relate to the focal role of the French state and state-driven paradigms of public policy, to the importance of ideas and political discourse, to the perceived inefficacy of social movements and political parties and to the role of France in the world.

We can identify several principal features of this traditional republican model of French politics and policies. The existence of a powerful central state was a legacy of the process of nation building, whereby centralisation and uniformity were imposed from above on rebellious provinces and local identities. This produced a model of Parisian centralisation, and – in comparative terms – a homogeneous political and administrative elite rigorously selected through a system of elite schools and competitive examinations. This pattern certainly became more visible after 1945, and the role of the *énarque* is a classic reference in any textbook on France, but it had long been preceded by the existence of a stable and relatively homogeneous political class during the Third Republic. Composed essentially of lawyers and other professionals, often with a strongly provincial flavour, it was able to establish a style of governance where Paris was the clear centre of decision, but where provincial interests were taken care of

Table 2.1 *The traditional (post-war) French model of politics and policies*

The focal role of the state
- A tightly knit politico-administrative elite believing in a strong central state and invested with a modernising policy style
- A powerful – or *dirigiste* – state in public policy formulation, especially in the economic and industrial sphere
- A top-down model of territorial administration (*la régulation croisée*): decisions made in Paris, implemented in provinces by an omnipresent state machinery, modified by local *notables*

The importance of referential frames and political discourse
- The importance of the discursive and ideological frames of equality, public service and the republican tradition
- The undivided nature of political legitimacy, as articulated in the One and Indivisible State

Dysfunctional representative processes
- A certain distrust by central elites of representative processes and a weak bargaining culture
- A tendency to popular rebellion against authority
- Partisan volatility, weak party organisation and the persistence of extra-systemic parties

France in the world
- A role for France as a great power in foreign policy
- Pretension to leadership within the EU

by a variety of means, crucial among which were the brokering skills of Deputies who often held local office in the practice known as *cumul des mandats*.

A natural corollary in the post-war period was the tradition of state interventionism in the economic and industrial sphere (*dirigisme*); the role of the state was to lead and to compensate for the lack of dynamism of domestic capitalism.

At the level of political representation, this traditional model vowed a distrust of intermediary institutions, such as parties, groups and regions, as unwelcome barriers between the state and the citizen. Though powerful provincial counterweights survived, these operated within the confines of Jacobin legality. There was a rather weak bargaining culture and divided, unrepresentative interest groups; the state determined which groups were representative. It should be said, however, that the pre-1939 parties, often derided for their weakness, were nevertheless able to broker many difficult issues in parliament, rather than in extra-parliamentary or neo-corporatist types of arrangement.[1] Whatever the success of such brokering may have been in the past, contemporary French politics repeatedly highlights the paradox of a weak bargaining culture producing strong social counterweights imbued with an ethic of direct action. The farming lobby acts as a particularly powerful domestic constraint in the French case that has no real equivalent elsewhere in Europe.

The Fifth Republic has generally had executive-dominated governments, relatively weak political and judicial counterweights to a powerful executive authority and a high territorial concentration of power. Even after the decentralisation reforms of 1982 and 2003–04, which first created, then strengthened, directly elected regions there is no equivalent of *Länder* governments, and metaphors of multi-level governance have more resonance in the German case than the French. Parliamentary counterweights to executive authority have generally been rather weak. The lower chamber, the National Assembly, enjoys limited constitutional sovereignty and exercises weak parliamentary scrutiny, though the institution has acquired more powers and prestige in recent years. Many commentators believe that the relative inefficiency of the National Assembly has less to do with its lack of statutory powers than with other constraining factors, such as the power of party managers (especially over members of the majority) or the wider attitudes of Deputies, who see the political process in winner-take-all terms. When one's own side has won power, then one is entitled to govern in the teeth of even the most sensible critiques from the opposition. Conversely, when one has lost an election, there is little possibility of constructive opposition, so one merely awaits, passively, the roll of the electoral dice.

The second chamber, the Senate, is an archaic and ineffective institution, overrepresenting rural and small-town France at the expense of the urban areas of population. The policy areas on which it is widely seen as competent – land or property law, family law, taxation – would tend to reinforce this view. Defenders of the Senate would point out that it is also a jealous watchdog of the rights of local authorities, reflecting the fact that its mode of representation is basically territorial.

By contrast, the rise of judicial and regulatory counterweights to executive authority has been a prominent feature of French politics since the 1990s.[2]

This traditional model of French politics and policies is an ideal type. It has been subjected to many pressures for change since the late 1970s. We can summarise the challenges to the traditional French model under six headings: changing institutional norms, changeable patterns of central steering, Europeanisation and globalisation, ideas and discourse, citizenship and identity, and the problem of political legitimacy.

Changing institutional norms

The study of political institutions is arguably the major growth area in contemporary political science. The 'new institutionalism', launched by March and Olsen as a reaction to behaviouralism and rational choice theory,[3] is still running strong in spite of its inherent limitations. We do not intend here to contribute explicitly to the rather circular debate about institutions, other than to note that the concept is frequently taken in a highly elastic way, according to the needs of the argument being presented. If used carelessly, this type of theory can present the institution as some kind of black box in which all kinds of processes are held to occur, thus dispensing the author from any further explanation. Whether we understand institutions in terms of organisations, beliefs, historical understandings, human action or forms of appropriate behaviour,[4] institutionalist frameworks, used subtly, do allow us to identify deep structural features of the French polity. In France, where there is a strong tradition of public law and of codification of human relations at all levels, interest in institutions has never waned.[5] We can understand institutions at two main levels: deep underlying structures and the institutions of the current political regime, the Fifth Republic. At both these levels, France provides an empirical terrain *par excellence* for the study of institutions. Deeper underlying structures are not specifically linked with a particular political regime, but in some cases pre-date the modern republican form of government. Vestiges of the Napoleonic state we referred to in Chapter 1, for instance, remain intact today. In Chapter 6 we examine the role of the powerful *grands corps* (especially the Council of State) that keep the French state tradition very much alive. Many Fifth Republic developments have their origins in the Fourth Republic or earlier. Political and ideological beliefs can span several political generations, or even regimes, as Tocqueville showed in his study of the *ancien régime* and the Revolution.

By institutions we also refer to the institutional structures and political rules of the game of the current regime, the Fifth Republic. The Fifth Republic can boast itself the second longest surviving political regime in post-revolutionary French history. In terms of this most basic measurement, the regime must be considered a success. Its longevity has rested upon a combination of (relative) political stability, institutional adaptability and democratic legitimacy that has provided a just equilibrium. The early Fifth Republic restored political stability from the chronic precariousness of the post-war Fourth Republic, benefiting from the solid social institutions established by its predecessor and the fact that by the late 1950s the Cold War had entered a more stable phase. This was its first claim to legitimacy. More recently the regime has proved flexible and adaptable, most particularly in the alternation in power between right and left in 1981, and the repeated experiences of *cohabitation* (1986–88, 1993–95, 1997–02). *Cohabitation* has proved that the political regime has the capacity to withstand systemic pressures that commentators such as Goguel had predicted would hasten its demise. Indeed, there is an argument that the hybrid nature of the regime allows the flexibility and adaptability required of modern political institutions.

By changing institutional norms we also allude to changing beliefs in relation to what institutions and political offices can achieve. There has been a weakening of hyper-presidentialism since the first *cohabitation* in 1986. This reduced capacity of presidential leadership has arguably been fortuitous, given the changing context of state activity both at a domestic and a non-domestic level.

Changing patterns of central state steering

The history of France is to some extent the history of the French state and there is still a widespread positive connotation of the state as an instrument of public service and a guarantor of equality between French citizens. The equality and neutrality of the state form an important part of the French republican tradition. The scope of the public sector is not static; it varies according to changing norms and domestic or international policy fashions. After the discredit of the wartime Vichy regime, the state discovered new roles in the post-war period as an economic agent, and as provider of social welfare. In some cases, experiments made in the Vichy years, particularly in the field of economic interventionism, sowed the seeds of successful post-war management.[6]

The state became a first-rank economic actor in its own right. Though the importance of the five-year economic plans was often exaggerated, the state affirmed its presence as a key actor in the sphere of industrial policy, and its control over much financial investment. As in other Western European nations, the extension of the state's activity went beyond the economic sphere to encompass social protection and welfare. The creation of a comprehensive social security system remains one of the achievements of the post-war tripartite government. French levels of social protection are among the highest in the world. Life expectancy, educational achievement and health standards have improved consistently. These public services were won as social and political conquests. Safeguarding public services is perceived as an electoral imperative – and not just by the left parties – as former premier Juppé discovered to his cost in 1997.

Challenges to the French state have come from several directions. The interventionist state has ceded ground under the combined pressures of fiscal austerity, European regulation and international benchmarking. In the domestic arena, decentralisation reforms from the 1980s onwards have altered the nature of centre–periphery relations. Certain traditionally pre-eminent policy actors (those in the *grands corps* especially) have had to re-evaluate their positions, faced with a changing domestic and international environment. Though there remain close links between government and business, the French state no longer has the capacity to call the captains of industry to obey its orders.[7]

State retrenchment is not the only side of the story. There are some areas where the state has assumed new functions, in the field of health and social security in particular. The French state remains massively present throughout French territory and any attempts to slim down the state are met with determined resistance from civil servants and public sector workers. The ideology of public service is a powerful barrier to the perennial demand from economists for reform of the state. A total of 9 million people are treated in one capacity or another as servants of the state (including those on public sector pensions). Staff costs account for 40 per cent of the total state budget. Though the French state has lost functions, through privatisations and decentralisation, the number of civil servants has actually increased. The sheer size of the state is at the heart of the burgeoning pension crisis and impacts directly upon France's relationship with the European Union and the European Central Bank (ECB).

French governments have adopted various strategies to try and reform the state, particularly through using methods of contractualisation, decentralisation and the creation of new regulatory agencies. In recent decades governments in all European countries have been confronted with a weakening capacity to steer society by proposing solutions to the problems they have identified. In France, as in the United Kingdom and other EU states, the state can no longer assume alone the management of complexity but has had to reformulate its role.

The end of ideology?

Another fundamental change relates to the diminishing, though by no means vanquished, power of ideology to mobilise political action. Despite the plurality within both left and right, until (and including) 1981 each political camp was able to mobilise by referring to distinct sets of values. Whichever side one was on, the sense of identity and of belonging to one camp or another was strong. Since the Socialist experience in office (1981–86, 1988–93, 1997–02), and especially since the end of the Cold War, the ideological bearings of left and right have far more become confused. Put simply, the left/right cleavage is of less significance in French politics today than it was in 1980. The general ideological climate has changed, both in France and elsewhere, as have perceptions of the possibilities of governmental action. Marxism in particular has lost its attraction for the French left, as have May 1968-inspired ideas of *autogestion* (self-management). Values have tended to become more instrumental, elections more prone to the exigencies of political marketing and the circumstances of particular elections. The famous *variables à papa*, those underlying structures – class, religious affiliation, geographical location – that were long believed to be the real determinants of electoral behaviour and on which generations of French electoral sociologists since André Siegfried have based their work, are losing their explanatory power, as French voters seem more prone to short-term pressures and issues when they cast their ballots.

There are limits to this weakening capacity of ideology to drive action. In comparative terms, the discursive register of politics in France remains more ideologically structured than in the United Kingdom or Germany. There are important areas of non-decision making, where no government dares venture until forced to by impending crisis, in the case of pensions or public sector reform, for instance. In comparison with earlier periods of French history, however, the capacity of ideas to drive politics has diminished.

The challenge to the state-centred model of public policy making we noted above has been accompanied by the development of a domestic consensus on many, though by no means all, of the most important issues of public policy.

This is particularly the case in relation to economic policy. After the left's abandoning of Keynesian-style reflationary policies in 1982–83, and its modification of its traditional statism, the dividing line between left and right became blurred. The monetarist policies engaged by the French Socialists after 1983 were at least as rigorous as those undertaken by conservative administrations in other European countries. External constraints weighed increasingly heavily on the freedom of manoeuvre of governments from the mid-1980s onwards. In key sectors of domestic policy, difficult choices were imposed upon governments of all political complexions. Differences between left and right – over issues of economic management, at least – are those of degree. In the run-up to the creation of the euro, for instance, successive governments of right and left were both content to accept the purging from the economy of inflationary tendencies and the reduction of public debt as a prelude to future economic stability and growth, even though this harsh medicine was estimated to have cost at least one percentage point in growth per annum and tens of thousands of jobs. With constrained convergence on issues of economic management, the battleground between left and right in France is increasingly fought in the area of social and employment policies, security and civil liberties (the *pacte civil de solidarité*, or PACS, being perhaps the major plank in the Jospin government's social legislation). The range of economic options has narrowed under the impact of Europeanisation and globalisation that we now consider.

France, globalisation and foreign policy

Both European integration and globalisation have called into question many features associated with the traditional model of French politics and policies. The theme of Europeanisation has been dealt with in some detail elsewhere.[8] We will focus here on the complex and paradoxical relationship with globalisation.[9] There is a mainstream ideological reluctance in France to accept the ascendancy of 'neo-liberalism', that is, economic liberalism and unregulated international free markets. The poor score achieved by Alain Madelin in the 2002 presidential election demonstrated that there is a weak constituency for explicit liberalism. Apart from the Madelin tendency, right-wing parties in France seldom openly espouse liberalism. Except for a brief period in the 1980s, Gaullism has eschewed any reference to economic liberalism, while the centre-right has at most advocated social liberalism, split as it is between one-time social democrats, outright liberals of the Madelin type and the remnants of the Christian democratic tradition in France. Within the left, there have only been a handful of avowed social liberals. Former Premier Laurent Fabius and former Finance Minister Dominic Strauss-Kahn are two cases in point. We note with interest, however, that the former has been leading opposition to French ratification of the European constitution in the name of defending social Europe, while the latter was instrumental in drawing up the very statist strategy of the last Jospin government (the thirty-five-hour week and job-creation schemes) to combat unemployment. Social liberalism is a difficult *creneau*, or slot, to occupy within the culture of the French left.

Globalisation challenges the traditional French model in several ways. The global – American – model poses an obvious threat to a French culture that has always proclaimed itself to be universalist, quite apart from the menace caused to the French language by rampant American English. In the economic arena, global capitalism lessens the reliance of French business on the French state and increases the importance of international capital flows, cross-shareholdings and the international strategies of French groups, themselves very proficient at playing the global card. Inward investment decisions taken by foreign companies can have a major impact on French employment levels, but foreign companies are not usually willing to channel their investment in accordance with French regional policy objectives. Globalisation also threatens well entrenched domestic interests, especially in two very influential areas: culture and agriculture. In culture, French governments fought long and hard to obtain a 'cultural exception' in the 1993 General Agreement on Tariffs and Trade (GATT) round and are resisting attempts to dilute it in the latest round of World Trade Organisation (WTO) talks. One of the few social movements to have experienced real growth in the past few years is the anti-globalisation movement, symbolised by ATTAC and by José Bové, each interpreted as a defence of a particular vision of the French model. In agriculture, French governments of all persuasions have fought a rearguard action in the European Union and the WTO to defend the interests of domestic farmers through export credits and production subsidies. In short, globalisation lessens not only the capacity of the state to act in a voluntarist manner but also its ability to protect its key client groups.

If globalisation is usually construed mainly in economic terms, any discussion of it runs inevitably on to wider questions of foreign policy. In the bipolar world system of the Cold War, France had manoeuvred adroitly to preserve maximum autonomy in its foreign policy. Fourth Republic governments had quickly recognised the need for protection against possible Soviet pressure and signed France up to the North Atlantic Treaty Organisation (NATO). Implicit in this was clear acceptance of US hegemony, at least so far as defence was concerned. Increasing dissatisfaction with the perceived inadequacies of American support over a variety of issues, ranging from German rearmament to the colonial wars in Vietnam and Algeria, created, however, an audience for those who argued against excessive dependence on the United States. Thus de Gaulle was able by the mid-1960s to reposition France on the world stage. By removing French forces from NATO's integrated command structure, building up an autonomous French nuclear deterrent, pursuing diplomatic openings towards selected members of the Communist bloc and attempting to create privileged links with Africa in particular and underdeveloped countries in general, de Gaulle was able to profile France as firmly rooted within the Western camp but enjoying relative autonomy from the United States and attempting, however faintly, to offer a role model for medium-sized states aspiring to greater autonomy in their foreign policies.

Crucial to this strategy was French policy in Europe. Integration was pursued slowly, and increasingly the special Franco-German relationship[10] was used as the motor of Europe building; probably its most spectacular success was the European Monetary System (EMS), inaugurated by Helmut Schmidt and Valéry Giscard d'Estaing, which opened the route to the euro. As European integration developed, French strategists could imagine a *Europe-puissance*; the economic giant which was clearly emerging might begin to use its weight commensurately in the sphere of international politics. It might be able to represent a distinct type of political society (referred to variously as a 'European social model' or 'social market economy'), qualitatively distinct from that found in the United States or emergent Asian economies. If any of this were true, the question of Europe's and France's relationship with the United States would clearly recur in more pointed form.

Such was the situation when the Communist regimes collapsed and the world system moved overnight from a situation of bipolarity to one where the one remaining superpower was clearly dominant. At the same time, the main type of potential conflict changed; scenarios of a clash between NATO and Warsaw Pact forces in Germany had to be abandoned for a looser vision of security. Henceforth crises were more likely to occur at the periphery, most likely in the 'arc of crisis' said to run from Rabat to Basra.[11] They were more likely to be about territory, ethnic or religious conflict, or control of resources, than about the confrontation of capitalism and socialism. These clashes were far away and in many cases posed no direct threat, yet they would require a response from the West, that might be part diplomatic or economic, but would also involve a military component, whether peacekeeping or peace-making. Hence the development by all Western powers over the past fifteen years of highly specialised, mobile armed forces which can be rushed into situations anywhere once the political decision to intervene has been taken. The crises in the former Republic of Yugoslavia in the 1990s provided an early illustration of these themes, revealing *inter alia* the lack of capacity, both political and military, on the part of European states to deal with such problems. Both in Bosnia and Kosovo, the United States clearly forced the issue via NATO as European attempts to broker a solution foundered.

While useful lessons could clearly be learned from the Balkans, the problems there were relatively small in scale and could not be said in any way to represent a threat to Western interests. Hence disagreement between Europeans and Americans remained at a low level. The case of another sensitive point on the 'arc of crisis', however, brought out dramatically into the open the latent tensions between United States and European, especially French, perceptions. France is still struggling to digest the consequences of the Second Iraq War.

French opposition to a pre-emptive strike against Iraq was consistent and firm. Even during the first Gulf War, François Mitterrand had tried until very late in the day to broker a peaceful solution with the Baathist regime, and although French forces duly participated in the war, some on the US side had reservations about the quality of the effort.[12] French opposition to a second war was logical. For decades France had invested heavily in its *politique arabe*, cultivating regimes irrespective of their democratic credentials in the Middle East in return for economic and diplomatic gains. The down side of this process was the maintenance of a critical distance with Israel and therefore, to an extent, the incurring of US displeasure. From such a long-standing French perspective it was unlikely that Iraq would be perceived as constituting any kind of threat; attempts to link the militantly secularist Baathist regime with fundamentalist terrorism were seen as laughable in a secular republic. US strategy in the Gulf could only be seen in France not as an attempt to counter terrorism but as a drive to impose a politico-economic restructuring of the Middle East as a whole, starting from Iraq. Such a project was intrinsically dangerous and not necessarily in French interests, however much it might serve those of the United States and its major ally in the region, Israel. Hence French attempts to deny the United States any legitimacy for an invasion from the United Nations (UN). George W. Bush and Colin Powell believed, when they failed to put a final resolution to the UN Security Council, that France would veto it, even if it were to win a majority in the first place. Jacques Chirac made it clear that France would use its veto if necessary.

Iraq was, of course, always going to be invaded, with or without UN approval. The diplomatic battle in New York in the weeks prior to invasion involved more than just a show of strength on the part of the French, however; it was a test of their whole foreign policy. For Europe lay at the centre of the French–US dispute. Clearly if a united European response to the emergent crisis could be agreed early, then it was possible that the United States' hand might just be stayed. Such was the challenge facing the quai d'Orsay. Gerhardt Schröder's Germany came out strongly against intervention, in unheard-of defiance of US wishes, proving that the Franco-German tandem could still produce more than quick fixes on the renewal of the Common Agricultural Policy (CAP). But, in terms of major players in Europe, the French position found little further support. The governments in the United Kingdom, Spain and Italy were headed by men possessed of an unusually high degree of Atlanticist conviction; allied to the grateful leaders of the new EU entrants, recently rewarded with NATO membership also, they soon formed a pro-American bloc that neutered any idea of a critical EU position on the Iraq issue. Donald Rumsfeld, US Defense Secretary, described this crowingly as a victory for new Europe over old Europe. Since then France has been able to do little more than criticise from the side-lines, as the United States and its allies have encountered predictable difficulties in Iraq. Anger at French attempts to block what broad swathes of US opinion, as well as most of the political class, considered a legitimate self-defence operation has surfaced in various ways, ranging from boycotts of French products to media attacks on France as a nation, which say more about those conducting them than about their ostensible target.

Franco-American relations are at a low ebb, then, but this situation only mirrors the generally poor position of French foreign policy generally in a globalised world. It is clear now that Europe cannot be mobilised as a significant actor on any major global issue where the United States has decisive unilateral views. The Franco-German axis has shown its limits, the more so as, cruelly, the enlarged Europe welcomed by so many has proved to be unruly and refractory to Franco-German leadership. The drift towards a much more intergovernmentalist Europe, with possible enhanced co-operation between groups of willing countries in selected issue areas, offers no prospect of greater unity in international affairs. Even the development of a common security policy, thought by some to offer one way towards more integrated action in foreign affairs, has received a huge setback from the Iraq crisis. In addition to the cost implications which already beset it,[13] it is now clear that the deadlock between those who, like France, seek the development of an integrated, autonomous European military capacity and those who, following the United Kingdom, insist on linking any European capacity firmly to NATO, cannot be resolved to the advantage of the autonomists. Faced with this bleak position, French policy makers could only cling to the slim hope that a change of presidency in the United States might show more desire for genuine multilateral consultation with European partners. But the future of French–US relations is likely to take place in a context where US power cannot really be modified significantly by a Europe which remains divided and which French or Franco-German leadership cannot pull together. *Europe-puissance* is no match for *Amérique-puissance*.

In their strongest definition, Europeanisation and globalisation both appear to challenge many traditional French public policy preferences. Rather than specific policies, however, Europeanisation and globalisation can both appear to go against the grain of *une certaine idée de la France*. The belief in the universal mission of French civilisation is menaced by European integration *and* by globalisation once European construction becomes a melting pot of European cultural influences rather than a mirror to reflect French grandeur or a policy space to regulate world capitalism.

Republicanism, social movements and the public sphere

Europeanisation and globalisation each pose questions that go the heart of the traditional republican model of citizenship, predicated upon a direct relationship between the national community and the citizen. At a different level of analysis, regionalism, group identities and multi-ethnicity raise similar questions. Postwar social change has tended to enhance the sense of national community – up to a point. As old cleavages based on class and subcultural identity have diminished, new ones have emerged, notably those tied to the advent of a post-industrial, cosmopolitan, spatially differentiated and ethnically more diverse society. They have given rise to a new pattern of social movement activity. We would highlight the importance of political and associative ecology, the women's movement and local groups of all shades and varieties. Whether the rise of new social movement activity is testament to a new style of civic participation or not is debatable, but it marks a noticeable shift in patterns of interest articulation.[14]

In spite of the rise in voluntary associations, the environment is not particularly conducive to the expression of difference. Equality is an important part of the French reference frame. A demand for equal treatment underpins the French republican model, the glue that binds the rich diversity of territories that together constitute contemporary France. We must not forget that the republican form of government itself was vigorously contested by powerful sections of French society for 150 years after the French Revolution. The efforts of republicans to inculcate a universal model of French citizenship were broadly inspired by ideals of the Enlightenment and the legacy of the French Revolution. The question today is not whether the republican founding fathers acted in good faith, but rather whether the defence of the Republic can continue to be used as a legitimate excuse to suppress any deviation from a centrally defined norm. The French model of republican citizenship has great difficulty in accepting diversity and hence in adapting to the reality of a multi-ethnic, regionally differentiated society.

The lay republican model posits an unmediated relationship between the citizen and the state. In the republican conception, all citizens are created equal and are members of a national political community. They owe their allegiance to the nation as a whole, rather than to ethnic or interest groups. From the republican perspective, intermediary associations are bearers of particularist agendas and pose a threat to national identity and cohesion. This spirit is exemplified by the Revolution's Le Chapelier laws of 1791 that banned most intermediary associations and was not repealed until 1905. Matters of personal belief are given constitutional recognition, but they are expected to be confined to the private sphere. The public sphere ought to be neutral, with no ties with religion. Initially anticlerical, in the sense of combating the negative influence of the Catholic Church, this belief has expanded to refer to all religious groups. Indeed, it has extended beyond religion to include minorities, and the specific recognition of identity-based group rights. If the French political community is open to all, regardless of ethnicity or origin, central to becoming 'French' is socialisation into French values, including respect of the neutrality of the public sphere. Faced with this powerful republican frame of reference, it has been difficult to ground an agenda of positive discrimination in France, even in the minds of feminist groups.[15] There is some sign that France is changing here; the parity reforms have forbidden sexual discrimination and created quotas for women on party lists. Measures in the field of education have also targeted resources to underprivileged areas and sought to create equal outcomes, rather than equality of opportunity.

As Gino Raymond demonstrates in Chapter 1, the French model of republican citizenship has been a dichotomous construction from its inception. In theory, there is a strict republican dichotomy between public and private spheres. In practice, there has been a long tradition of formal rules and negotiating exceptions to rules. While formal rules stress uniformity, exceptions to rules have allowed a state-centric polity to adapt to territorial, social and religious pressures. While public schools are seen to embody republican citizenship, for example, ever since the Debré law of 1959 there has been a *de facto* compromise between Church and State. The Republic has shown itself to be much more flexible in practice than in theory to its various religious groups, demonstrated by public support for mosque-building programmes or by the practice of 'contracted-in' Catholic schools.

The headscarves affair of 2003–04 symbolised these conflicting pressures. On the one hand there were those who championed the Jacobin notion of the one and indivisible Republic and the concept of secularity. The principle of secularity is one traditionally espoused by the left, and this dates back to the Third Republic, when, as a result of the laws of 1881 and 1882, national unity was cemented by a system of secular schools. The separation of Church and State became law in 1905. According to the partisans of this vision of society, Muslim girls wearing the veil at school were negating republican values, since they were visibly differentiating themselves from other pupils and in so doing drawing attention to their religion. The secular school should permit no distinct sign indicating the religious denomination of the pupil. Instead, the defenders of the traditional republican vision argued that Islam, and indeed any religion, should be practised in private, and that preferably Muslims should be persuaded to endorse secular values. The supporters of the notion of secularity included many Socialist MPs and intellectuals of the left such as Elisabeth Badinter.

In the opposing camp are those who have forged close links with minority groups in French society, or who believe that the Jacobin vision no longer corresponds to the realities of life in contemporary French society and most certainly does not reflect the diversity of its population. According to the proponents of this vision, Islam ought not to be considered incompatible with the rules, institutions and values of French society. These positions are not clearly demarcated along lines of left and right. Former Interior and Finance Minister Nicolas Sarkozy was one of the leading opponents of the 2004 law: President Chirac its leading protagonist. Perhaps the most fundamental point raised by the 2003–04 debate on *laïcité*, however, was that left and right are now closer to each other in relation to defining the conditions of French citizenship than is either with the domestic far left or the far right, or, indeed, with rival English-speaking or Germanic notions of citizenship. The French polity more explicitly demands respect for a form of 'thin universalism' than do others, though this is to some extent a matter of degree.

The problem of political legitimacy

The 2002 electoral series posed starkly the issue of political legitimacy.[16] Let us recall some simple facts. Jacques Chirac and Lionel Jospin, the announced second-round contenders, obtained only just over one-third of votes and one-quarter of registered electors between them. France's historic political families were each challenged on 21 April 2002: Communists, Socialists, Gaullists, Liberals, Christian Democrats, even Greens. None of these candidates performed as well as they might have expected and many electors were dissatisfied with all of them. The strong performance of the far-left and far-right candidates, the high abstention rate (at 28.3 per cent, a record in any presidential election) and the general dispersion of votes to candidates not generally considered to be genuine presidential contenders, such as St Josse, Chevènement and others, were all part of this trend. Once again, the election went against the incumbent government, as has every decisive election since 1978, except where, as in 1981, 1988 and 2002, parliamentary elections have followed shortly after the presidential contest. The exceptional nature of Chirac's second-round victory on 5 May 2002 could not conceal his poor performance on 21 April 2002 (19.1 per cent), and this provided a narrow basis for holding all the key offices of the Republic. While clarifying institutional practice in a pro-presidential sense, the electoral series of 2002 left many questions unanswered, the most important of which was whether France's new rulers would be able to build bridges with that sizeable proportion of the electorate that appears alienated from political processes and takes refuge in support for extremes.

The emblematic event of the 2002 presidential election was the breakthrough of the far-right Front national candidate Jean-Marie Le Pen to the second round. As ever, Le Pen offered a real choice. Taken together, the two candidates of the far right – Le Pen and Megret – polled 19.2 per cent, which, put in context, was more in mainland France than Jospin and the Communist Robert Hue combined. Le Pen's accession to the second round was the story of the election. By comparison with his past demagogic campaigns, in 2002 Le Pen adopted the mantle of elder statesman, confidently expecting that events and the security-focused campaigns fought by most of the other candidates would play into his hands. Le Pen's electorate embodied a popular France down on its luck. It was more masculine than feminine and older rather than younger. More than ever, the Le Pen electorate was over-representative of those suffering from the most acute sentiments of economic and physical insecurity. It is the least well educated electorate of the three main candidates. Le Pen was the favoured choice of the lower middle classes (31.9 per cent) and of workers (26.1 per cent), far outdistancing both the Socialist Jospin and the Communist Robert Hue in working-class support. The French electorate's vote on 21 April 2002 suggests an unresolved tension between French identity, the implicit promises of French citizenship (including the economic promises) and the uncertainty provoked by Europeanisation, globalisation and an unpredictable future.

The 2002 electoral series articulated, in an exaggerated manner, trends that have become increasingly apparent since 1981. While the early Fifth

Republic could claim to have restored political stability, there has developed a tendency for incumbent governments to lose elections, a new 'iron law of anti-incumbency'. Governments have once again become short-lived and *cohabitation* has become an increasingly regular occurrence. Alongside a pattern of increased electoral volatility (each election since 1978 going against the incumbent government), we observe a disaffection towards traditional politics, as demonstrated in higher abstention rates and the weakening of the mainstream parties. Both the regional and the European elections of 2004 continued the habit of punishing the incumbent government but did show some movement away from the smaller protest parties and back towards the mainstream. It is unclear how far the tightening up of the electoral law was responsible for this or how far it represents a more resigned or realistic mood on the part of voters. Certainly, over recent years, the main developments in the French party system confirm these trends.

Institutions, ideas and interests: the continuity of the French model

We have insisted in this chapter on the changing French polity, upon challenges to the traditional French model by a combination of external and internal forces. The other side of the coin of change is that of continuity. We set out in Table 2.2 areas of continuity and change in the contemporary French polity.

The continuity of the French model is provided by an interconnecting set of institutions, interests and ideas that provide long-term cohesion and allow internal and external changes to be interpreted in ways that are comprehensible to the French. In relation to institutions, we revisit the distinction we drew above between the Fifth Republic and deeper institutions that are not specific to a particular regime. As far as the Fifth Republic is concerned, the converging of the presidential and parliamentary majorities in the 2002 elections and the subordinate relationship of the latter to the former would appear to signal a return to a pre-eminently presidential practice. After the experience of the third *cohabitation* from 1997 to 2002, presidentialism was reaffirmed as the key organising principle of the Fifth Republic in 2002. The underlying legitimacy of the system is shaped by the choices made by all key actors in favour of the presidential election as the decisive election in the Fifth Republic. A President genuinely representing the French nation was provided by the electorate with a 'clear and consistent' majority, as he had requested. Better still, the electoral series was crowned by an overall majority in seats for the new-style presidential party, the best performance of a right-wing presidential rally since the heyday of Gaullism. Excepting unforeseen circumstances, the five-year Parliament elected in 2002 will coincide with a five-year term in office for President Chirac.

The case for continuity is strengthened once we move from the formal institutional superstructure to deeper institutions, those which go to the heart of the state and which defend the French state tradition. These institutions are the civil service (*fonction publique*) and the interests to which this gives rise, the

Table 2.2 *Continuities and changes in the Fifth Republic*

Continuities	Changes
Executive bias in the 1958 constitution. Parliament subordinate. Weak checks and balances	Emergence of counterweights to executive power (judicial, electoral, social)
Principle of presidential initiative (except *cohabitation*)	Adaptability and flexibility of the institutional architecture: *cohabitation*
Institutional 'rules of the game' intact: electoral system; separation of presidential/parliamentary mandates	Reduction of presidential mandate to five years
Tradition of top-down policy making: remnants of *dirigisme* (e.g. aerospace, pharmaceuticals)	End of heroic policy making and industrial *dirigisme*? Impact of Europeanisation/globalisation. Acceptance of privatisation
Formal, bipolar party system	Party system change: emergence of new parties, especially FN; decline of PCF
French state tradition remains strong, especially elite recruitment (ENA, *grandes écoles*)	Political and administrative decentralisation; reshaping of the French state. Weakening of *grands corps*
Processes of socialisation; centralised education system, pedagogic uniformity	Timid decentralisation and Europeanisation in this sphere
Political discourse based on general will	Less scope for political voluntarism
French 'leadership' in Europe	Changing equilibrium within EU, notably within the hollow core of the Franco-German partnership

Council of State and the Constitutional Council. In September 2002 the national statistical office INSEE published a report concluding with the impossibility of controlling the size of the civil service and the public sector in general. The number of civil servants had increased by 10 per cent over the last ten years, in spite of a permanent campaign to reduce their number and the creation of a division specifically designed to achieve that effect. The number of employees of the Education Ministry is now 1,200,000, a number inflated by the Jospin government's youth employment programme and the decision to reward a number of these employees with permanent tenure. The same conclusion could be applied to the police, a predicable consequence of the concern of public opinion with security. These internally driven, path-dependent processes render more difficult the reform of the state to which all politicians are, in theory, committed. The other institutions mentioned – the Council of State and the Constitutional Council – act as real brakes on change, or least the type of change that concerns us in this chapter. The problem lies not just with the institutions but with the constitution they are sworn to uphold. The creation of new regulatory agencies in spheres such as telecommunications is certainly important, but the overarching existence of a system of public law closely monitored by a rather conservative Council of State is probably more significant. These institutions too often reject changes that challenge a rather conservative republican uniformity.

Continuity is provided not just by institutions but also by interests and ideas. Existing institutions are defended by sets of interests that occupy a precise position within the French state (and which rely on the state to promote their interests in Brussels and elsewhere). The role of the farm lobby is very well documented in shaping the position adopted by French governments of all persuasions in international arenas, whether the European Union, the WTO or elsewhere. The farmers are an easy target, as is the teaching profession, routinely fingered as the culprit for preventing any profound reform of the Education Ministry. Equally remarkable has been the role of the medical profession, at the heart of the efficient functioning of the French social security system. Suleiman demonstrated years ago how the *notaires'* profession has resisted with ease various attempts at reform by governments of left and right.[17] In short, powerful interests in the state and civil society generally frustrate reform, as repeatedly demonstrated during the Jospin and Raffarin governments. Established positions are very difficult to challenge, hence reinforcing the model of routine authoritarianism and sporadic direct action much beloved of the classical commentators. Underpinning institutions and interests are a set of well defined ideas, about the appropriate relationships between politics and economics, about the role of the individual and society and about the need for equal treatment, to which political discourse needs to appeal. These ideas generally consolidate existing preferences and practices. Ideas, such as the general will, equal treatment, solidarity, support the concatenation of interests and institutions that promote stability, to the extent that sectional groups seek to capture these ideas in order to defend their own causes.

Conclusion

France has been subject to intense pressure for change since the late 1970s. As a leading European nation with a particular state tradition and historical legacy, endogenous and exogenous pressures have challenged the traditional French model at least as much as in any comparable country. French politics and public policy making have become far less introspective. The strains and stresses within French politics itself have produced some seismic shocks. On the other hand, there is also much evidence of French resistance to unwelcome external ideas such as 'neo-liberalism'. There are deep obstacles to reform from entrenched domestic interests, as illustrated during the Jospin and Raffarin governments by the difficulty of implementing policy reforms in the education or fiscal administrations. The French polity has indeed mutated under the combined impact of internal and external pressures for change. But, in many important respects, French elites have dealt with external and internal challenges in ways that are consistent with the overarching national traditions explored earlier. The institutions, interests and ideas that together comprise the French model of politics and policy-making have proved remarkably resilient in the face of so many challenges.

The orthodox model has been challenged from numerous directions that we develop in successive chapters. As France moves into the twenty-first century we can safely predict that the French polity will continue to adapt to processes of domestic and external change and slowly transform itself in the process.

Notes

1 D. Hanley, *Party, Society, Government: Republican Democracy in France* (London: Berghahn, 2002).
2 A. Knapp and V. Wright, *The Government and Politics of France*, 3rd edn (London: Routledge, 2001).
3 J. March and J. Olsen, *Rediscovering Institutions* (New York: Free Press, 1989).
4 G. Peters, *Institutional Theory in Political Science: The 'New Institutionalism'* (London: Cassell, 1999).
5 R. Elgie, *Political Institutions in Contemporary France* (Oxford: Oxford University Press, 2003).
6 R. Kuisel, *Capitalism and the State in Modern France* (Cambridge: Cambridge University Press, 1981).
7 V. Schmidt, *From State to Market? The Transformation of French Business and Government* (Cambridge: Cambridge University Press, 1996); V. Schmidt, *The Futures of European Capitalism* (Oxford: Oxford University Press, 2001).
8 A. Cole and H. Drake, 'The europeanisation of French polity? Continuity, change and adaptation', *Journal of European Public Policy*, 7:1 (2001), 26–43; A. Smith, *Le Gouvernement de l'Union européenne : une sociologie politique* (Paris: LGDJ, 2004).
9 M. McClean and S. Milner (eds), 'France and globalisation', special issue of *Modern and Contemporary France*, 9:3 (2001).
10 A. Cole, *Franco-German Relations* (Harlow: Longman, 2001).
11 G. Joffé and C. Gastgeier, *European Security and the new Arc of Crisis*, Adelphi Paper 265 (London: IISS, 1991–92); E. Mortimer, *European Security after the Cold War*, Adelphi Paper 271 (London: IISS, 1992).
12 L. Fawcett and R. O'Neill, 'Britain, the Gulf crisis and European security', in N. Gnesotto and J. Roper (eds), *Western Europe and the Gulf* (Paris: West European Union Institute of Security Studies, 1992), pp. 141–58.
13 P. Buffotot (ed.), *La Défense en Europe : nouvelles réalités, nouvelles ambitions* (Paris: Documentation française, 2001).
14 S. Waters, *New Social Movements in France* (London: Palgrave Macmillan, 2003).
15 A. Mazur, 'Gendering the Fifth Republic: new beginnings or the legacy of the past?', in A. Cole, J. Levy and P. Le Galès (eds), *Developments in French Politics III* (Basingstoke: Palgrave, 2005).
16 J. Gaffney (ed.), *The French Presidential and Legislative Elections of 2002* (Aldershot: Ashgate, 2004).

17 E. Suleiman, *Private Power and Centralization in France: The Notaires and the State* (Princeton NJ: Princeton University Press, 1987).

Select bibliography

P. Buffotot (ed.), *La Défense en Europe : nouvelles réalités, nouvelles ambitions* (Paris: Documentation française, 2001).

A. Cole, *Franco-German Relations* (Harlow: Longman, 2001).

A. Cole and H. Drake, 'The europeanisation of French polity? Continuity, change and adaptation', *Journal of European Public Policy*, 7:1 (2001), 26–43.

R. Elgie, *Political Institutions in Contemporary France* (Oxford: Oxford University Press, 2003).

J. Gaffney (ed.), *The French Presidential and Legislative Elections of 2002* (Aldershot: Ashgate, 2004).

D. Hanley, *Party, Society, Government: Republican Democracy in France* (London: Berghahn, 2002).

G. Joffé and C. Gastgeier, *European Security and the new Arc of Crisis*, Adelphi Paper 265 (London: IISS, 1991–92).

A. Knapp and V. Wright, *The Government and Politics of France*, 3rd edn (London: Routledge, 2001).

R. Kuisel, *Capitalism and the State in Modern France* (Cambridge: Cambridge University Press, 1981).

J. March and J. Olsen, *Rediscovering Institutions* (New York: Free Press, 1989).

M. McClean and S. Milner (eds), 'France and globalisation', special issue of *Modern and Contemporary France*, 9:3 (2001).

E. Mortimer, *European Security after the Cold War*, Adelphi Paper 271 (London: IISS, 1992).

G. Peters, *Institutional Theory in Political Science: The 'New Institutionalism'* (London: Cassell, 1999).

V. Schmidt, *From State to Market? The Transformation of French Business and Government* (Cambridge: Cambridge University Press, 1996).

V. Schmidt, *The Futures of European Capitalism* (Oxford: Oxford University Press, 2001).

A. Smith, *Le Gouvernement de l'Union européenne : une sociologie politique* (Paris: LGDJ, 2004).

A. Stone, *The Birth of Judicial Politics in France: The Constitutional Council in Comparative Perspective* (Oxford: Oxford University Press, 1992).

E. Suleiman, *Private Power and Centralization in France: The Notaires and the State* (Princeton NJ: Princeton University Press, 1987).

S. Waters, *New Social Movements in France* (London: Palgrave Macmillan, 2003).

3

Politics on the periphery: Brittany and republican France

Alistair Cole

In the opinion of one Breton autonomist interviewed in the summer of 2001, the French nation-state was imposed by 'blood, sweat and tears'. Through a gradual and uneven process of territorial aggrandisement and military conquest France was constructed as a state-nation, with a determined central authority gradually imposing a single national identity upon various territorial, linguistic and religious identities. French nationhood was imposed upon mainly unwilling provinces by a succession of kings, and later by the Revolution. The French Revolution gave rise to a universalist concept of citizenship and nationhood, postulating equal rights and duties for all French citizens. The classic republican tradition modelled France as a nation which is one and indivisible, made up of a politically homogeneous citizenry. As it emerged historically – and as certain politicians would like to restore it today – the French republican tradition did not easily accommodate difference, especially at regional level. In one version of the republican tradition, territorial (especially regional) identities are considered a threat to the direct relationship between citizens and the nation.

In this chapter we focus upon Brittany, one of France's most easily identifiable regions. Through intensive interviews with around eighty actors in 2001 and 2002, and a mass survey carried out in 2001, we seek to provide answers to a number of pertinent questions that relate to the overarching themes of this book. How is the French tradition of unitary government mediated by local and regional variations? Why are successful forms of regional advocacy successful? How do citizens reconcile their multiple and overlapping identities? What does the treatment of regional minorities tell us about the construction of the French republican state itself? Before addressing these questions, however, we begin with a presentation of the French unitary state model.

In his conceptual map of Europe, Stein Rokkan identified three types of European state: the strong empire-nations of the Atlantic west; the economically weaker states of the eastern plains; and the states of imperial central Europe, unified only in the nineteenth century.[1] Like the United Kingdom,

France formed part of the Atlantic seaboard states, with a strong central authority and powerful economic resources. France is usually considered as the archetype of the unitary state, with a coherent doctrine of undivided political sovereignty that breaks decisively with the federal tradition. Modern France also contains several regions with highly distinctive identities of which Brittany, Alsace, the Basque country, Corsica and Savoy are the most obvious examples. France is not alone in this respect. Most European Union (EU) states were created through the triumph of one ethnic group over another. Nations were built by core hegemonic groups, such as the Piedmontese in Italy, the English in Britain, the Castilians in Spain, the Franks in France, the Prussians in Germany, the Walloons in Belgium. Consistent with Rokkan's schema, minority 'nations', such as the Bretons, were assimilated by the dominant group in the early sixteenth century, at the early modern stage of state formation.

In France the idea of the nation was driven from the fifteenth century onwards by an ambitious, theoretically absolutist monarchy, which succeeded in imposing its control on a large number of previously independent principalities (in Normandy, Brittany, Aquitaine, Burgundy, Provence, Savoy and so on). In spite of military conquest, diplomatic manoeuvre and civil war, the pre-revolutionary French monarchy kept the form of a union state, its constituent parts (such as Brittany) being incorporated by means of treaty and agreement and being guaranteed certain privileges. The convoking of the provincial *parlements* until 1789 embodied these rights, though in practice the power of the *parlements* had waned since the absolutist monarchy of Louis XIV (1648–1715). The French Revolution of 1789 swept away all vestiges of provincial autonomy and created a sophisticated administrative infrastructure whereby the French state penetrated down to the smallest towns and localities. Post-revolutionary France constructed powerful homogenising institutions, with an egalitarian institution-focused appeal (the public schools, the army, the Republic). In this way, French nationalism proved highly attractive, including in 'peripheral' regions such as Brittany where state modernisation offered the prospect of social mobility.[2] The French state project was based on transcending 'archaic', pre-modern identities and building a modern, unified nation-state, based on respect for universal values. Irrespective of their origins, citizens had a duty to conform to central norms, as they would become peers with equal access to a set of universal rights and obligations. The state project was deliberately designed to be attractive to provincial elites, for whom ascending to Paris was the height of social achievement.

The traditional French unitary state model has become much less pertinent since the decentralisation reforms of the early 1980s, a theme we develop elsewhere.[3] Even today, for many French citizens, ideas of decentralisation are synonymous with social regression, unequal provision and a return to a pre-republican social order. Upstanding republicans equate territorial uniformity with notions of progress, equal opportunity and citizenship. The building of France as a modern nation-state provides the key to understanding this

equation of territorial identity and political reaction. Regional political forma-
tions are, almost by definition, suspected by a certain brand of republican of
anti-republican intent. The French state-building enterprise has, historically
speaking, been remarkably successful in inculcating deeply rooted beliefs
linking the national territory with social progress. We touch here at the core of
state sovereignty which, in the French case, is intimately tied in with perceptions of national prestige and territorial hierarchy. It is against this powerful
institutional legacy that we consider the case of the French region of Brittany.
In this chapter we investigate themes of multiple identities, institutional loyalties and the advocacy of Breton interests. We focus successively upon French
and Breton political and cultural movements, upon the 'policy community' in
Brittany and upon public opinion. Underpinning our investigation of regionalism in Brittany lie more fundamental questions of identity, citizenship and post-
republican realities in contemporary France. We begin by presenting a short
history of Brittany.

A short history of Brittany

One of the most distinctive regions of France, Brittany has a strong sense of its
specific position within French society.[4] First an independent monarchy
(845–938), then a duchy (938–1532), then a French province with special
prerogatives (1532–1789), reduced for long to being a collection of disparate
départements before becoming an administrative then political region in 1982,
modern Brittany is a French region with a difference. Unlike many other French
regions, Brittany can look to its past existence as an independent duchy, with
its own institutions and founding myths. Though the symbols of statehood
have long been suppressed, the region retains many distinct characteristics.
The Breton language is the European continent's only Celtic language. The
enduring symbolic importance of the Catholic religion is ever present physically in the architecture of Breton villages, as well as in higher than average
rates of religious practice. The spectacular growth of Breton cultural movements (music, dance, theatre, costume) is testament to a revival of Breton
values and consciousness. At a more abstract level, observers have noted the
capacity of Breton actors to join forces to promote their common interests and
to defend Brittany against attacks from the outside world.[5] Breton solidarity can
also be gauged more intuitively by the effectiveness of Breton elite-level networks in Paris and Brussels, and by the importance of the Breton diaspora in
retaining a sense of distinctiveness.

Brittany is sometimes taken as a litmus test of the health of regional identity
within France. In historical terms, Brittany corresponds well to one of those
regions, identified by Rokkan and Urwin,[6] in which the development of
regional consciousness is a function of economic dependence and the persistence of a strong cultural identity. Bretons speak with pride of their nation as a
prosperous maritime power from the fifteenth century to the eighteenth, an

outward-looking region/nation with an important position along the Atlantic trading routes. The prosperity of Breton ports was testimony to its maritime vocation. Brittany also had a thriving business culture, centred around textiles and commerce.[7] The decline of Brittany from the eighteenth century onwards is sometimes linked with its political and economic union with France. Brittany was integrated into the French tariff system under Louis XIV in the late seventeenth century. As a result of integration into French markets and French protectionist economic policies, Brittany was cut off from its main trading partners, notably the British Isles and the Caribbean. By the end of the nineteenth century Brittany was the poorest mainland French region, and also the one with the highest level of emigration. With few natural resources, Brittany missed out on the industrial revolution. It was forced back into subsistence agriculture, notwithstanding the poor quality of most arable land. There were no large cities and only a few medium-sized towns. There was a weak indigenous bourgeoisie, with no financial or human capital concentration. Brittany became a reservoir of labour for the more industrial regions. The ideology of republicanism itself favoured emigration away from peripheral areas such as Brittany and drained the most productive forces to Paris.

This legacy of impoverishment and internal colonisation remains very present in the minds of the Bretons today (especially the Paris-based diaspora), as illustrated by the following testimony from a former (Breton) president of a Parisian higher education institute:

> Brittany has a strong sense of its identity, which is by no means dead. It is a region that was for long despised and mocked from outside (the region of 'Becassine', the stupid domestic help). It gave the impression of being a backward zone, a place where half the people were always drunk and the other half were suffering from a hangover. Back then Brittany was a poor region, marked by an exodus from rural areas to Paris. Bretons would enter domestic service for Paris households. This gave a very unfavourable image of Brittany, an image in which the inhabitants had great difficulty in understanding French and were in thrall to the Catholic Church.[8]

The rapid demographic and economic expansion of Brittany during the post-war years has been all the more remarkable. From being the poorest French region in 1945, Brittany had climbed much closer to the national average by 2003.[9] The post-war period has been marked by heavy inward investment into the region, first from the French state in the 1950s and 1960s and, more recently, from foreign direct investment. Brittany has enjoyed strong rates of economic growth (testament to the modernisation of its agricultural sector), external investment in high-technology sectors such as telecommunications, defence and health and a specific pattern of multipolar spatial development. These developments have been facilitated by the reputation for conscientiousness of a well trained work force and by the Brittany region regularly boasting the highest educational standards in France at age eighteen. External stimuli have combined with an original model of indigenous economic development, in part based upon the co-operative mode of governance we identify below.

At the core of this spatial network is the city of Rennes, the capital of the administrative region of Brittany. Pre-1945 Rennes was a modest regional capital, dominated by the army, the legal profession, the regional offices of government departments and Rennes University. Rennes expanded very rapidly during the post-war period, with its population doubling from 100,000 to 200,000 inhabitants between 1950 and 1980, the population of the wider Rennes metropolitan district increasing to 333,000 in the 1999 census. Rennes is an important centre of public sector employment as a result of housing the city's university and research institutes, its large hospital serving the Brittany region and its status as a regional capital. Rennes has a modest industrial sector (the car manufacturer Citroën and the publisher Ouest-France are the two main private employers), offset by a large and diversified small and medium business culture, with particular strengths in transport, food processing and telecommunications. Even after continuous post-war growth, Rennes remains only one of several medium-sized Breton towns operating within a larger regional and national context. According to Phlipponeau[10] the specificity of the Breton industrial model lay in its multipolar nature. Post-war economic development involved a dense network of medium-sized towns, alongside the growth of the capital Rennes. These small and medium-sized towns included Redon, Vitré, Lannion, Brest, Morlaix, Vannes, Quimper and Lorient. Much of the more dynamic growth was concentrated in towns smaller than Rennes, of which Lannion provided the model.[11]

Rennes is also a contested regional capital. Breton autonomists are dismissive of Rennes as the 'first station on the Paris Metro' and argue strongly that the historic capital Nantes should be recognised as the Breton capital. The competition between Rennes and Nantes clouds somewhat the issue of whether Brittany should recover its the fifth 'lost' department, the Loire-Atlantique and its capital Nantes. Many, perhaps most, Bretons do not simply identify their region with the geographical boundaries of the current regional institution, but see it also as including the fifth 'lost' *département* of Loire-Atlantique (removed from Brittany by Marshall Pétain in June 1941). Our survey in June 2001 revealed powerful public support for the reunification of historic Brittany (over 62 per cent strongly in favour or in favour), a sentiment shared across the political and geographical spectrum, with only minor variations according to *département*, partisan allegiance or other variables.[12] On 30 June 2001 – sixty years after the division of historic Brittany – a mass demonstration took place in Nantes in favour of reunification. The Loire-Atlantique departmental council then unanimously voted a motion in favour of being incorporated into Brittany. Unanimity was short-lived, however, as in October 2001 the Rennes municipal council opposed unification; a reunified Brittany would challenge the leading role of the Breton capital.

One of the most remarkable features of post-war Brittany has been the transformation of the Catholic Church. While the Church had been closely associated with anti-republicanism, in the post-1945 period there was a major shift. As part of the reconciliation with republican democracy and modern society that culminated in Vatican II in 1964, the Church created a dense network of youth organisations that had a massive impact in Catholic Brittany. The Young Christian Farmers association (Jeunesse agricole chrétienne, JAC) in particular had a major influence in Brittany and became one of the channels through which farm leaders became convinced of the importance of modernisation and technical progress. In the appreciation of one interviewee:

> Everything is linked with the transformation of Catholicism. The silent revolution in farming is at the heart of post-war economic development. The leaders of the young Christian organisations [JEC/ JOC/JAC] played a very important role here, not least in creating the FNSEA as a modern farming union and in convincing Breton peasants to espouse modern farming techniques. In turn, Brittany produced its own very powerful agri-business. The Church fully supported this effort of economic and social modernisation. Brittany is today one of France's principal farm export regions and a leader in agri-business.

The Breton miracle has turned a little sour since the mid-1990s. Heavy investments in telecommunications or defence have produced excess capacity. Medium-sized towns such as Lannion have paid the price for the dot-com collapse in 2000–01, while defence cut-backs from the early 1990s onwards have hit Brest and Lorient hard. The core farming communities in central and west Brittany have suffered from reforms of the Common Agricultural Policy (CAP) and the drying up of EU subsidies. And yet the picture presented by Brittany in 2005 is starkly different from that in the 1950s. The legendary Breton pessimism has given way to a sense of achievement and regional pride. We now consider how the party system in Brittany has facilitated the construction of a regional belief system based upon the value of cross-partisan consensus and the advocacy of the Breton cause in higher arenas.

The party system in Brittany

If all main political tendencies have been well represented in post-war Brittany (except the Front national, FN) the prevalent post-war political tradition is best described as one of political centrism. In the immediate post-war period Brittany was the birthplace and one of the bastions of French Christian democracy and, though in decline, powerful vestiges remain. With the creation of the Fifth Republic, Brittany could not resist the national pull of Gaullism, and the region's first three presidents were all Gaullists. Brittany also contributed markedly to the rise of the new Socialist Party (PS) from the 1970s onwards, with the Socialist Party in Brittany subtly imbued with values representative of the underlying Breton political culture, notably left Catholicism and social partnership.[13] The French Communist Party (PCF) also established its own strongholds in the 'red triangle' of north-west and central Brittany and was supportive from an early date of many of the Breton movement's 'anti-colonial' demands.[14] Long resistant to national trends, the decline of the PCF in Brittany has threatened the survival of an original model of rural Communism, largely to the benefit of the PS. Only the far-right FN has failed to establish solid bases in Brittany, outside one or two pockets of support (notably in La Trinité sur Mer, birthplace of Jean-Marie Le Pen, leader of the FN). The case of the FN illustrates well the innate cohesion of Breton political culture. Having been spared the ravages of excessive urbanisation, industrial decline and unemployment, Brittany's social networks have remained largely intact, providing a barrier to the breakthrough of the far right movement.

Political traditions in Brittany have been deeply influenced by Catholicism, by the Catholic Church and by Christian democratic ideas. A local branch of the Catholic union, the CFTC, was created in Rennes as early as 1925.[15] The city became one of the citadels of Christian democracy; in 1945 four out of seven Ille-et-Vilaine Deputies belonged to the Christian democratic Popular Republican Movement (MRP). The decline of French Christian democracy since the 1960s has favoured both the Gaullists and most especially the Socialists. In the 1970s the Socialists made considerable local inroads, with the PS winning a string of town halls in 1977 (in Rennes, Brest, Lorient, Saint-Brieuc), most of which have remained with the party ever since. The PS in Brittany in the 1970s appeared as the inheritor of the reformist tradition that had been alive in the left wing of the MRP. The PS was renovated in Brittany by forces from outside the old Socialist Party, the SFIO: these included former PSU activists, members of regionalist political clubs and associative movements, left Catholic groups and new party members influenced by the ideals of May 1968. These groups had a marked interest in local economic development, encouraged by the regionalist traditions of Breton Socialists. Many local Socialists were (and remain) active in the Breton regionalist movement, which had an important influence on the local political community. Breton Socialists were also heavily influenced by the 'Grenoble' model of local municipal activism, with its belief in decentralisation, its disdain for traditional *notables* and its advocacy of new forms of political participation.

Breton politicians of all parties, however divided they are internally, tend to close ranks against threats from the outside. In a rather paradoxical manner, Breton political capacity is strong because of the weak intensity of domestic cleavages, confirmed in our survey findings.[16] There is a distrust of political extremes, except in specific subcultural circumstances. In the 2004 regional election the FN obtained less support in Brittany than anywhere else in France, less than the UDB/Green list (though more than the far left). If Brittany has not produced significant regionalist parties (a theme we develop below), it is in part because national political parties are infused with Breton cultural values, at least when they are in Brittany. This is even true of the Gaullist RPR and the former president of the Brittany region, Josselin de Rohan, who adopted a much more regionalist tone in Brittany than in Paris. This pattern of influence bears certain similarities with traditional models of cross-regulation whereby influence in Brittany is above all dependent upon the quality of networks in Paris (and Brussels), hence de Rohan's combination of the presidency of the Brittany region with a seat as Senator.

In post-war Brittany there has been a strong political consensus among the regional elites in favour of enhanced regionalisation. This pattern of cross-partisan regional advocacy has been partly instrumentalised. Entering into a dialogue with the French state was, for most regionally minded politicians, the only way forward after the bitter divisions of the inter-war and wartime period. Breton-style identity politics were discredited by the collaborationist activities of a minority of Breton activists during the war, a theme we develop below. The prevailing post-war model of political activism has been one of territorial solidarity aimed at procuring material advantages for Brittany, namely through raising living standards in what had been France's poorest region in 1945.

From 1950 onwards, Breton actors of all political persuasions co-operated closely in the CELIB (Comité de d'étude et de liaison des intérêts bretons), the archetype of a post-war regional advocacy coalition. The CELIB brought together politicians from all parties, along with professional and economic interests, to promote the interests of the region. Under the impetus of CELIB, Brittany was the first French region to publish a regional plan in 1953, calling for industrialisation and improved transport facilities. The CELIB served as a model for post-war French planning. The activities of CELIB inspired the French state to launch its first regional plan in 1956. The logic was an instrumental one: to bring a backward region into national productivity. The lobbying activity was crowned with success, as the French state poured massive resources into Brittany in the 1950s and 1960s. The CELIB could certainly claim the credit for many of the improvements in transport infrastructure conceded to the Brittany region in the 1960s and 1970s and remains a powerful reference point today.

Interviews with surviving actors and published historical accounts demonstrate that instrumentalist ends coexisted within the CELIB with a high degree of regional consciousness and a desire for powerful regional political institutions. How to affirm Breton identity continues to be a source of division. The mainstream view has been to lobby for increased state and EU resources to rescue Brittany from its isolated geographical position and to assure its integration with the rest of France (and Europe). Looking to the state, whether for industrial investment or for support for a fledgling intensive agriculture, has been a favoured tactic, one pursued on a cross-partisan basis. The leader of the Breton Socialists, now president of the Regional Council, expressed it thus in 2001: 'In Brittany, we all believe in the merits of the Breton compromise. Left and right are perfectly capable of coming together and agreeing on the big questions that concern the region'. The (then) Gaullist president of the Brittany region shared this analysis.

This regional advocacy position has always been contested by an autonomist minority, more concerned to safeguard and strengthen Breton identity than to promote the integration of Brittany within the French nation. This dichotomy was illustrated in interviews by the case of the high-speed train (TGV). Most interlocutors favoured extending the high-speed train to Brest, in the far west of Brittany. Messrs de Rohan (president from 1998–2004) and Le Drian (president since April 2004) combined their efforts to plead Brittany's case in Paris, on this issue and several others. A minority of cultural activists were opposed, however, in the name of defending Breton identity. This example demonstrates why most regionally minded politicians have distanced themselves from the Breton movement. The regional cause has been much more effectively pursued by Christian Democrats, Socialists, and even Gaullists, than by the Breton regionalist or nationalist parties. We now consider cultural and political movements in Brittany, addressing the underlying question: *why has the Breton movement, which has made such far-reaching cultural advances, been so stagnant politically?*

Cultural and political movements in Brittany

Historical trajectories

In the Rokkan and Urwin schema, Brittany, combining economic underdevelopment with a strong cultural identity, ought to be a prime contender for a region that develops a strong regionalist movement. Though the Breton nationalist/regionalist movement has made far-reaching cultural advances, however, it has been stagnant politically. In this section we address the apparent paradox of a strong Breton identity coexisting with a weak regionalist or nationalist movement.

Emsav ('the movement' in Breton) is the term used to designate the whole of the Breton regionalist/nationalist movement, which spans from the far left to the far right of the political spectrum. It is customary to distinguish three distinct phases of Emsav: a literary and cultural awakening during the nineteenth century; a more assertive nationalist movement during the inter-war period; the diffuse but powerful and effective cultural movement that dominates Breton expression today. A brief overview of these three phases of Emsav highlights the fundamentally ambiguous character of Breton regional advocacy. The first phase of Emsav, which can be traced to the late nineteenth century, was essentially a literary and cultural phenomenon. The cultural revival was rooted in the literary renaissance of the nineteenth century (the *Barsaz Breizh* of 1839) and was based around defence of the Breton language. The first regionalist movement was recognisably a right-wing creation: in 1898, a royalist Deputy created the Union régionaliste breton, a movement that called for administrative decentralisation while defending the idea of monarchy, the aristocracy, the Catholic Church and the Breton language. The Catholic Church initially supported this strategy of preserving Brittany from capitalism and defending the rights of the Church. Most of the early cultural associations had a religious connection. In 1905, for example, the Catholic association Bleun-Brug, created by the Abbé Perrot, was dedicated to spreading Breton through the Church and private schools.

The First World War represented a major turning point in Breton history.

Bretons were mobilised *en masse* to fight in the war. With the loss of 150,000 lives, twice as many as the average for the rest of France, Bretons suffered enormously.[17] The First World War also socialised the young Breton generation into the French national community and inculcated daily use of the French language. In 1918 Brittany emerged emotionally and physically exhausted by the First World War,[18] its economy structurally damaged and economically underdeveloped, its future compromised by the massive emigration of young people. The second phase of Emsav occurred during the inter-war period, when there was a strengthening both of the cultural movement and of political nationalism. Cultural manifestations continued to focus upon the language, gradually divorced from the defence of the Catholic Church. In 1933 an important secular movement, Ar Falz, was created by schoolteachers committed to teaching in Breton. More explicitly political movements developed also, strongly influenced by the Irish uprising of 1920–21 and the conception of the Irish Free State. Breizh Atao ('Bretagne toujours'), created in 1920, presented a platform for Breton autonomists from across the political spectrum, an ideological and political precursor to the Breton Autonomist Party (Parti autonomiste breton, PAB), formed in 1927. The PAB was increasingly split between a pro-European, federalist left and a hard-line nationalist right, which eventually won out. Dissolved in 1939, the PAB reappeared as the Breton National Party (Parti national de Bretagne, PNB) in 1940 under the Occupation. A number of leaders of this nationalist party collaborated with the Germans. Around a hundred of the most committed nationalists formed the Breton *brigade*, the *bezenn* Perrot, which fought as part of the German army.

The war had a devastating, probably fatal effect on the Breton autonomist movement. Though Breton nationalists had also been very active in the resistance, the activities of the pro-Nazi minority discredited the Breton movement for a generation and precluded the emergence of a powerful regionalist/nationalist party. Interviews within the Breton political and policy communities in 2001 underscored the debilitating effect of past Breton engagements. One prominent figure in the Breton autonomist movement recognised the liability of this period, in a nation (France) still struggling to come to terms with its own past: 'Then there was the war. Breton political activists fought with the Germans during the war! There were not many of them, but all the same ... We have been suffering the indignity of this collaboration ever since. The Breton people distrust political parties that specifically refer to Breton autonomy. I don't know how long this will last ...'

Post-war Brittany

There is an essential source of tension within the Breton movement. There is a vibrant Breton cultural movement, on the one hand, centred on the revival in Breton music, dance and language. On the other hand, there has been limited political space for the development of a Breton regionalist movement. Let us investigate further this apparent paradox.

A very dense tissue of cultural associations exists in Brittany. For over thirty years, for example, the Inter-Celtic Festival in Lorient has attracted 150,000 paying visitors every year. Though most of these associations are explicitly apolitical, their existence testifies to an enduring sense of regional identity and patrimony. The main cultural federations – such as Dastrum or Tiavro – certainly consider themselves part of the broader Breton movement (Emsav). These associations operate at various levels. Most are local, limited to a neighbourhood or a town (such as the myriad Breton music groups and dance troops in Quimper). Some operate at a departmental level. Few are genuinely regional, but the most important are regrouped into two major federations at the all-Brittany level: the Brittany Cultural Institute (ICB), based in Vannes, and the Brittany Cultural Council (CCB) in Rennes. These organisations maintain rather antagonistic relations with their main sponsor, the Brittany Regional Council.

The powerful Breton cultural movement, while not explicitly focused on language issues, has done much to revive interest in the Breton language. We identify elsewhere[19] a language advocacy coalition that draws its strength from a shared belief in the need to safeguard the patrimony represented by the Breton language and from the capacity to mobilise the powerful Breton cultural movement. If it is impossible to detect any single actor, we can identity a constellation of individuals, semi-official agencies and voluntary associations, gravitating for the most part around the Brittany Regional Council. This advocacy coalition includes actors within local and regional authorities, semi-autonomous agencies such as the Breton Language Office (Ofis ar Brezhonneg) and the cultural federations regrouped in the ICB and the CCB.

We drew above a distinction between cultural and political regionalism, but there are some organisations that act as a bridge between the two. The strongest symbol of the intersection between the political and cultural movement is the Diwan association, which runs a network of Breton-medium schools. The history of Breton-medium language teaching is one of successful and sustained social mobilisation. The first Breton-language school was opened in Finistère in 1977 by a group of Breton language activists, determined to provide a Breton-medium education for their own children. These parents created the Diwan association. The first few Diwan schools were concentrated in the nursery and primary sector, with one, then several, *collèges* and, finally, a *lycée* in Carhaix. By 2002 Diwan was in charge of the education of 2,768 pupils (2,127 in primary and infant schools, 504 in *collège* and 137 in the *lycée*). From its origins, *Diwan* was at the centre of a tightly knit Breton cultural network. It drew its support not only from the dedication of its activists but from their involvement in a series of interlocking cultural networks, centred around the revival of traditional Breton music and dance, and the renewed interest in Breton language and history. Each of the critical junctures of Diwan's history has been marked by the social mobilisation of this cultural network. In the early years, Diwan relied almost entirely on the devotion of its activists and the parents of its pupils (usually one and the same) for raising finance. The powerful Breton cultural movement has always answered the call when Diwan has needed it. In 1999, for example, when the regional prefect attempted to prevent the opening of the first Diwan *lycée* in Carhaix, there were mass demonstrations followed by a discreet climb-down by the state's representative.

From being an undoubted source of strength, the cultural movement became, for many within Diwan, an obstacle to the survival of the Breton-language schools. The Diwan movement split in 2002 over whether or not to support the integration of the Diwan schools into the public education system. In favour were those rallied behind Andrew Lincoln, the architect of an agreement with the French Education Ministry in 2001. Lincoln argued that the long-term future of Diwan could be secured only by fully integrating the schools into the public education service, even if it meant making some compromises on teaching methods. Opponents of the Lincoln stance regarded an agreement with the French state as a betrayal, given the state's treatment of Brittany in the past. There remains an aspect of the 'counter-society' among the most fervent supporters of Diwan. Any contact with the French state would dilute the purity of the Breton language cause and lead to betrayal. Some went so far as to call for historical reparations from France, clearly identified as a foreign country. All in the movement advocated genuine regional control over education. The divisions between pragmatists and purists began to weaken the movement, but the achievements of Diwan are very considerable indeed. To argue that Diwan has reversed linguistic decline would be excessive. But there has emerged a new generation of fluent Breton speakers that is beginning to enter into professional life.

Why is there no significant Breton political movement?

There is a great deal of ambiguity in the interplay between the political and the cultural movements. There are two contrasting readings, one that stresses the continuity between the political and cultural movements, the other that emphasises cultural investment as a means of avoiding a political expression of being Breton. In support of the first interpretation, though cultural activists have kept their public distance from the Breton regionalist or nationalist movements, they often belong to both: 'many very well known Breton cultural activists are also openly nationalist. But they wear two hats and are careful, for funding reasons, not to confuse political and cultural demands.' Another correspondent affirmed that the cultural activists are essentially acting politically, as 'any regional culture in France is a political statement, a challenge to the centralised Paris-based culture of the Republican state'. A less sanguine view stresses the tendency for autonomists to take their desires for reality: 'I have the impression that the Bretons are very apolitical. They are not interested in politics. As they have a strong identity, they over-invest their energies in the cultural sphere. Elsewhere, in other countries with minority languages (Ireland, Corsica, the Basque country, Wales), there is no equivalent of the Breton cultural effervescence, but there are strong nationalist movements'.

Conscious of the damage done to their reputation, early post-war Breton movements positioned themselves as legitimist and apolitical. The first of these was the Breton Organisational Movement (Mouvement d'organisation de la Bretagne, MOB), which situated itself as being neither on the left nor on the right. The apolitical strand represented by the MOB sat well with the traditions of the Breton political movement; one of its former activists dismissed left and right as 'French' concepts, not appropriate to Brittany, with a more inclusive political culture. In practice the MOB was a right-of-centre movement. At its height the MOB counted a few hundred activists and we were certainly less than a hundred in the student organisation. As was the case with the main French parties, the Breton regionalist/nationalist movement was deeply divided by the Algerian war. The leadership of the MOB emphasised its sympathy for the French settlers in Algeria, or *colons*, envisaging a realignment of France as a fully federal state with a statute of autonomy for Algeria and Brittany. The student section was hostile to this position. Adopting Marxist theses of 'internal colonisation', the MOB student section came out against the Algerian war and in favour of Algerian independence. By 1964 the left of the MOB had split off to create the Breton Democratic Union (UDB) that we consider below. The modern inheritor of the MOB, the POBL, is a small splinter party with, at most, a hundred activists. POBL is allied with two even smaller *groupuscules* ('Co-ordination Bretagne' and Breizh Nao) in the Entente fédéraliste Breizh (EFB).[20]

The Breton Democratic Union has been the most influential autonomist movement in Brittany. For the first two decades of its existence the UDB placed the Breton regionalist movement firmly on the left. It espoused Marxist analyses of internal colonisation and adopted a Leninist mode of internal party organisation. Though it eschewed political violence, there were links between certain UDB activists and the Breton Liberation Front (Front de la libération de la Bretagne, FLB), the armed wing of the Breton nationalist movement that modelled itself on the Irish Republican Army (IRA). This stance rapidly ensured insignificance and unpopularity for the Breton autonomist movement. Breton regionalist forces drifted away from the UDB and sought refuge in either the Unified Socialist Party (Parti socialiste unifié, PSU) or the new Socialist Party (Parti socialiste) in the 1970s. In 1982 a major split occurred when the historic leader Ronan le Prohon and a group of activists quit the UDB and rallied to the PS in government. The 1980s were a very difficult decade, as the Socialist government delivered a number of regionalist promises, for many weakening the rationale of an autonomist movement. By the early 1990s the UDB had gained a new lease of life as the Socialist government and party moved further and further away from the regionalist agenda. The 1990s saw numerous advances and the arrival of many new activists. Since the regional elections of 2004 the UDB has formed part of the Regional Executive.

In addition to the UDB there are a number of tiny *groupuscules*, such as POBL, Frankiz Breizh and the Parti breton. There are also movements on the extreme left and the extreme right. Emgann, which advocates complete independence for a socialist Brittany, is the best structured of the extreme left movements. Emgann is believed by police to be the political wing of the Revolutionary Breton Army (Armée révolutionnaire bretonne, ARB), assumed to be behind the bomb attack on a McDonald's restaurant in the town of Quévert in April 2000. On the extreme right, two small movements, Adsav and the MRB, are in the tradition of the PNB and right-wing Breton nationalism.

Several traits characterise all these movements. First, they are extremely small. The best organised, the UDB, counts at best 3,000 activists, and most of the others have fewer than 100. Second, attempts to create a pan-Breton, cross-partisan party (such as MOB or POBL) have failed, leaving the Breton movement to exhaust its meagre forces in an astonishing array of minor causes. Some of these groups have adopted verbally violent stances that sit uneasily with the prevailing legitimist representations of Breton political culture. Apart from one or two individuals (such as the autonomist mayor of Carhaix, Christian Troadec, or Jean-Yves Cozan, the vice-president of Breton Identity in the 1998–04 majority), only the UDB has any sizeable presence. Since the regional elections of March 2004, at which the UDB/Green list obtained 9.7 per cent, there are three 'autonomist' councillors in the Socialist-led majority, occupying important positions of responsibility.

The vitality of the cultural movement stands in contrast to the emasculation of a genuine political regionalist movement. There are two main explanations for the weakness of the regionalist movements in Brittany (and more generally in France). First, Bretons have refused to support in meaningful numbers any movement that calls into question Brittany's belonging to the French Republic. One expert explains the weakness of the indigenous Breton political movement as a consequence of the deeply rooted legitimist strand within Breton public opinion.[21] Imbued by a Catholic, conformist ethic, the Breton public is not prepared to support pro-independence or pro-autonomist parties. This conformist sentiment is reflected in the modest scores obtained in elections by the UDB and the smaller Breton regional or autonomist parties. Second, the political opportunity structure in the Fifth Republic is so resolutely Paris-centric that Breton forces have adapted accordingly. There is an underlying consensus among the 'French' parties to defend Breton interests to the outside world and limit political conflict. This consensual model is broadly shared within Breton public opinion, where there is a high degree of trust in the regional council, a belief that the region defends Brittany's interest well in other arenas and a preference for the region over other arenas in many important areas of public policy.[22] The annual surveys on Brittany carried out by the Paris-based OIP confirms these findings, as does comparative work with other French regions.[23]

The idea of region has a strong moral authority in the case of Brittany, the birthplace of regional consciousness and identity in France. We now continue this overview of regionalism in Brittany by venturing further within the Breton policy community.

Inside the community: cultural identity and political ambiguity

We engaged in intensive interviews in Brittany in 2001 and 2002. Most interviews were conducted from April to September 2001, when the Socialist government led by Jospin promised to lead France down the path of asymmetrical devolution. Follow-up interviews occurred in July–September 2002, with the Raffarin government preparing to introduce the major new constitutional reform embedding regions in the constitution. We can regroup the answers from these free-flowing interviews under a number of broad themes: the future of decentralisation and the regional institution; the policy challenges facing Brittany; the operation of the Breton policy community and Brittany, France and Europe.

The future of decentralisation and the regional institution
There was very strong support in the interviews for strengthening the regional political institution and for vesting the Brittany regional council with a leadership role in relation to other sub-national authorities. We have to interpret these findings with some caution. Interviews took place principally with members of the regional political and policy communities, rather than with local or departmental politicians. Having said this, most of the politicians interviewed combined a regional with a local, departmental or national mandate. There was no blanket support for the regional level. Even the leader of the UDB, for example, refuted the suggestion that there could be a regional police force, or that the social security system should be regionalised. But there was widespread support for enhanced regional powers in the spheres of education, culture, historic monuments, transport, training, regional languages and, to a lesser degree, health. Almost everybody interviewed in the summer of 2002, irrespective of party, was favourable to the extension of the policy responsibilities of the regional councils then proposed by the Raffarin government. Our structured questionnaire backed up the findings of the interviews. This general support for the regional level was also confirmed in our public opinion survey. There is a high level of regional consciousness in Brittany, in a manner that is not obvious in other French regions.

The policy challenges facing Brittany
There was a remarkable cohesion between the attitudes expressed rather informally in interviews, the findings from our elite questionnaire and evidence from our public opinion poll survey about the nature of the policy problems facing Brittany. All interviewees were asked what they considered to be the main policy problems facing Brittany in the years ahead, a question repeated in the elite questionnaire. Three types of response came way ahead of all others: first, problems related to the environment and, specifically, to water provision and pollution of water supplies; second, the need for more regional economic development and, third, the need for a strengthening of the powers

of the regional council. How should we interpret these findings? To take the last one first, informed opinion in Brittany supports more regional responsibility to tackle deeply rooted problems that, in face-to-face interviews, were often attributed to distant decisions taken by technocratic Parisian elites. We identified a certain amount of blame avoidance in the facility with which Breton decision makers attributed Brittany's malaise to outside forces, a phenomenon typical of a region with a consciousness of being on the periphery. Upon further prompting, several interviewees acknowledged that environmental pollution was made worse by the intensive farming model and practices associated with Breton farmers during the post-war economic miracle. Alongside deep environmental concern, there was also strong support for regional economic development and for help for the agricultural sector. The paradox was not lost on decision makers themselves. Awareness of the environmental damage caused by intensive farming (pollution, water contamination, soil erosion) has been painful for one of France's main agricultural regions. The policy priorities of environmental policy and economic development illustrate a certain dilemma and uncertainty that Bretons face. On the one hand, they wish to continue their story of the Breton 'economic miracle'. On the other hand, this very success, based as it was on intensive agricultural methods, has endangered one of Brittany's greatest assets, its reputation for unspoiled natural produce.

If there was much support for enhanced regional governance, little direct linkage was made between the objectives of political governance and the symbols of Breton identity such as language or culture. Support for regionalisation was rather more instrumental (the region as the appropriate level for good services) than identity-based (the region at the service of a distinct identity, separate/adversarial from that of the rest of France). We should qualify this conclusion. There *was* general support in the interviews, the questionnaire and the opinion poll for allowing more regional influence over the definition of language policy and for more public support for Breton-language education. But the salient issues of concern were those of economic development, agriculture, the environment and education, rather than those of language.

The operation of the Breton policy community

Yes, in Brittany, as in Wales, we have a strong sense of identity. You refer to a national sentiment, we call this regional, but it is the same thing. We've even copied your national anthem. Unfortunately, in other parts of France, the region is meaningless. Elsewhere they are quite happy with their *départements*. But here, the *départements* are meaningless . . . We are able to come up with Breton compromises that are impossible elsewhere.

A number of interviewees spontaneously volunteered the information that, in the words of one, 'in Brittany we do things differently'. They referred to a Brittany effect, particularly in relation to the outside world. Though conflicts within Brittany could be fierce, there was a common front presented to the outside world, whether the French state, the European Union or other regions and countries. Some interviewees referred to Brittany's past as an independent duchy, a degree of autonomy they equated with pre-unification Scotland. There was some nostalgia about pre-1532 Brittany, a 'prosperous maritime trading state larger than Belgium or the Netherlands'. Unlike Scotland, however, Brittany had had to face a formidable centralising machine in the form of the post-revolutionary French state. In order to defend Breton interests in a hostile environment, Bretons of all persuasions had developed powerful codes to recognise each other across formal divides. More than one interviewee spoke of a Breton 'network' in Paris, linking key positions in the Ministries with the defence of Breton interests. Whatever the nostalgia for the past, there was a general feeling that the existing pattern of representing Breton interests had served Brittany fairly well, though this coexisted with a demand for more regional autonomy.

Brittany, France and Europe

Bretons are distinctive not only because of the strength of their regional sense of belonging but also by their European attachment. Pro-European sentiment is stronger in Brittany than in most French regions. This European identity has been identified in numerous monographs and was graphically illustrated by the results of the 1992 referendum on the Maastricht Treaty. Along with Alsace and Lorraine, Brittany was the strongest pro-Maastricht region in France, with the three peripheral regions securing the victory of the Yes vote. This evidence is supported by elite-level surveys in which the peripheral status of Brittany is identified as a major obstacle to future prosperity and closer European integration as a major opportunity.[24] Brittany was for a long time the main French beneficiary of European structural fund grants (in the 1960s and 1970s) and has always benefited from the CAP.[25] On the other hand, the reform of the CAP in the 1990s, and the introduction of milk quotas and set-aside in particular have hardened the opinion of some Breton farming organisations against 'Brussels'.

Many interviewees stressed the fundamentally pro-European sentiment existing within Brittany. Europe is part of the 'Christian democratic' stock in trade, which remains alive in Brittany, despite the creation of a unified conservative party in November 2002 (the UMP). Several interviewees also linked the pro-European sentiment in Brittany with the peripheral location of Brittany at one of the westernmost points of continental Europe. Bretons looked to the European Union, as much in faith as in expectation, as the best guarantor of their future prosperity. On the other hand, a number of interviewees expressed frustration at the tight control over European issues exercised by the French government, while secretly congratulating Bretons for maintaining networks in Brussels that allowed local and regional politicians to sidestep the French state.

From this overview of interviews within the Breton political and policy communities we conclude in the simultaneous existence of a high degree of elite-level regional identity and acceptance that efforts to better Brittany are best focused upon Paris, where they are most likely to make a difference. We now engage in a similar exercise in relation to public opinion in Brittany.

Multiple identities in contemporary France: some findings from Brittany

The problem of political and national identity is revealed as an essential problem throughout most of French history. Identity is a compound, not to say a nebulous concept. Identity can be personal, social or collective. Political identity can be understood as 'common purpose', something that persists through time. It consists of a combination of myths, symbols, rituals and ideology. In the French case, several centuries of political engineering were required to create the myths, symbols, rituals and ideologies that underpin contemporary French identity. In this final section we present some empirical evidence about multiple identities in Brittany. The data presented are drawn from a mass survey and interviews carried out in Brittany in 2001 and 2002.

Does identity matter? Efficience 3 conducted a mass survey on our behalf with a representative sample of Breton public opinion in June 2001.[26] We asked respondents in the survey to state whether they considered themselves to be Breton, not French, more Breton than French, equally Breton and French, more French than Breton, or French, not Breton. The results, presented in Table 3.1, are highly revealing. In Brittany the sense of regional identity is strong, but this is not considered as being in opposition to an overarching French nationhood.[27] Regional identity is not a surrogate nationality. Interestingly, these findings were backed up by interviews and by a questionnaire we distributed to members of the Breton policy community. Our findings highlighted the paradoxes and limitations of the Breton autonomist cause. Even those working for greater Breton autonomy (the case with many of our sample) felt a deep sense of their French identity and declared themselves proud to be French. The French state-building enterprise has been thorough.

Table 3.1 *Multiple identities in Brittany*

Do you feel yourself to be	%
Breton, not French?	2
More Breton than French?	15
Equally Breton and French?	57
More French than Breton?	17
French, not Breton?	8
Don't know/Other	1

Around three-quarters of Bretons feel a sense of regional identity that is at least as powerful as their pride in being French. On balance, these figures suggest that there is a fairly comfortable linkage between regional identity and regional and national political institutions in the case of Brittany, testament in the long run to the efficacy of the French state project.

Conclusion

In our introduction, we set out to provide answers to several related questions. How is the French tradition of unitary government mediated by local and regional variations? Why are successful forms of regional advocacy successful? How do citizens reconcile their multiple and overlapping identities? What does the treatment of regional minorities tell us about the construction of the French republican state itself?

The above survey strongly suggests the following conclusions, in order of increasing importance. First, the French tradition of unitary government is certainly mediated by local and regional traditions. In the case of Brittany there is a 'regionality effect', though this is, by and large, played out within the parameters of traditional republicanism. Second, regional advocacy in Brittany has been so effective because it has combined heightened regional consciousness with an awareness of the most effective modes of operation offered by the political opportunity structure of the French polity. Other French regions are much less likely to combine regionality and regional advocacy in this way. Third, regional advocacy is successful because of the activities of mainstream French parties; the political opportunity structure is not conductive to political regionalism, though, in the case of Brittany, a powerful cultural movement provides an influential milieu for both regionalist and French parties. Fourth, though Bretons are supportive of a more thoroughgoing regionalisation, this choice in no sense limits their attachment to the broader French nation. As there is little or no conflict between local, regional and national identities (with the exception of Corsica), the French government ought to be able to devolve more responsibilities to localities and regions with a clear conscience. The final conclusion is a more normative one: only outright autonomists and traditional republicans (for opposing reasons) are likely to find such a pattern of intermediated regional influence intolerable. If it is to survive and prosper, French republicanism needs to recognise post-republican realities, one of the most important of which relates to accommodating varying forms of territorial distinctiveness.

Notes

1 P. Flora, S. Kuhnle and D. Urwin, *State Formation, Nation Building and Mass Politics in Europe* (Oxford: Oxford University Press, 1999).

2 C. Ford, *Creating the Nation in Provincial France: Religion and Political Identity in Brittany* (Princeton NJ: Princeton University Press, 1993).

3   A. Cole and P. John, *Local Governance in England and France* (London: Routledge, 2001).
4   F. Favereau, *Bretagne contemporaine : langue, culture, identité* (Morlaix: Editions Skol Vreizh, 1993); P. Flatres, *La Bretagne* (Paris: Presses Universitaires de France, 1986); M. McDonald, *We are not French* (London: Routledge, 1989); Y. Le Bourdennec, *Le Miracle breton* (Paris: Calmann-Lévy, 1996); R. Le Coadic, *L'Identité bretonne* (Rennes: Presses Universitaires de Rennes, 1998).
5   R. Pasquier, *La Capacité politique des régions : une comparaison France/Espagne* (Rennes: Presses Universitaires de Rennes, 2004).
6   S. Rokkan and D. Urwin, *The Politics of Territorial Identity* (London: Sage, 1982).
7   Pasquier, *La Capacité politique des régions : une comparaison France/Espagne.*
8   From 2001 to 2003, 101 interviews were carried out in Brittany as part of an ESRC-funded project on 'Devolution and decentralisation in Wales and Brittany', part of the Devolution and Constitutional Change programme (grant No. L219252007). Alistair Cole thanks the Council for its support. As part of the research ethics statement, all interviewees were guaranteed anonymity. The anonymised interview transcriptions can be consulted in the Essex Data Archive (www.data-archive .ac.uk). Study No. 4802, *Devolution and decentralisation in Wales and Brittany* (2001–02).
9   INSEE, *Tableaux de l'économie française* (Paris: Documentation française, 2003).
10 M. Phlipponeau, *Le Modèle industriel breton 1950–2000* (Rennes: Presses Universitaires de Rennes, 1993).
11 *Ibid.*
12 A. Cole and J. Loughlin, 'Beyond the unitary state? Public opinion, political institutions and public policy in Brittany', *Regional Studies*, 37:3 (2003), 265–76.
13 D. Hanley, *Keeping Left: CERES and the French Socialist Party* (Manchester: Manchester University Press, 1984); F. Sawicki, 'La structuration du Parti socialiste : milieux partisans et production d'identités', PhD thesis (University of Paris 1, 1993).
14 M. Lebesque, *Comment peut-on être breton?* (Paris: Seuil, 1970).
15 P. Le Galès, *Politique urbaine et développement local* (Paris: Harmattan 1993).
16 Cole and Loughlin, 'Beyond the unitary state?'
17 Lebesque, *Comment peut-on être breton?*
18 Le Coadic, *L'Identité bretonne.*
19 A. Cole and C. Williams, 'Institutions, identities and lesser-used languages in Wales and Brittany', *Regional and Federal Studies*, 14:4 (2004), 1–26.
20 E. Chartier and R. Larvor, *La France eclatée?* (Spézet: Coop Breizh, 2003).
21 Le Coadic, *L'Identité bretonne.*
22 Cole and Loughlin, 'Beyond the unitary state?'
23 M. Nicolas, 'Breton Identity highlighted by European Integration', paper in European University Institute Conference on 'Nations, Minorities and European Integration', Florence, Italy, 7–8 May 2004; C. Dargent, 'Identités régionales et aspirations politiques : l'exemple de la France aujourd'hui', *Revue Française de Science Politique*, 51:5 (2001), 787–806.
24 Cole and John, *Local Governance in England and France.*
25 Phlipponeau, *Le Modèle industriel breton.*
26 Mass survey carried out by the polling organisation Efficience 3 in Brittany in June–July 2001, with a representative sample of 1,007 individuals. The Economic

and Social Research Council funded this research project on 'Devolution and Decentralisation in Wales and Brittany' (grant No. L2152092007). We thank the Council for its support.
27 Cole and Loughlin, 'Beyond the unitary state?'

Select bibliography

E. Chartier and R. Larvor, *La France éclatée?* (Spézet: Coop Breizh, 2003).

A. Cole and P. John, *Local Governance in England and France* (London: Routledge, 2001).

F. Favereau, *Bretagne contemporaine : langue, culture, identité* (Morlaix: Editions Skol Vreizh, 1993).

P. Flatres, *La Bretagne* (Paris: Presses Universitaires de France, 1986).

P. Flora, S. Kuhnle and D. Urwin, *State Formation, Nation Building and Mass Politics in Europe* (Oxford: Oxford University Press, 1999).

C. Ford, *Creating the Nation in Provincial France: Religion and Political Identity in Brittany* (Princeton NJ: Princeton University Press, 1993).

D. Hanley, *Keeping Left: CERES and the French Socialist Party* (Manchester: Manchester University Press, 1984).

Y. Le Bourdennec, *Le Miracle breton* (Paris: Calmann-Lévy, 1996).

R. Le Coadic, *L'Identité bretonne* (Rennes: Presses Universitaires de Rennes, 1998).

P. Le Galès, *Politique urbaine et développement local* (Paris: Harmattan, 1993).

M. Lebesque, *Comment peut-on être breton?* (Paris: Seuil, 1970).

M. McDonald, *We are not French* (London: Routledge, 1989).

J. Martray, *Vingt ans qui transformèrent la Bretagne : l'épopée du CELIB* (Paris: France Empire, 1983).

Y. Morvan, *Demain la Bretagne* (Rennes: Éditions Apogée, 1997).

R. Pasquier, *La Capacité politique des régions : une comparaison France/Espagne* (Rennes: Presses Universitaires de Rennes, 2004).

M. Phlipponeau, *Le Modèle industriel breton 1950–2000* (Rennes: Presses Universitaires de Rennes, 1993).

S. Rokkan and D. Urwin, *The Politics of Territorial Identity* (London: Sage, 1982).

4

Urban governance and local democracy in France

Susan Milner

> After twenty years of decentralisation, of 'power to the locality', the idea has emerged that one can and one must govern differently.[1]

In Chapter 4 we discuss recent moves undertaken by France's local (municipal) councils to promote local democracy. Until recently France appeared to lag behind the United Kingdom in terms of local participation initiatives. Its hyper-centralised political system and the dynamics it produced have been the subject of sustained commentary.[2] Liberated in part by the decentralisation reforms of the early 1980s, as well as by subsequent legislative initiatives of the 1990s, France's municipal councils have been very active in promoting initiatives to enhance local democracy, raising questions about whether a general trend towards 'new urban governance' may now be observed in France as in other Western countries. In this chapter we review recent trends towards local governance. We focus upon the specific case of Lille, where the council has experimented with, and institutionalised, a particular form of consultation, a '*concertation* committee'. This case is discussed with reference to the concepts of local democracy, social capital and urban governance. We begin by presenting an overview of developments in local and regional governance over the past two decades, developments that have called into question important assumptions of the classical French republican model.

Cross-regulation and the republican model of territorial administration

The pattern of central–local relations known as the French 'system of territorial administration' was a key feature of the traditional French model of policy and politics.[3] It rested upon the principle of administrative uniformity across the nation. It recognised the superiority of central state interests over those of parties, regions, interest groups and localities. It formed part of a hierarchical mode of top-down organisation, whereby public policies originated within government departments or administrative corps, were implemented in localities by state field agencies and local authorities and were co-ordinated by the prefect, the representative of the French state in the departments. The model of 'cross-regulation' applied mainly to rural and small town France, however. Large cities, undertaking cohesive public policies from the early twentieth century in some instances, fell outside the cross-regulation model. The model of cross-regulation depended in part on the weakness of political parties and upon the *notable*'s dominance of his local political community. While this was an accurate description of politico-administrative relations throughout most of the country, certain types of municipal government never corresponded to the model. Those cities (especially in the Paris region and northern and southern France) controlled by the left (particularly the Communists) became citadels of opposition to government policy, with the municipality subject to tight control by a disciplined party organisation. Party politics was always far more important in large cities, where the left-wing parties had a weighty presence. Rapid post-war urbanisation and industrialisation created more complex cities and produced more specific politics in the large cities.

Even in the pre-decentralisation period, local influences could be brought to bear more obviously in large cities than in small towns. City case studies, such as those on Lyons and Lille, on Rennes and on Lille and Rennes,[4] all emphasised the importance of city-based actors in developing territorially specific public policies. Encouraged by the decentralisation reforms of the early 1980s (and propelled by broader European political and global economic trends), in the last decade medium-sized regional capitals such as Nantes, Rennes, Strasbourg, Montpellier, Toulouse, Grenoble and Nice have become booming cities, enjoying considerable economic and demographic growth. Cities, metropolitan areas and regional councils are becoming more important sites for the organisation of interests, for decision making, for the implementation of public policy and for the creation of collective strategies.

When considering the development of patterns of French sub-national administration over the past twenty-five years or so, we agree with Le Galès that a more complex picture of local government has emerged,[5] a mosaic-like pattern resembling the situation in other countries throughout Europe and very different from the previous well organised state view of local government: uniform, controlled by civil servants and enshrined within financial and legal constraints set by the state. Notwithstanding the existence of institutional competition between rival layers of public administration and the sub-optimal policy outcomes this produces, there are underlying sources of cohesion. We can make a strong case for the emergence of a qualitatively different pattern of sub-national politics and administration in the past two decades or so.[6] This case rests upon a series of interlocking phenomena: the rise of city governments; the strengthening of local political leadership, the development of more interdependent forms of policy making, more dense local policy networks and the development of a regional public sphere.

Amongst these developments, there has been a rise in city governments. The 1990s witnessed a major legislative effort to strengthen further inter-communal structures, particularly through developing the inter-communal public corporations (*établissements publics de co-opération intercommunale*, EPCIs), especially in French cities. In French public law the EPCI has the statute of a public corporation. It is not a fully constituted local authority, such as a commune, department or region, but it has an independent executive and certain tax-raising powers. The principal EPCIs are the urban communities, urban districts and the new city-wide communities (*communautés d'agglomération*). Important moves were made to strengthen the EPCIs during the 1990s, through a series of landmark reforms (the Joxe law of 1992, the Voynet and Chevènement laws of 1999). These reforms were driven by the desire to discourage local tax competition, to ensure a more equitable distribution of resources and to promote appropriate structures for tackling the organisational weakness of the communal structure.

More cohesive local government structures are addressing the problems of extreme institutional fragmentation. The new French local governance also rests upon the strengthening of local political leadership, the mobilisation of much broader coalitions of actors in pursuit of collectively defined local objectives, the institutionalisation of more interdependent forms of policy making and the emergence of new players in French localities.

City case studies have long demonstrated the importance not only of the local environment in shaping the character of local political leadership, but also of the ability of local leaders to shape their environments. Decentralisation enhanced the power of urban mayors by loosening tight state controls on their financial decision making and by increasing their legal and political scope for policy innovation. Today's mayors are as likely to be judged as effective by their ability to build horizontal relationships with other public and private sector actors as they are by their lobbying of central government. Problems of co-ordination and leadership are the natural corollary of an increasingly complex charge. Successful mayors have become more entrepreneurial, determined to implement local public policies, preferably within the space of one term in office. Across France, mayors have also placed themselves at the head of new-style development coalitions, mobilising large-scale public and private resources for ambitious development projects.

We should note, also, that the local government route can produce political leaders with international reputations, such as Bernand Delanoë in Paris. Direct election of French mayors ensures that the mayoral office, rather than the presidency of a departmental or a regional council, continues to be the most coveted among politicians with a base in local government. The developments we have analysed above are not necessarily to the detriment of France's regional councils. The ability of a regional council to articulate an overarching territorial vision might be enhanced by strengthening inter-communal collaboration, for example. Inter-communal structures, usually based on employment or training zones that are substantially larger than traditional communal boundaries, are generally consistent with the region's own planning on a sub-regional level. More cohesive local government structures also allow meaningful negotiations to take place between the regional council and the varied territorial interests in their midst. Finally, we identify the development of a local public sphere as an important feature of the new French governance. By local public sphere we signify an arena in which a plurality of organisations interact: local and regional authorities, state field services, public–private partnerships, firms and local associations. Whether the local public sphere enhances democracy, however, is a cause of vigorous debate, a discussion we now develop.

Three reference frames for neighbourhood democracy

These general themes are important for our understanding of the context in which local democracy has developed in France. Before considering our case study of Lille in more depth, we present three reference frames for understanding 'neighbourhood democracy'.

Local democracy

Local democracy is a normative concept which has been promoted by national politicians in France and in other European countries. It rests on two main arguments. First, politicians see a need to counter the decline in civic participation at national level, as seen in falling turnout at national elections since the 1970s, particularly in large cities.[7] Since turnout at local elections has remained relatively stable, it follows that the local level of government has retained or even gained legitimacy and therefore needs to acquire more political powers.[8] Hence local democracy ought to be boosted by further decentralisation of decision-making.

Decentralisation in France (and elsewhere) has sometimes been justified in terms of bringing decisions closer to the people, of connecting with the grass roots. The 'grass roots' metaphor is useful as an attempt to capture one dimension of decentralisation, namely the concern for proximity as a principle of decision making. Consideration in depth of the history of decentralisation in France over the past two decades lies outside the scope of this chapter. The three major trends have been: embedding regional political and institutional capacity, supporting new forms of city governance, and timid moves towards strengthening neighbourhood democracy. Having considered the regional level in Chapter 3, in Chapter 4 we focus more squarely upon neighbourhood democracy in an urban context by means of a case study of the northern city of Lille. We begin by introducing some broader contextual themes, in order to familiarise the reader with patterns of local (especially city) government in France.

Second, local government is the most appropriate level for direct and participative forms of democracy. Decentralisation therefore needs to be supported by new forms of civic participation such as referendums and citizens' juries (particularly youth forums and shadow councils) as well as more widespread information and consultation. The creation and institutionalisation of neighbourhood associations have been encouraged in a number of European countries. Populist alternatives to representative democracy could be divided into three main categories: communitarianism (e.g. neighbourhood councils), deliberative democracy (for example, citizens' juries) and direct democracy (e.g., referendums).[9] To these we might add Hirst's call for associative democracy.[10] The main purpose of such initiatives, echoing the social capital literature, is to promote greater participation among citizens at all levels and to generate a virtuous circle in terms of affect, legitimacy and efficiency of outcomes. Deliberative democracy is seen as responding to the perceived legitimacy problems of representative democracy,[11] whether as a complement or an alternative.

On the other hand, local democracy is contested by a political current within France which remains loyal to the republican tradition of the egalitarian state[12] Local democracy initiatives, it is argued, will fail because they undermine the elective principle and open political institutions to private interests.

French political scientists have also questioned the beneficial effect of consultative mechanisms on civic participation. Sceptics point out that they are likely merely to reinforce existing trends towards the polarisation of the electorate between the politically engaged and the abstentionists. Mabileau argues that local democracy is undermined by a 'culture of non-participation' and that local residents are happy to leave decision making to elected representatives,[13] whilst Sadran notes that citizens limit themselves to 'consumerist and intermittent' access to local power.[14] Pierre and Peters outline potential disadvantages to all three types of 'proximity' politics: these relate to the weak representativeness of community and interest groups and to the differential distribution of power, resources and influence among groups which may lead to the replication or even amplification of inequalities.[15]

Social capital

Following Putnam,[16] it is argued that reciprocal relations among citizens (usually formalised in voluntary associations of various kinds) can promote general trust and therefore strengthen civic participation and contribute to the stability of political institutions, even when they are newly established. This creates a virtuous circle whereby the outcomes (in terms of efficiency as well as affect) are improved. The social capital literature has therefore been embraced by national policy makers keen to legitimise policy and enhance performance. The strengthening of civil society is seen as having broader, if difficult to quantify, social and political benefits.

Political scientists have contested or qualified Putnam's arguments on several key points. First, some scholars argue that the link between associationism and civic behaviour is not automatic and have sought to identify which types of voluntary association are likely to modify the behaviour and/or attitudes of participants. Putnam himself has acknowledged the differential outcomes of membership of different types of association. However, at local level there is a strong risk that the activism of interest and pressure groups takes on a defensive, parochial and even exclusive nature.

Second, there is a broad institutionalist approach which sees the interactions between political authorities and grass-roots associations as the key to understanding outcomes. These interactions form the political opportunity structures which determine the extent of associations' influence over decisions taken and can also help to shape the configuration of the associations themselves. Institutional design may also influence outcomes, for example, in providing co-ordination mechanisms that can amplify the voice of community associations or mechanisms for conflict resolution. Policy priorities may also influence the behaviour of associations, for example, in giving certain groups privileged access to policy makers. The institutional approach takes us closer to concepts of urban governance, discussed below.

Urban governance

The urban governance literature in political science places shifts in political arrangements within the context of local society and economic change.[17] According to Bagnasco and Le Galès,[18] governance is defined 'as a process of co-ordinating actors, social groups and institutions in order to reach objectives which have been collectively discussed and defined in fragmented, even nebulous environments'. Economic governance has thus been shifted from national to local or regional level in order to fulfil efficiency objectives. This can lead in some cases to city 'boosterism', where local social capital is harnessed to meet the demands of specific economic groups (whether property developers, manufacturers or financial interests, etc.) and which is usually characterised by a shift towards public–private partnerships. However, there does not seem to be one model of urban governance in Europe, rather differentiated patterns of local interests (where the dynamics of local society is the main variable) and political intervention (where institutions and ideology play a part). Comparatively, it has been argued that urban governance is still relatively underdeveloped in France and Britain, where economic competition is dominant and local political authorities are weak.[19]

Besides economic development, changes in social policy have modified urban governance patterns through similar instruments, for example, partnership with voluntary associations, although usually involving different sections of local society and with differential outcomes. The European Union has itself promoted such partnerships.[20] Some attempts to theorise local partnerships have looked to the American concept of the urban regime. Urban regime theory identifies new coalitions of actors at the heart of the governance of American cities. In his detailed study Clarence Stone described the long-term governance of Atlanta by a stable coalition of local political and economic leaders, with business playing the leading role.[21]

The urban regime literature, imported from the United States, may be less applicable to Europe. If, however, as Stoker and Mossberger suggest,[22] the concept of urban regime is widened to include community interests and the professionals employed by local agencies or government, it makes sense in the context of a shift from public provision to anti-poverty strategies based on the contracting out of services to voluntary bodies. In the French case, the territorialisation of state action took place first within the context of the city contracts (*politique de la ville*) introduced by the Rocard government in the 1990s. City contracts bring together political (i.e., local government and state field agents), associative and sometimes economic actors in pursuit of commonly agreed objectives. Together with priority education zones (*zones d'education prioritaires*, ZEPs), they represent a form of territorialised social policy, the closest approximation to positive discrimination one can imagine in the French context. Territorial social policy has been extended to areas such as employment and is characterised by a complex web of contractual relationships. New social policies are in the process of creating new urban regimes – in the sense of coalitions between private actors and local authorities – whereby state action modifies the environment for voluntary associations and, conversely, makes interactions with certain types of voluntary association necessary for local government to be able to carry out its service obligations. In the British case, partnerships are likely to be between public authorities and private economic actors around economic development issues. In the French case, public–private partnerships are more likely to occur around the deconcentrated action of the state in social policy areas,[23] though there has been a growth of public–private partnerships in the economic development field as well.

The urban governance literature therefore posits that new forms of relationship are emerging between local authorities and private actors. Civil society, in the sense of organised groups of interests, has become part of a shifting regime of urban governance, and local councils need to invent new ways of working with it. What is of interest from this viewpoint is the local society (in terms of groups of interests, and power relations between them) and the institutional arrangements which might facilitate contacts. However, the shift towards urban governance may not necessarily increase the democratic space open to citizens. In the British case, the transfer of planning and other responsibilities to non-elected agencies has been criticised for diminishing democratic accountability, let alone participation. In the French case, the addition of a new layer of local administration grouping together authorities within an urban agglomeration (*intercommunalité*) in order to counter territorial fragmentation has also decreased the opportunities for democratic participation. It may be argued that this is the least democratic layer of local government in France (because only indirectly elected).[24] The 2002 law (*loi* No. 2002-276, 27 February 2002, known as the 'Vaillant' law) failed to remedy this situation (see below).

There is also a fear in some quarters that the shift towards partnerships and the creation of networks of voluntary groups undermines traditional, bottom-up concepts of civil society in favour of a technocratic disempowering of local citizens. This may be seen for example in some criticisms of French urban policy, notably by anti-racist activists. In the next section, our essay will review recent developments in France before focusing on the claims made by Lille municipal council that it is pioneering new forms of local democracy.

The legislative framework of local democracy in France

Local democracy has been promoted by the central state since the early 1980s, as well as being the focus of local experiments in the same period. As indicated earlier, this has not been without problems or controversies; the law of 27 February 2002 took a year to reach the statute book and underwent many substantial amendments along the way.

One of the stated objectives of the 1982 ('Defferre') decentralisation laws was to strengthen local democracy by legitimising the commune as a space for political action. The idea was mainly that this would lead to a renewal and extension of local elites, making them more representative of local citizens at the same time as their powers were increased. Some local councils (particularly Communist and Socialist-led, and with support from Green councillors), anxious to retain electoral support, began to put in place new mechanisms for informing citizens while some also experimented with new forms of civic consultation. Central government supported these initiatives in a series of laws, such as the 1992 law encouraging the creation of consultative councils based on local interest groups and the 1995 law giving residents the right to demand a referendum on council projects if supported by at least a fifth of registered voters. The effect of these laws seems to have been to encourage such initiatives where local authorities were already in favour (as in the case of Lille regarding consultative councils, discussed below), but they lacked teeth where councils were less enthusiastic. Moreover, they were too vague in terms of implementation to have much effect. For example, in a case of conflict between the council and community groups demanding a referendum, the law had little to say on how the referendum should be organised or how its results should be handled. (In fact, they can simply be overridden.)

The 2001 Bill on local democracy was based on a report by former Prime Minister and then mayor of Lille, Pierre Mauroy, and had three main components.[25] First, the Bill sought to bridge the democratic deficit by introducing direct elections for inter-communal bodies (ECPI); however, this clause was dropped in the Senate, which removed much of the substance from the law. Second, the Bill further encouraged local democracy by making *conseils de quartiers* (neighbourhood councils) obligatory in communes with over 20,000 citizens. In the event, these clauses were adopted, but only for communes of over 80,000 residents, neighbourhood councils being optional in communes of between 20,000 and 80,000 residents. Nonetheless, these moves represent a significant innovation in local democracy. Third, the Bill sought to revitalise local politics by giving new rights to municipal oppositions; these provisions were adopted and may prove to have a significant impact on local politics over the longer term, since, as Assens and Phanuel argue, the lack of a coherent opposition may be the biggest factor in allowing 'autocratic' modes of local government to persist.[26]

The major innovation in the 2002 law was to devolve decision-making powers downwards by placing the neighbourhood (*quartier*) at the heart of the participative process, particularly in the biggest cities. However, whether this represents real empowerment of local communities remains unclear, particularly as under this scheme half the members of neighbourhood councils would be elected local citizens, with the other half being councillors designated by the city council. The city council therefore retains an important power of nomination and practical control of the neighbourhood council's business. For this reason the law was criticised by Green councillors.[27] The proposal to allow districts (*arrondissements*) to organise their own referenda on council projects was scrapped by Parliament. The law has also been widely criticised as falling significantly below existing arrangements in many larger towns and cities.[28] For this reason, its impact has been seen as limited. A study carried out in 2003 found that 57 per cent of communes (large and medium-sized) had a *conseil de quartier* in place, nearly all of which had been set up well before the law or in anticipation of it.[29]

In addition to the 2002 law, the state has directly promoted partnerships with local associations through its economic development and anti-poverty strategies. The 1999 framework law on territorial development and sustainable development made it obligatory to set up development councils in the 175 recognised *pays*.[30] However, again the legislation has been too loose to make much impact. Most of the development councils are composed of representatives designated by local councils; links between the development councils and grassroots associations are weak, and the development councils themselves have very few powers and even fewer resources.[31]

This brief review highlights two main points. First, institutional design matters and the French lawmakers have created a hybrid system which includes significant innovations but lacks overall coherence and allows a large amount of local discretion in the implementation of participative mechanisms. Second, this situation is likely to lead to greater differentiation of models of urban governance rather than the diffusion of one particular model. Just within central Paris a 2002 study noted that, although all twenty *arrondissements* had set up *conseils de quartier*, the bodies differed significantly in terms of mode of designation of members and mode of operation.[32]

Even though it was watered down in Parliament, the 2002 law owed its initial framing to the ideas of Pierre Mauroy, a powerful mayor with a highly localised view of local politics. Commenting on the law, and particularly on the provisions relating to neighbourhood councils, the Greens of Roubaix (close to Lille) bemoaned the triumph of the 'Lille model' of neighbourhood councils over others: 'Are [neighbourhood councils] in Lille not institutions rather than agents of social transformation?'[33] Whilst I have argued above that the laws are unlikely to lead to any across-the-board adoption of the Lille model in France, there is a competition between left-wing councils to become the most participative city in the country. Lille is proud of its model and claims to be a pioneer in France, actively responding to requests from other councils for advice on how to set up similar initiatives. It has been the subject of numerous press articles and, in 1999, it was awarded the title of most democratic local council in France by the magazine *L'Express*. In the next section I will present the main characteristics of the Lille model.

Lille, neighbourhood councils and the *concertation* council

The main characteristics of Lille have been discussed elsewhere and we will simply outline them briefly here.[34] It should be noted that accounts of Lille emphasise the distinctiveness of its style of governance, due to its geographical situation, economic problems and strategies, and political-ideological factors:

Lille itself is a smallish city (212,000 inhabitants after the incorporation of Lomme in 2000) but the conurbation (1.2 million inhabitants) is large by French standards, a medium-sized city by European standards (on a par with Leeds). Lille is surrounded by many smaller cities and towns with strong local identities and political cultures. These have created tensions over resource distribution, which coexistence in inter-communal and regional structures has brought to the fore (and tended to force to resolution in recent years). Lille's inter-communal structure is a leading one in France and has been pioneering in some areas, for example with regard to anti-poverty and urban regeneration.

Lille is a rare example of an 'industrial city' in France (Saint-Étienne being the other obvious example, on a smaller scale). Its regeneration problems are therefore, in many ways, more acute than those of more diversified cities. Lille has, until recently, suffered from an image problem in attracting new kinds of economic activity to the area. It has other advantages in its proximity to northern Europe, however, and its economic fortunes have been transformed in the past decade, not least as a result of its equidistant position from the three European capitals of London, Paris and Brussels and its role as a hub of French and European high-speed train networks. City actors (political, economic and associative) in Lille have also made important and impressive efforts to transform the city's negative image by promoting cultural activities, a mission rewarded with Lille becoming the European Capital of Culture in 2004.

The city was closely linked for several decades (1973–2001) with its energetic mayor, Pierre Mauroy, a heavyweight within the Socialist Party (Parti socialiste, PS) and the first Prime Minister of the Mitterrand years. Under Mauroy in the 1980s, the city council continued to prioritise social welfare but also reached out to private capital in a series of prestige projects designed to raise the city's profile nationally and internationally as well as improving infrastructure: the Channel tunnel, the TGV and Euralille commercial centre were the most important of these. In spite of its economic development, the area is historically associated with the development of socialism in France and the north continues to be a bastion of traditional workerist socialism. As a result, the area is rich in *associations* and may be seen as possessing high levels of social capital. As a result of these factors, Lille is characterised as having 'more complex' networks than the typical French city.[35] These tend to revolve around the central figure of the mayor (and the mayoral team) and shift according to the municipal council's priorities; in turn, the mayor's political longevity depends on his ability to manage these shifting networks.

In 2001 Mauroy handed over to his successor, Martine Aubry, having already announced his preferred replacement in 1994. The former Prime Minister did retain the presidency of the Lille Urban Community (Communauté urbaine de Lille, CUDL), the city's inter-communal structure, however, and was re-elected Senator for Nord/Pas-de-Calais in September 2001. Aubry's grip on the local political networks is considerably weaker than Mauroy's, which had already diminished since the glory days of the 1980s. Despite intense local campaigning, her electoral list gained only 34.5 per cent of the first-round vote in the March 2001 municipal elections, compared with Mauroy's 40.8 per cent in 1995 (already down from 43.1 per cent in 1989). The Greens, on the other hand, continued to improve their electoral fortunes, with 15.5 per cent of the first-round vote in March 2001. They used their new bargaining strength within the mayoral coalition to promote participative democracy, securing a political agreement with Aubry (hastily concocted between the two rounds) on reform proposals for the designation of local residents' representatives, in order to increase political diversity in local consultation forums (the Greens pushing for something more like standing 'citizens' juries').

Major city-wide and conurbation-wide projects have been driven by the mayor, harnessing local business interests, as with the pioneering 'mixed economy society' SEM Euralille in the 1980s. Economic development has led to the formation of a diverse coalition of business interests and the city council which, however, has not been particularly stable over time and seems to have broken up as the prestige projects have given way to smaller-scale initiatives (such as the City of Culture project for 2004). At the same time, partnerships with voluntary associations for anti-poverty measures under the inter-communal Grand Urban Project have increased in number and in stability, particularly in the areas of employment and anti-racism. The council is at the heart of a web of contracts with voluntary social service providers, all more or less dependent on these state-financed contracts.

Local democracy has been promoted in a more bottom-up way, although it has been boosted by the intervention of key actors within the city council, notably the Greens and independents. The *concertation* council is the brainchild of an independent councillor, Michel Falise, a former university lecturer.[36] Neighbourhood councils have existed since the 1970s and are the result of local activism in areas which have guarded their independence from the larger city, such as the working-class suburbs of Fives and Hellemmes.

Their links with the formal decision-making structures and processes of local government were strengthened in the 1990s by the institutionalisation of consultation in the *concertation* council as an 'interface' between civil society and municipal power.[37] Initially brought together as a loose grouping for consultative purposes, the *concertation* council was formalised by a municipal decision in June 1996 and given the status of a public interest group (GIP). In 1999 at the end of the first three-year mandate, the first direct elections to the council took place and the second at the end of 2002. Representatives are divided between the major interest groups such as businesses, professional bodies and trade unions. The bigger groups are invited to send a representative automatically; a third of seats are open to designation by groups, the remaining seats are filled by election among all the associations recognised by the municipal council. The groups are organised into sectors of activity: economic, social, cultural, sporting, and also some seats are reserved for particular territories (e.g. Hellemmes). The model for the *concertation* council is claimed to be the Porto Alegre model of 'participative budgets', although in practice the work of the council appears to be more routinised and more circumscribed. Nevertheless, its remit covers most of the main sectors of municipal council activity.

Moreover, the ability to intervene at its own demand (*auto-saisine*) has been available since 1999 and has been used assertively, in relation to the council's educational strategy, its urban regeneration strategy and plans for the European Capital of Culture in 2004. *Auto-saisine* is a powerful tool and has the potential to free the council from any fear of instrumentalisation by the municipal council as well as extending its role beyond simple *ad hoc* consultation.

At times, members of the consultative council have shown frustration with their role, particularly in relation to the neighbourhood councils and the intercommunal structure.[38] They have expressed complaints about municipal hijacking of the neighbourhood councils and some associations have accused the municipal council of 'clientelism'. Fears have repeatedly been expressed about the relationship between the city and the intercommunal structure (CUDL), with which the *concertation* council has no direct link. These relate to urban regeneration and economic development planning, which increasingly fall to the conurbation rather than the city.

In terms of the influence of the *concertation* council, there is little evidence of Lille council having to amend its decisions to take account of views expressed by the elected representatives of neighbourhoods and interest groups. On the one hand, there are anecdotal suggestions that the *concertation* council has forced open debates in areas where the municipal council would have carried on regardless. There is little doubt that the *concertation* council has opened up the space for outside interventions and, in this sense, increased transparency and the possibility of participation.

On the other hand, both the municipal council and the representatives on the *concertation* council are aware that *concertation* concerns only a minority of the citizenry. Whilst making local government more accountable and providing a space to challenge decision makers, the *concertation* council can contribute to a wider democratisation of public life only if the associations involved include its action in their own everyday activities. To date there is little sign of this happening, although it may take time for such practices to become established.

As with the 1982–83 reforms, the danger exists of the capture of 'participative' mechanisms by existing political parties. Neighbourhood councils appear to have become embroiled in partisan spoils systems.[39] In France as a whole, the rule seems to be that neighbourhood 'councils' correspond to a top-down logic, whilst neighbourhood 'committees' or 'unions' are more spontaneous, less institutionalised and correspond to a 'bottom-up' approach.[40] More generally, participative democracy seems to have become a central issue in the party political struggles within the city council, as socialist hegemony gives way to a more negotiated, 'plural left' style of decision making.

Finally, there are some limited signs that the *concertation* council has contributed to the renewal of local politics by giving expression to interest-based conflicts. The *concertation* council decides by consensus, that is, there is broad agreement on statements of policy whereby one or two groups can disagree on a specific point (rather than on the whole proposition) and in that case the dissenting or alternative view is attached in appendices. Consensus appears to be reached without too much difficulty on most policy areas. However, a classic business–labour conflict has emerged in relation to business opening hours, with business interests using the *concertation* council to argue that Lille's new status as a tourist city (specifically in relation to the European city of culture project) not only allows but requires longer opening of shops and other businesses than is allowed by the national regulations. To date, the business interests on the *concertation* council have been in the minority, but the debates have provided a focus for the campaign for longer business hours, which political leaders could use if they wished.

Discussion and conclusion

On-going observation of participation in French towns and cities has uncovered a large variety of practices.[41] Almost all the local councils observed had consultation and/or information mechanisms in place, but participation (deliberative) and *concertation* (associative) practices also appear to be very widespread, occurring in 60 per cent and 52 per cent of cases respectively. At the broad level, then, it would appear that a new pattern of urban governance is emerging, although with strong local specificities depending on the contours of local society and political networks. In this context, the Lille model does not stand out as particularly atypical, although associative democracy there has taken on a more institutionalised form.

The Lille model of neighbourhood councils and a formal *concertation* council provides an example of how interest and community groups can use participative mechanisms to create a space to make municipal councils more accountable and transparent. Over time, the behaviour of the elected representatives of the *concertation* council will help to shape the parameters of local decision making and may well extend the public space for participation, even though the mode of decision making in the *concertation* council itself does not increase participation.

Institutional design clearly matters. The direct election of representatives gives them a legitimacy which designated community representatives would not have. In particular, the ability to initiate opinions increases the power of the *concertation* council relative to the municipal council. The power to intervene on any issue marks a difference between the Lille structure and the consultative mechanisms observed in other municipalities such as Meylan,[42] which has an elaborate *concertation* structure based on specialism, giving the municipal council the power to determine the agenda of the *concertation* groups.

On the other hand, as already noted, simply involving grass-roots associations more closely in public policy is not likely to enhance wider civic behaviour, since, if it affects the relationship between associations and members at all, it is likely to be negatively. Despite efforts at local democracy, Lille municipal council has not been able to encourage greater participation at elections. Indeed, turnout at the 2001 municipal elections was low (just over 47.3 per cent in both rounds), down over ten percentage points from 1995, and among the lowest of all the French cities. It may be that 'proximity politics' detracts from traditional representative politics rather than sustains it, although research to date does not provide any evidence either way.

Finally, the shift towards a participative model needs to be seen as part of wider shifts which may be characterised as 'urban governance' but which are more complex than a simple alignment on an Anglo-American model of privatised service provision. The central state and other territorial units remain important actors. But in the case of the neighbourhood councils and the *concertation* council, shifts within the political class itself help to explain why modes of governance are changing and why those changes pose a fundamental challenge to the classic paradigm of the centralised and 'uniformising' Republic. Though their functioning may be imperfect, the example of neighbourhood councils and the '*concertation* council' in Lille demonstrates the importance of locality, of locally defined institutional structures and of local civil society as a political actor in post-republican France.

Notes

1 'Après vingt ans de décentralisation, de « pouvoir au local », émerge l'idée qu'on peut, qu'il faut, gouverner autrement'. Marie-Pierre de Liège, General Secretary of the Conseil national des villes, 2002.

2 A. Marbileau *et al.*, *Local Politics and Participation in Britain and France* (Cambridge: Cambridge University Press, 1989).

3 P. Sadran, *La Démocratie locale* (Paris: Les Cahiers Français, 1996), pp. 115–18.

4 S. Biarez, *Le Pouvoir local* (Paris: Economica, 1989); M. Phlipponneau, *Changer la vie,*

changer la ville : Rennes 1977 (La Baule: Breiz, 1976); A. Cole and P. John, *Local Governance in England and France* (London: Routledge, 2001).

5 P. Le Galès, *European Cities: Social Conflicts and Governance* (Oxford: Oxford University Press, 2002).

6 Cole and John, *Local Governance in England and France*.

7 V. Hoffmann-Martinot, 'Les grandes villes françaises : une démocratie en souffrance', in O. Gabriel and V. Hoffmann-Martinot (eds), *Démocraties urbaines* (Paris: Harmattan, 1999).

8 S. Collins, 'Beyond the "crisis of representation"? Experiments with local democracy in French cities', in S. Milner and N. Parsons (eds), *Reinventing France: State and Society in the Twenty-first Century* (Basingstoke: Palgrave, 2004), pp. 97–109.

9 P. John, 'Central–local relations in the 1980s and 1990s: towards a policy learning approach', *Local Government Studies*, 20:3 (1994), 412–36.

10 P. Hirst, *Associative Democracy: New Forms of Economic and Social Governance* (Oxford: Polity Press, 1994).

11 A. Bevort, *Pour une démocratie participative* (Paris: Presses de Sciences Po, 2002); J. Parkinson 'Legitimacy problems in deliberative democracy', *Political Studies*, 51:1 (2003), 180–96.

12 D. Collin, 'Crise et réforme de l'État', in T. Andréani and M. Vakaloulis (eds), *Refaire la politique* (Paris: Syllepse, 2002), pp. 91–116.

13 A. Mabileau, *Le Système local en France* (Paris: Montchrestien, 1991).

14 Sadran, *La Démocratie locale*.

15 J. Pierre and B. G. Peters, *Governance, Politics and the State* (Basingstoke: Macmillan, 2000).

16 R. D. Putnam (ed.), *Democracies in Flux* (Oxford: Oxford University Press, 2002); R. D. Putnam and S. J. Pharr (eds), *Disaffected Democracies* (Princeton NJ: Princeton University Press, 2000).

17 Le Galès, *European Cities: Social Conflicts and Governance*.

18 A. Bagnasco and P. Le Galès, *Cities in Contemporary Europe* (Cambridge: Cambridge University Press, 2000), p. 25.

19 *Ibid.*, p. 28.

20 John, 'Central–local relations in the 1980s and 1990s: towards a policy learning approach'; D. Mezzana and M. Cacace, 'Partnership and governance: towards overcoming the crisis of the state?' www.europeansynthesis.org (2003).

21 C. Stone, *Regime Politics: Governing Atlanta, 1946–1988* (Lawrence KS: University Press of Kansas, 1989).

22 G. Stoker and K. Mossberger, 'Urban regimes in comparative perspective', *Government and Policy*, 12:2 (1994), 195–21.

23 Mezzana and Cacace, 'Partnership and governance: towards overcoming the crisis of the state?'

24 Le Galès, *European Cities: Social Conflicts and Governance*; Cole and John, *Local Governance in England and France*.

25 P. Mauroy, *Refonder l'action publique locale : rapport au Premier ministre* (Paris: La Documentation française, 2000).

26 C. Assens and D. Phanuel, 'Les modes de gouvernement de la démocratie locale', paper for the IV Rencontres Ville–Management, Nancy, 16–17 November 2000.

27 Les Verts de Brest, 'Pour une véritable démocratie de proximité', www.verts-brest.infini.fr/Brestou-Vert.article.php?idarticle=26 (20 March 2002').

28 Réseau initiatives et citoyenneté (RIC), 'Les conseils de quartier sont-ils un outil de proximité?' Summary of seminar discussions, Paris, 7 June 2002.
29 Cap'Com, 'La démocratie de proximité vue par les communicants publics', report, November 2003.
30 *Pays* are yet another layer of territorial administration (although not local administration as such) for the promotion of even economic development. They cover large, mainly rural areas with similar physical characteristics.
31 S. Costanzo, 'Conseils de développement : vers un outil de démocratie locale', *Territoires*, 430 (2002).
32 I. Lévy, 'Le Paris des conseils de quartier', *Territoires*, 427 (2002).
33 M. Cau, 'Démocratie de proximité : en Vert et vu d'ici', www.vertsderoubaix .org.article.php3?id_article=54 (23 March 2002).
34 Cole and John, *Local Governance in England and France*, pp. 122–4.
35 *Ibid.*, p. 128.
36 M. Falise, *Démocratie participative : promesses et ambiguïtés* (Paris: L'Aube Essais, 2003).
37 Conseil communal de concertation, 'Concertation', *Bulletin du CCC*, 3 (1999).
38 Conseil communal de concertation, 'La démocratie participative à Lille–Hellemmes–Lomme : perspectives et propositions', text adopted by the plenary session, 20 November 2000.
39 A. Laurent, 'Lille : de Pierre Mauroy à Martine Aubry, la transition inachevée', in B. Dolez and A. Laurent (eds), *Le Vote des villes : les élections municipales des 11 et 18 mars 2001* (Paris: Presses de Sciences Po, 2002), pp. 211–28, for discussions between the Greens and the Socialists after the second round in March 2001.
40 G. Gontcharoff, 'Le renouveau des comités de quartier', in CRAPS/CURAPP, *La Démocratie locale : participation et espace public* (Paris: Presses Universitaires de France, 1999), pp. 305–27.
41 'Dossier : les habitants dans la décision locale, politique de participation et participation au politique', *Territoires*, 399 *bis* (1999).
42 Assens and Phanuel, 'Les modes de gouvernement de la démocratie locale'.

Select bibliography

T. Andréani and M. Vakaloulis (eds), *Refaire la politique* (Paris: Syllepse, 2002).

A. Bevort, *Pour une démocratie participative* (Paris: Presses de Sciences Po, 2002).

M. Cau, 'Démocratie de proximité : en Vert et vu d'ici', www.vertsderoubaix.org .article.php3?id_article=54 (23 March 2002).

A. Cole and P. John, *Local Governance in England and France* (London: Routledge, 2001).

S. Costanzo, 'Conseils de développement : vers un outil de démocratie locale', *Territoires*, 430 (2002).

B. Dolez and A. Laurent (eds), *Le Vote des villes : les élections municipales des 11 et 18 mars 2001* (Paris: Presses de Sciences Po, 2002).

M. Falise, *Démocratie participative : promesses et ambiguïtés* (Paris: L'Aube Essais, 2003).

O. Gabriel and V. Hoffmann-Martinot (eds), *Démocraties urbaines* (Paris: Harmattan, 1999).

G. Gontcharoff, 'Le renouveau des comités de quartier', in CRAPS/CURAPP, *La Démocratie locale : participation et espace public* (Paris: Presses Universitaires de France, 1999).

P. Hirst, *Associative Democracy: New Forms of Economic and Social Governance* (Oxford: Polity Press, 1994).

P. Hirst and S. Khilnani, *Reinventing Democracy* (Oxford: Blackwell, 1996).

P. John, 'Central–local relations in the 1980s and 1990s: towards a policy learning approach', *Local Government Studies*, 20:3 (1994), 412–36.

P. Le Galès, *European Cities: Social Conflicts and Governance* (Oxford: Oxford University Press, 2002).

Les Verts de Brest, 'Pour une véritable démocratie de proximité', www.verts-brest.infini.fr/Brestou-Vert.article.php?idarticle=26 (20 March 2002).

I. Lévy, 'Le Paris des conseils de quartier', *Territoires*, 427 (2002).

M-P. Liège, 'Gouverner autrement : ou, les nouvelles façons de faire de la politique', *Territoires*, 428 (2002).

A. Mabileau, *Les Élites politiques locales* (Paris: Montchrestien, 1999).

A. Mabileau, G. Moyser, G. Parry and P. Quantin, *Local Politics and Participation in Britain and France* (Cambridge: Cambridge University Press, 1989).

P. Mauroy, *Refonder l'action publique locale : rapport au Premier ministre* (Paris: La Documentation Française, 2000).

D. Mezzana and M. Cacace, 'Partnership and governance : towards overcoming the crisis of the state?' www.europeansynthesis.org (2003).

J. Parkinson, 'Legitimacy problems in deliberative democracy', *Political Studies*, 51:1 (2003), 180–96.

J. Pierre and B. G. Peters, *Governance, Politics and the State* (Basingstoke: Macmillan, 2000).

R. D. Putnam (ed.), *Democracies in Flux* (Oxford: Oxford University Press, 2002).

R. D. Putnam and S. J. Pharr (eds), *Disaffected Democracies* (Princeton NJ: Princeton University Press, 2000).

P. Sadran, *La Démocratie locale* (Paris: Les Cahiers Français, 1996).

G. Stoker and K. Mossberger, 'Urban regimes in comparative perspective', *Government and Policy*, 12:2 (1994), 195–21.

5

From margin to mainstream? Establishing a community of gay citizens

Steve Wharton

Paragraph 2 of Penal Code Article 331 is repealed.[1]
    The politicisation of homosexuality is incontestably one of the key points of the last decade.[2]
    It is simply the claims we are making, our demand not for special rights but equal rights, which upset things.[3]
    The PACS . . . is not simply a matter of the fate of certain individuals, it marks an evolution of society as a whole . . . [T]he demand for equality between sexualities also begs questions which impinge on the very definition of society.[4]

The decision of the Bordeaux *tribunal de grande instance* on 29 July 2004 to declare invalid France's first gay marriage between nursing auxiliary Stéphane Chapin and shop owner Bertrand Charpentier performed in Bègles by its Vert (Green) *député-maire* Noël Mamère on 5 June that year, on the grounds that the *Code civil* makes it clear in paragraphs 74, 144, 184 and 190 that marriage is between male and female, reiterated the pre-eminence of the Republic over the individual and, more important, of the *République une et indivisible* over any concept of gay community which might have been deemed to arise from confirmation that Mamère had acted correctly.[5]

And so, twenty years on from the publication of the law erasing the last traces of Vichy's homophobic legislation, with a gay Maire de Paris, Bertrand Delanoë, and a PACS[6] which grants certain fiscal and inheritance rights to same-sex couples, has the notion of a more tolerant French society been dealt a blow by such a decision? When 64 per cent of *Elle* readers declare themselves in favour of gay marriage, alongside 57 per cent of those of the readership of LGBT[7] magazine *Têtu* and even 50 per cent of the readership of the traditionally conservative *Valeurs actuelles*,[8] in taking the action it has over Bègles is the state reflecting the concerns of the citizen or those for its own continued and unaltered existence?

There have undoubtedly been major milestones in the history of the LGBT community in France over the last two decades. In answering the foregoing questions this chapter is not, however, the place to revisit the particular historical events of those decades in great detail, but rather to seek to explore whether, in the light of the 'developments', we have seen a move for *le pédé* from margin to mainstream in France. Although the LGBT community is more visible and arguably more tolerated than it has been in the past, the Bègles case clearly demonstrates that further progress remains to be made, not only in tolerance but in potentially positing a re-evaluation of the notion of *La République une et indivisible* which has characterised France since the Revolution and which we have seen increasingly questioned elsewhere, for example in the light of France's immigrant population. Although there is to be no exhaustive chronology, there is of course a general requirement to provide the odd historical signpost, together with some theoretical background.

Theory and practice

From the theoretical point of view, especially within a French context, we cannot discuss sexuality and identity without briefly mentioning the F-word: Michel Foucault. His *Histoire de la sexualité*[9] (among other work) prompted a rethink of our traditional appreciations of sexuality and the normative processes it operates. In the context of the PACS such work gives major pause for thought. If we accept Foucault's vision of the paradigm of sexuality, then our awareness of sexuality begins to crystallise only in the eighteenth century (at which time it became a point of discussion; until then it was something which did not form part of everyday discourse). By the same token, although homosexual practice existed since before then, it was not until the medicalist categorisation of the term in the nineteenth century (the word was invented only in the 1860s, and then it was the medical and not the social which obtained); references to homosexuality saw it as a disease (or dis-ease) rather than a state of self.[10] As such, it fell to the state to regulate diseased action. (We shall see below how the state criminalised homosexuality and finally reversed that discrimination.) It therefore follows that the subsequent literal *fin de siècle* (*dernier*) incorporation of explicit state recognition of homosexuality through the PACS leaves us with a sort of 'same difference'; since the state recognises same-sex relationships and affords them financial and inheritance rights similar (though not identical) to those of heterosexuals, that is in essence a similarity of treatment to relationships of a sexuality different from what has hitherto been regarded as the norm. The deviant thus joins the mainstream. Or does it? And who has the authority to pronounce on or define which is the mainstream and which is the 'deviant'? Similar questions are present within the LGBT community itself, be it in France or elsewhere, as (for example) the debate around separatism versus assimilationism; should gays and lesbians celebrate their difference, or should they 'conform' and not 'disturb'? 'We want the right to difference in order to enjoy the right of indifference' as one slogan from the 1980s has it.

Certainly in the 1950s in France the self-styled 'homophile' organisation Arcadie was keen to conform, eschewing the word 'homosexual' in any description of itself, ensuring no physical contact between its members at meetings, a stressing of 'normality' described in the mid-1990s as 'Act in a dignified manner and you'll be respected'.[11] This was in stark contrast to the revolutionary activities of organisations such as CAPR (the Comité d'action pédérastique révolutionnaire, or Committee for Revolutionary Pederastic Action) and FHAR, the Front homosexuel d'action révolutionnaire, or Homosexual Front for Revolutionary Action in the 1960s and 1970s, and more recently the activities or 'zaps' of ACT-UP, a direct action group drawing its inspiration from those of the same name with their origins in the United States.[12] Just as opinion in the LGBT community was divided over ACT-UP's tactics and its anti-assimilationist discourse, the 'fault lines' in the LGBT community which have been thrown into prominence over Bègles and further 'equal treatment' issues arising therefrom (adoption, assisted fertility treatment), indicate precisely how disunited the 'community' actually is.[13]

The issue of community is at the heart of the work of British author and academic Jeffrey Weeks, who did much to establish the framework for the discussion of questions around identity and image within the United Kingdom. His comments are equally valid for France, and he succinctly outlined the paradoxical status of sexuality *per se* when he said that 'As a contemporary phenomenon [it] is the product of a history of autonomous and interacting traditions and social practices: religious, moral, economic, familial, medical, juridical.'[14] And yet, as Georges Canguilhem indicates, such traditions and social practices ('norms' if you will) are clearly the result of invention rather than of inherence: 'If social norms were as clearly observable as organic norms, humankind would be mad to conform to them. As humanity is not mad and there are no Great Wise Ones, *this means that social norms are something to be invented and not to be observed.*'[15]

And taking the term 'gay', as Eribon says in a summary *reprise* of a key element of Foucault's extensive work on the subject, 'Language is never neutral, and the act of naming has consequences which are social: those consequences define images and representations. To choose the word "gay" is to recognise the legitimacy and need of the movement of self-affirmation which established it.'[16]

Affirmation de soi also encompasses groupings of that *soi*, groupings which may in certain circumstances be considered communities. American academic Margaret Cruikshank takes Dennis Altman's suggestion that the notion of gay community depends on a gay culture, since homosexuals have no common country or language to bind them. In her eyes, therefore, '"gay community" refers to the lesbians and gay men who consider themselves part of a political movement. *Membership of the community is thus chosen rather than automatic.*'[17]

Use of the word 'gay' as an adjective or noun in France is also arguably a potential problem in a country in which the state through the Académie française seeks at every turn to ensure the purity of its language and measures such as the loi Toubon require percentages of French music to be played on national radio. The word 'gay', written with no concession to its use in a country so proud of its linguistic traditions, is clearly an 'Anglo-Saxon' import and, furthermore, arguably encompasses the communitarian concepts which it connotes. As such it immediately encounters the problem of accommodation within *la République une et indivisible* to which we have already referred and which does not admit of separate communities within the state monolith. Moreover, debates in France among the 'gay community' itself have in some quarters been resistant to the communitarian model precisely because it is seen as American or 'Anglo-Saxon' and therefore against those republican ideals. The argument runs that, since the universal Republic provides for equality between its members' communitarian (self)-differentiation, rather than engaging with the need to treat everyone equally within that republican model, it sets the members of that community apart and prevents them from engaging with the fundamental 'given' that universalism has always shifted to accommodate different groups.[18]

There is however one such republican ideal which unites Weeks's social and juridical in France: the *loi du 1 juillet 1970* (Article 9 of the *Code civil*) which guarantees the right to a private life. In consequence, an individual's gender object choice is a matter for the individual and that gender object choice, and the media or another individual should not interfere. Mention of an individual's sexuality without that individual's permission renders the transgressor liable to prosecution, and ironically was a weapon used against those wishing to out the gay Gaullist *député* who was active in opposing the PACS. Paradoxically, however, the state intervenes in the individual's private life with its prescriptions in respect of the recognition of same-sex relationships. And, as we have observed, state recognition of different *identities* within the Republic – religious,[19] sexual or other – is practically impossible. Indeed, it was this very republican ideal of non-recognition of separate identities, together with reluctance on the part of the gay community in France to 'surrender' its liberties and become more concerned with safer sex practices, which arguably delayed the targeting of AIDS-related information campaigns in the 1980s.

The simple fact remains that, without some legal reform or recognition of a cohabitative status, same-sex couples are prevented from benefiting, for example, from rights in the fields of inheritance and taxation. Following a 1989 decision that Air France had been wrong in not according partnership travel rights to an air steward's partner, the *cour de cassation* on 11 July that year determined on appeal that *concubinage* (cohabitation, a kind of French common-law partnership) applied only to heterosexual couples,[20] even though those *concubins* themselves were denied specific inheritance rights under the law. In objective terms, a legal framework predicated on marriage and the family *within a context of equality* should not of itself discriminate against unmarried couples (in French, *concubins*) either. The machinations of the Christine Boutin-led coalition against the PACS had intended to preclude the need for a PACS by introducing same-sex *concubinage* instead; its eventual incorporation in the

PACS legislation had the ironic outcome of benefiting heterosexual *concubins* whilst also permitting same-sex *concubinage* alongside the PACS (rather than stopping it).

That said, equal rights in the general context of the shorthand definition of 'gay marriage' is in itself problematic by its very terminology. From a religious perspective, marriage is predicated on procreation; as a biologically non-productive union it has no place in a Judaeo-Christian value set which elsewhere condemns the homosexuals who would constitute it.[21] The feminist critique of marriage as reinforcing patriarchy and its structures of submission has further repressive characteristics when applied to 'gay marriage', since here again the mainstream interpretation of masculinity and sexuality drawn from patriarchy is homophobic. A Foucauldian reading of the situation would further problematise the concept; in adopting/adapting marriage, homosexuals are conforming within the very socially reproduced models their (externally defined) sexuality should be seeking to undermine or destabilise.

Indeed, criticisms of the PACS in France from within the LGBT community itself hinge around their aping of marriage. And what of the 'logical' corollary, the reproductive imperative? Opponents outside the LGBT community seize on this, speaking of its undermining marriage and the family, that it is the first step towards adoption and *in vitro* fertilisation; the end of 'civilisation' as seen by the traditionalists (both political and religious). Yet, with the PACS enshrined in law,[22] there is a new area of debate building on these criticisms: how does one cut the Gordian knot which says that, although there are some similarities of treatment for the heterosexual and same-sex communities, there cannot be identity of treatment, for example in the field of adoption?

Turning to the question of similarity of treatment and the role of the state, it was not until 1982 that homosexuality was finally decriminalised for men over the age of fifteen in France. When Charles de Gaulle replaced the constitution of the Fourth Republic with that of the Fifth in 1958, he retained one particular piece of Vichy legislation that had not been repealed at the Liberation with other Nazi-inspired measures; Article 331-2 of the new Republic's Penal Code continued Vichy's *ordonnance* of 6 August 1942 (Vichy's Penal Code Article 334) criminalising same-sex activity between males under the age of twenty-one. Political backing for its abolition was slow in coming despite regular campaigning. During the 1981 presidential campaign, candidate François Mitterrand openly expressed support for the abolition of the discriminatory paragraph only tardily; invited to a meeting at the Palais des Congrès on 28 April 1981, shortly before the presidential elections, he was asked questions on homosexuality by *Le Monde* journalist Josyane Savigneau. Although reported as 'Homosexuality should cease to be a crime,'[23] the actual response was typically *mitterrandien* and evasive: in response to the question 'Should homosexuality cease to be a crime?' his response, 'Absolutely,' was followed by 'within the framework of normal relationships falling within the purview of those laws which should nonetheless provide for the organisation of society'.[24]

As we shall see later, this issue of 'normality' is to the fore over the PACS. It displays the latent fear in a heteronormative society in which 'normal' and 'organisation' are to the fore, with the counterpart (as expressed in Fortin's opening quote) that anything else disturbs, is disruptive and (in the words of its defensive extremists) could ultimately lead to the destruction of this 'normal' society. Despite these fears, the removal of the discriminatory paragraphs (together with a 1985 law preventing workplace discrimination on the grounds of sexual orientation) did not lead to the collapse of French civilisation. And although there has been criticism of the PACS and its probable undermining of marriage, figures from INSEE show that, for example,

> 303,500 marriages were celebrated [in France] in 2001. . . . The appearance of the [PACS] has not had a negative effect on the marriage rate: the PACS came into effect at the end of 1999, a period in which we see a rise in the number of marriages. . . . *For every hundred marriages we see eight PACS entered into.* Current available statistics do not allow an assessment of whether [the PACS] is primarily a matter for homosexuals, or whether it is seen as an alternative to marriage by certain heterosexual couples.[25]

'Presidentiables et pédés'

The PACS (or, more correctly, its role in the case of equality of treatment) was an issue during the presidential elections, albeit on a minor scale; readers of the April 2002 issue of *Têtu*[26] may have been surprised to see the cover and article inside: 'Le duel: Chirac/Jospin'. As the publication itself stated, the reasoning behind the President and Prime Minister directly addressing the gay community was clear:

> This double event is a direct political effect of the law establishing the Civil Solidarity Pact. By having a vote on the first legislation to recognise homosexual couples, Lionel Jospin has obliged the entire political class to make its views known on issues as diverse as homosexual parenting, the rights of homosexuals in the world, homophobia or the difficulties of young gays and lesbians.[27]

Interestingly, a poll for *Têtu* had shown (in February 2002) that 73 per cent of French people would not be shocked if a homosexual were elected *Président de la Republique*.[28] When asked directly why he has chosen to answer questions from a magazine targeting the homosexual community, Chirac's reply is 'Why should I have turned down such a request? I am very worried by the development of disrespect in France. . . . I never fought against the PACS. At the time, certain individuals approached me with a request to commit myself in opposition to it; I always refused.'[29]

Of course, there is another, more cynical, reason for these interventions by both politicians: since it is generally accepted that some 10 per cent of any given population is gay, it follows that for any politician wishing to swing an overall vote it would be foolish in the extreme to ignore such a constituency. And yet, despite Chirac's apparent support for PACS, he is a firm proponent of children being raised by a mother and father: 'The overriding factor before all other considerations should be that of the interests of the child.'[30] Such comments are eerily similar to those of Jospin: 'Everyone's right to their own individual sexual choice should not be confused with some hypothetical right to a child. A child has the right to a father and a mother.'[31] This apparently heteronormative approach ignores other comments made by Chirac himself within the article and elsewhere, that the situation of the family now has many forms, e.g. one-parent families, divorced couples with children, etc. It is, however, similar to the decision of the *cour de cassation* in 1993 not to allow a single gay man to adopt,[32] a decision confirmed by the European Court of Human Rights (26 February 2002) when it stated that it was the duty of member states to decide for themselves how best to interpret such cases; the dismissal came since discrimination on grounds of gender was not proven.[33] Such a decision appears strangely at odds with the clauses of the Amsterdam Treaty excluding prejudice on the grounds of sexual orientation, which saw themselves transformed in part into an EU directive which is being implemented by all member states[34] and which was the subject of protracted debate in the United Kingdom with regard to its actual protection of LGBT employees.[35]

L'État s'impose: equal rights, unequal wrongs?

And it is again to the question of equal treatment that we must turn in a closer examination of the Bègles gay marriage of 5 June 2004, providing a wider context. 16 January 2004 saw a homophobic attack on thirty-five-year old Sébastien Nouchet in the northern town of Noeux-les-mines which left him with third-degree burns. Within a month activist groups had begun to respond with a call for legal protection against such homophobic acts, and the Collectif pour l'égalité des droits (Collective for Equal Rights) was born; its key principle was that the starting point for combating homophobia was equality between homosexuals and heterosexuals. On 16 March philosopher Didier Eribon and jurist Daniel Borillo published their *Manifeste pour l'égalité des droits*, which invited French mayors to celebrate gay marriage. Within a month a number of mayors and their deputies had committed themselves to the pursuit of such requests. Some tension arose when the gay mayor of Paris, Bertrand Delanoë, declared himself opposed to such unilateral moves on 4 April, stating, 'Yes to a debate to see whether the law has to be changed in Parliament, but while we're waiting we shan't solve the problem by organising three "gay marriage media events".'[36] Eighteen days later, Noël Mamère announced that he was intending to marry two men in Bègles. Political opponents were quick to criticise such an announcement and even to seek Mamère's dismissal from office. Reiterating a theme on which he had touched in his February 2002 *Têtu* article, on 29 April Chirac declared himself opposed to same-sex marriage. The same day the *député-maire* of Villeneuve-lès-

Avignon, Jean-Marc Roubaud, proposed a law stating that marriage was designed for heterosexual union,[37] and Dominique Perben announced that the President and Prime Minister had asked him to undertake an assessment of the PACS. In the coming months the issue became a political football, each side lining up to defend the current institution of marriage or even to propose constitutional changes providing for equality before the law in the case of sexuality and transgender matters.

Another announcement of future marriage came on 19 May when Noël Caru, mayor of Caudebec-lès-Elbeuf, made clear his intention to celebrate a gay marriage. One of the members of that couple was physically attacked by members of the CFTC union and accused of a mediatisation of the marriage in a manner which was 'detrimental to the union'. On 24 July a 'symbolic' marriage was performed by Caru, though no official badges of office or registers were used, the 'married couple' simply leaving the ceremony with a document signed by witnesses but nothing 'official'.

The state intervened in the Bègles affair on 4 June when the State Prosecutor challenged Mamère's right to marry the couple on the grounds that there were residence irregularities. Mamère replied that documentary evidence existed, that he would proceed, and that the State Prosecutor, the Ministry of Justice and the Prime Minister were harassing and intimidating the couple.

The marriage went ahead as planned on 5 June, with a dozen or so protesters outside the *Mairie*. As, inside, Mamère had tears in his eyes and announced that he had never been so proud to be mayor of Bègles, slogans outside included 'Yesterday the PACS, today marriage and adoption, tomorrow incest and paedophilia' (*Hier le PACS, aujourd'hui le mariage et l'adoption, demain l'inceste et la pédophilie*).[38] Two days later, on 7 June, Mamère and Paris *député* Martine Billard put forward a proposal to open marriage to same-sex couples, she having worked with the same lawyers behind the *Manifeste des égalités*.

Despite its misgivings over his actions, the state would not dismiss Mamère, though a thirty-day suspension of mayoral duties was imposed on 15 June, since he had failed to follow the instructions of the State Prosecutor in pursuing the marriage despite instruction to the contrary. That in turn was challenged by Mamère's lawyer, revoked, and the revocation dismissed on appeal on 9 July, the same day that a proposal for another same-sex marriage in the nineteenth district of Paris was formally opposed by the State Prosecutor

In parallel with the debates around the issue of gay marriage the government majority in Parliament put forward proposals to enshrine in law sanctions against homophobia, and Raffarin met representatives of the LGBT community on 24 June, three days before Paris Gay Pride 2004, to discuss this and related issues. However, the anti-homophobia proposals were attacked by Philippe de Villiers (who was present at Bègles in June to protest against the wedding) as a possible means of depriving opponents of same-sex marriage of a means of expressing their opposition.

'Ultimate' state intervention in the gay marriage debate came on 14 July when, during a televised interview to mark Bastille Day, Chirac spoke in favour of improvements in the PACS but against same-sex marriage:

> Obviously it appears that the PACS could be improved and I would wish to see it improved in such a way that the rights and responsibilities of same-sex cohabitors . . . are protected in the same way as those of others. This should not lead to a parody of marriage . . . We should not confuse two different things. There are problems which require resolution. The PACS has been established and that's perfect.[39]

As incarnation of the state, the President ensures the *status quo* and thereby provides support for the anti-homophobia proposals of his Prime Minister.

The final state blow to the Bègles marriage came on 29 July, when, as has already been indicated, the marriage was annulled. The following day the extreme right-wing group Bloc identitaire, itself present among the protesters in Bègles on 5 June, issued the following statement: 'Elected officials and representatives tempted by such veiled invitations from an increasingly self-assured and overbearing gay lobby need to know that they will regularly have to face up to, even at home, militants from the Bloc and its youth wing.'[40] Clearly an indication of the potential violence inherent within homophobia, against which the state appears to wish to act through its proposals for a new law. Such state protection is necessary – the Nouchet case is hardly an isolated incident, and the group SOS Homophobie records regular attacks, physical or verbal, on the LGBT community. Even gay mayor of Paris Bertrand Delanoë is not immune from homophobic comment within his own *conseil général:* in June 2001 its president, Jacques Larché accused him of being unable to reply to his mail since he was parading at the head of a Gay Pride march.[41]

And even when the state does legislate, as for example it did with the PACS, that legislation must in turn be interpreted according to the opinions of judges and jurists, themselves perceived by some as emanations of the state. Not all are in favour. Indeed, the following quotations from more hard-line jurists indicate arguably that gays are still more margin than mainstream:

> With regard to society . . . there is an irreducible difference which hangs, whether we like it or not, upon *the nature of things:* knowing that the shared lifestyle of a homosexual couple is at best socially neutral whereas that of a heterosexual home brings hope and stability for society. Unfit for ensuring the renewal of the members which make up that society, *homosexuality is by its nature a way of living which is fatal to society.* Such a comment is not a subjective, moral appreciation but an *elementary biological statement.*[42]

> If it is to be welcomed that the right of respect for private life *a priori* excludes any reproach to homosexuals over their lifestyle, it does seem on the other hand legitimate to refuse them the right to take advantage of their situation to bring a child into the world: even if it is commonplace, *homosexuality is still not yet a 'normal' lifestyle* which can offer a child the guarantees of personal development which comes from parents; the interest of a child being born into such a family is therefore not self-evident.[43]

These views may be justifiably characterised as personal opinion masquerading as legal judgement. Since some jurists are already opining that there are dangers in a legal definition of homophobia, since the net may be thrown too wide, and bearing in mind the difficulties over the preparation and passage of the PACS, it is not difficult to imagine precisely how that anti-homophobia legislation will be drafted and interpreted. The PACS itself (or at least, the concept of state recognition of same-sex relationships which was to culminate in the PACS in 1999) took nearly ten years to become law, and its passage through Parliament was subject to misinformation, disinformation and homophobic discourse both outside and within Parliament. In this latter connection, for example, according to the *Observatoire du PACS*, 'At the final reading of the PACS in the Senate, on 30 June 1999, the Gaullist Senator for the Rhône Emmanuel Hamel rose and proposed that the PACS be renamed the "Pact for AIDS Contamination".'[44]

Conclusion

Such a comment as the one made above, from a legislator charged with promoting the interests of the Republic and its citizens, serves, together with the issues raised and discussed here, to demonstrate clearly that the state monolith is slow to acknowledge the rights of certain of its citizens whose existence has until recently been relatively low-profile but which is becoming less so. The republican ideal, seeking to avoid the recognition of anything communitarian, something which is not simply *and singly* French, further slows the process of tolerance, understanding and acceptance which is so necessary here. EU directives, presidential candidates and laws by themselves do not change society; it is a question of education and the eventual changing of mind-sets. Certainly, although there is a PACS, although there is indeed a gay mayor and some other mayors are willing to consider extending the rights of marriage to members of the LGBT community, and although decriminalisation has finally come, the Judaeo-Christian foundations of French society, its general heteronormative approach, the *polémique* and the *politique*, are such that the *pédé* remains largely marginalised through continued insistence on *la République une et indivisible*.

Notes

1 All translations are my own unless otherwise stated. The original reads as follows: 'L'alinéa 2 de l'article 331 du *Code pénal* est abrogé.' Loi L82-683 du 4 août 1982, *Journal officiel* (1982).
2 'La politicisation de l'homosexualité est incontestablement l'un des faits saillants de la dernière décennie.' F. Devoucoux du Buysson, *Les Khmers roses : essai sur l'idéologie homosexuelle* (Paris: Editions Blanche, 2003), p. 71.
3 'Nos revendications toutes simples, notre exigence non de droits particuliers mais d'une égalité de droits, dérangent l'ordre des choses.' J. Fortin, *L'Homosexualité : l'adieu aux normes* (Paris: Textuel, 2000), p. 9.

4 'Le PACS n'est . . . pas seulement le sort de quelques-uns, c'est l'évolution de la société dans son entier . . . [L]a demande d'égalité entre les sexualités pose ainsi des questions qui touchent à la définition même de la société'. D. Borillo and E. Fassin, *Au-delà du PACS : l'expertise familiale à l'épreuve de l'homosexualité*, 2nd edn, Politique d'aujourd'hui (Paris: Presses Universitaires de France, 2001), p. 4.

5 'We are not talking here about the legitimacy or illegitimacy of homosexual marriage . . . It is not a social, moral or philosophical matter, but a simple matter of law' ('Il ne s'agit pas ici de parler de la légitimité ou de l'illégitmité du mariage homosexuel . . . Ce n'est pas une question de société, de morale, ou de philosophie mais une question pure de droit'), as the lawyer for the government put it (http://tetu.com /infos/lire/7062), thereby rehearsing legal arguments made a century earlier.

6 *Pacte civil de solidarité* or Civil Solidarity Pact, legislation enacted in November 1999 permitting couples of the same or either sex to register their 'civil solidarity' and eventually to benefit from inheritance and other financial rights. Some commentators view the PACS as the ultimate republican form of marriage, since they argue that even the civil ceremony retains the biblical injunction to reproduce; the PACS, having no such imperative but being the Republic's recognition of mutual cohabitative status, is more *laïc*, or lay, and therefore more appropriate to a secular republic.

7 Lesbian, Gay, Bisexual, Transgender. Although the term LGBT is used here, many of the following references are predominantly male. This does not mean any value judgement of the role of lesbians or trans in French society; rather, in the 'LGBT community' as in society in general, their role has been under-investigated and does not fall directly within the remit of this chapter, written as it is by a gay man.

8 *Elle* poll published 10 May 2004, *Têtu* and *Valeurs actuelles* the following week, details quoted in *Libération* on 4 June 2004.

9 M. Foucault, *Histoire de la sexualité* (Paris: Gallimard, 1976).

10 As we see below, there is a distinction between homosexuality (medical term) and being LGBT (more a political act, an *affirmation de soi*); in simple syllogistic terms, all LGBT people are homosexual, though not all homosexuals are LGBT. In medical terms it was not, for example, until 1973 that the American Psychological Association removed homosexuality from its official manual listing as a mental illness.

11 'Soyez dignes et on vous respectera.' J. Le Bitoux, 'Le mouvement homosexuel français : politique ou socioculturel ?' *Politique*, 5 (1997), 28.

12 For further information on ACT-UP see S. Wharton, 'Progress, what progress? Lesbian and Gay Liberation under the Fifth Republic', in M. Allison and O. Heathcote (eds), *Forty Years of the Fifth French Republic: Actions, Dialogues, Discourses* (Berne: Peter Lang, 1999).

13 ACT-UP Paris was particularly critical of the 'normalising', non-troubling aspects of the mid-1990s AIDS awareness campaigns from organisations such as AFLS.

14 J. Weeks, *Coming out: Homosexual Politics in Britain from the Nineteenth Century to the Present* (London: Quartet Books, 1983), p. 6.

15 'Si les normes sociales pouvaient être aperçues aussi clairement que les normes organiques, les hommes seraient fous de ne pas s'y conformer. Comme les hommes ne sont pas fous, et comme il n'existe pas de Sages, *c'est que les normes sociales sont à inventer et non pas à observer.*' S. Prokhoris, 'L'adoration des majuscules', in D. Borillo and E. Fassin, *Au-delà du PACS : l'expertise familiale à l'épreuve de l'homosexualité*, 2nd

edn (Paris: Presses Universitaires de France, 2001), p. 145; G. Canguilhem, *Le Normal et le pathologique* (Paris: Presses Universitaires de France, 1994), p. 194.

16 'Le langage n'est jamais neutre, et les actes de nomination ont des effets sociaux : ils définissent des images et des représentations. Choisir le mot « gay », c'est reconnaître la légitimité et la nécessité du mouvement d'affirmation de soi qui l'a institué.' D. Eribon (ed.), *Les Études gays et lesbiennes* (Paris: Editions du Centre Georges Pompidou Supplémentaires, 1998), p. 23.

17 M. Cruikshank, *The Gay and Lesbian Liberation Movement* (New York: Routledge, 1998), pp. 118–19. My emphasis.

18 See Le Bitoux, 'Le mouvement homosexuel français : politique ou socioculturel ?'; L. Bersani *et al.*, *Les Études gay et lesbiennes* (Paris: Editions du Centre Georges Pompidou Supplémentaires, 1998).

19 See for example, the controversy over the enactment of a law forbidding the wearing of any 'ostentatious religious symbol' following on from the original *affaire du foulard*, when female Muslims at school were forbidden to wear the traditional *chador* or headscarf, since for them to do so would be contrary to the secular state's refusal to recognise any separate religious community within the one and indivisible Republic.

20 More recently, in 1997, Air France itself reversed its decision of eight years previously and now offers partnership travel.

21 Even though it is the articulation of a lay state, the republican civil ceremony repeats the biologically reproductive imperative.

22 Figures have risen from 23,718 in 2000 to 31,500 in 2003, with total numbers over the four-year period of 100,320 (*Le Monde*, 5 June 2004).

23 'L'homosexualité doit cesser d'être un délit.' F. Martel, *Le Rose et le noir : histoire des homosexuels en France depuis 1968* (Paris: Seuil, 1996), p. 142.

24 'Should homosexuality cease to be a crime?' 'Absolutely . . . within the framework of normal relationships falling within the purview of those laws which should none the less provide for the organisation of society.' *Ibid.*

25 'En 2001, 303 500 mariages ont été célébrés. . . . L'apparition du pacte civil de solidarité (PACS) n'a pas eu d'effet négatif sur la nuptialité : le PACS est entré en vigueur à la fin de l'année 1999, date qui correspond à la hausse du nombre de mariages. . . . *Pour cent mariages célébrés, huit PACS sont signés.* Actuellement, les données disponibles ne permettent pas de déterminer si ce contrat concerne essentiellement les couples homosexuels ou s'il constitue plutôt une alternative au mariage pour certains couples hétérosexuels.' www.insee.fr/fr/ffc/pop_age4.htm. My emphasis.

26 The very LGBT monthly which started its life as a clarion call to seize the moment and the initiative by Didier Lestrade, founder member of ACT-UP. Lestrade formally broke with ACT-UP on 9 June 2004 and now works with The Warning, 'Un nouveau groupe de pédés qui n'aiment pas le sida' (a new group of gays who don't like AIDS). *Le Monde*, 12 June 2004.

27 'Ce double événement est un effet politique direct de la loi instituant le pacte civil de solidarité. Lionel Jospin, en faisant voter le premier texte de loi qui offre une reconnaissance juridique aux couples homosexuels, a contraint l'ensemble de la classe politique à se prononcer . . . sur des questions aussi diverses que l'homoparentalité, le droit des homosexuels dans le monde, l'homophobie ou les difficultés des jeunes gays et lesbiennes.' T. Barbe Doustaly, 'Chirac et Jospin sortent du placard', *Têtu*, 66 (2002), 3.

28 http://infos/tetu.com/lire/2161.

29 'Mais pourquoi aurais-je refusé ? Je suis très préoccupé par le développement de l'ir-respect en France. . . . Je n'ai jamais combattu le PACS. A l'époque, certains m'ont sollicité pour que je m'engage contre le texte : je m'y suis toujours refusé.' T. Barbe Doustaly *et al.*, 'Chirac/Jospin : duel pour le vote homo', *Têtu*, 66 (2002), 57–66.

30 'Le facteur qui doit prévaloir avant toute autre considération est celui de l'intérêt supérieur de l'enfant'. *Ibid.*, p. 60.

31 'Le droit de toute personne à avoir la vie sexuelle de son choix ne doit pas être con-fondu avec un hypothétique droit à l'enfant. Un enfant a droit à un père et à une mère.' *Ibid.*, p. 63.

32 Pronouncing on this case in 1996, the Conseil d'État stated that 'In respect of [the appellant's] circumstances, and despite clear human and educational qualities, he does not present sufficient guarantees in the family, educational and psychological spheres to take an adopted child into his home' ('[l']appellant], eu égard à ses condi-tions de vie et malgré des qualités humaines et éducatives certaines, ne présentait pas de garanties suffisantes sur les plans familial, éducatif et psychologique pour acceuillir un enfant adopté'). M. Gross, *L'Homoparentalité*, Que-sais-je ? (Paris: Presses Universitaires de France, 2003), p. 40.

33 Until the proper implementation of comprehensive legislation preventing discrimi-nation on the grounds of sexual orientation occurs, the only recourse available to LGBT individuals in cases of discrimination is on *gender* grounds under the substi-tution principle which normally obtains in such cases. That is, replace the appellant with someone of opposing gender and, if they would be treated differently in iden-tical circumstances, then discrimination has been proved.

34 The Amsterdam Treaty added Article 13 to the EC Treaty, 'reinforcing the principle of non-discrimination, which is closely linked with equal opportunities. Under this new article, the Council has the power to take appropriate action to combat discrim-ination based on sex, racial or ethnic origin, religion or belief, disability, age or sexual orientation. It contains the injunction on members to act to combat discrim-ination against citizens of the Union on the grounds of sexual orientation' (http://europa.eu.int/scadplus/leg/en/cig/g4000e.htm#e9). That said, it is, how-ever, interesting to note that the European Court has stated that discrimination against unmarried *heterosexual* couples in terms of pension entitlement is permis-sible.

35 The Equal Treatment (Sexual Orientation) Regulations 2003, for example, exempt religious organisations from compliance with the requirement not to discriminate in the workplace on grounds of sexual orientation. Further, the regulations refer only to the workplace; discrimination against members of the LGBT community in the provision of goods and services remains possible.

36 'Oui à un débat pour savoir si la loi doit être changée au Parlement, mais en atten-dant, on ne va pas régler le problème en organisant trois mariages gay médiatisés.' Quoted in *Têtu en ligne* (http://sd407.sivit.org/tetu.com/index.php?set language +en&cccpage).

37 His words to the newspaper *Midi libre* were 'Marriage is one thing, the PACS another. The PACS exists for homosexual couples and for heterosexual couples who do not wish to contract a marriage. You can't have your cake and eat it. Marriage is a strong value in our society; it must not be sullied' ('Le mariage, c'est une chose. Le PACS en est une autre. Le PACS existe pour les couples homosexuels et les couples hétérosexuels qui ne souhaitent pas contracter dans le cadre du mariage. On ne peut

pas avoir le beurre et l'argent du beurre. Le mariage est une valeur forte dans notre société. Il ne faut pas la galvauder'). *Ibid.*

38 *Ibid.* The shorthand of equating homosexuality with incest and paedophilia has long been a key element of the homophobic arsenal, with Christine Boutin writing in her book on the PACS that 'The age of sexual majority being fifteen in France, where will the boundary be placed for an adopted child between homosexuality and paedophilia? . . . How can we protect adolescents who are sensitive or fragile from the influence of men or women of whom we know that attraction to minors is frequent?' ('L'âge de la majorité sexuelle étant de cinquante ans en France, où placera-t-on la frontière, pour un enfant adopté, entre l'homosexualité et la pédophilie ? . . . Comment protéger les adolescents, qui sont fragiles, contre l'influence d'hommes ou de femmes dont on sait que l'attirance pour les mineurs est fréquente ?') C. Boutin, *Le 'Mariage' des homosexuels ? Cucs, Pic, PACS et autres projets législatifs* (Paris: Critérion, 1998), pp. 95–6.

39 'A l'évidence, il apparaît que ce PACS pourrait être amélioré et je souhaite qu'on l'améliore de façon à ce que les droits et les devoirs des personnes de même sexe qui vivent ensemble . . . soient respectés au même titre que ceux des autres. . . . Cela ne doit pas nous conduire à une parodie du mariage . . . Il ne faut pas mélanger les genres. Il existe des problèmes qui doivent être résolus, on a créé le PACS, c'est parfait.' TFI, 14 July 2004.

40 'Les élus qui seraient tentés par de tels appels du pied à un lobby gay sans cesse plus sûr de lui et dominateur doivent savoir que, systématiquement, ils vont trouver face à eux et dans leurs propres murs les militants du Bloc et des Jeunesses identitaires.' Quoted in *Têtu en ligne* (http://sd407.sivit.org/tetu.com/index.php?set language +en&cccpage).

41 See www.france.qrd.org/assocs/sos/actu.html.

42 'Il existe . . . au regard de la société, une différence irréductible qui tient, qu'on le veuille ou non, à la *nature des choses*: savoir que la communauté de vie d'un couple homosexuel est, au mieux, socialement neutre, tandis que celle d'un ménage hétérosexuel est porteuse d'espoir et de longévité pour la société. Impropre à assurer le renouvellement des membres qui composent celle-ci, *l'homosexualité est par nature, un comportement mortel pour la société.* Ce n'est pas là une appréciation d'ordre moral et subjectif, mais une *constatation biologique élémentaire.*' J-L. Auber, 'Note sur arrêt Cour de Cassation, 3e Civ. du 17 décembre 1997', *Recueil Dalloz*, 9e Cahier Jurisprudence (1998), 114–15. My emphasis. Borillo and Fassin, *Au-delà du PACS : l'expertise familiale à l'épreuve de l'homosexualité*, p. 165.

43 'S'il est bienvenu que le droit au respect de la vie privée exclut *a priori* qu'il soit reproché aux homosexuels leur mode de vie, il paraît, en revanche, légitime de leur refuser le droit de se prévaloir de leur situation pour faire venir un enfant à la vie: même banalisée, *l'homosexualité n'est pas encore un mode de vie « normal »* qui puisse offrir à l'enfant les garanties d'épanouissement que l'on peut escompter des parents, l'intérêt de l'enfant à naître dans une telle famille n'est donc pas manifeste.' F. Terré and D. Fenouillet, *Droit civil : les personnes, la famille, les incapacités* (Paris: Précis Dalloz, 6th edn, 1996), p. 799; Borillo and Fassin, *Au-delà du PACS : l'expertise familiale à l'épreuve de l'homosexualité*, p. 167. My emphasis.

44 'Lors de la dernière lecture du PACS au Sénat le 30 juin 1999, Emmanuel Hamel (RPR, Rhône) se lève et propose que le PACS soit rebaptisé « pratique de la contamination sidaïque »' (www.prochoix.org/).

Select bibliography

M. Allison and O. Heathcote (eds), *Forty Years of the Fifth French Republic: Actions, Dialogues, Discourses* (Berne: Peter Lang, 1999).

L. Bersani *et al.*, *Les Études gay et lesbiennes* (Paris: Editions du Centre Georges Pompidou Supplémentaires, 1998).

D. Borillo and E. Fassin, *Au-delà du PACS : l'expertise familiale à l'épreuve de l'homosexualité*, 2nd edn (Paris: Presses Universitaires de France, 2001).

C. Boutin, *Le « mariage » des homosexuels ? Cucs, Pic, PACS et autres projets législatifs* (Paris: Critérion, 1998).

M. Cruikshank, *The Gay and Lesbian Liberation Movement* (New York: Routledge, 1998).

F. Devoucoux du Buysson, *Les Khmers roses : essai sur l'idéologie homosexuelle* (Paris: Editions Blanche, 2003).

D. Eribon (ed.), *Les Études gays et lesbiennes* (Paris: Editions du Centre Georges Pompidou Supplémentaires, 1998).

D. Eribon, *Réflexions sur la question gay* (Paris: Fayard, 1999).

J. Fortin, *L'Homosexualité : l'adieu aux normes* (Paris: Textuel, 2000).

M. Gross, *L'Homoparentalité*, Que-sais-je ? (Paris: Presses Universitaires de France, 2003).

F. Martel, *Le Rose et le noir : histoire des homosexuels en France depuis 1968* (Paris: Seuil, 1996).

C. Mercary and G. De La Pradelle, *Les Droits des homosexuel/les*, Que sais-je ? (Paris: Presses Universitaires de France, 1998).

J-F. Pillebout, *Le PACS* (Paris: Litec, 2000).

J. Weeks, *Coming out: Homosexual Politics in Britain from the Nineteenth Century to the Present* (London: Quartet Books, 1983).

R. Wintermute and M. Andanaes (eds), *The Legal Recognition of Same-sex Relationships* (Oxford: Hart, 2000).

6

The citizen and the Subject

Nadia Kiwan

France has a long history of immigration, dating back to the nineteenth century. It has traditionally relied on a republican conception of integration into the nation through education, military service, trade union membership but, most important, through naturalisation and citizenship. Citizenship, in this context, has been essentially political and immigrants would be integrated into the body politic by transcending their 'origins' and participating in the workplace and political process as universal and culturally 'neutral' citizens. However, the last thirty years have seen the decline of industrial society and traditional modes of social conflict and political participation. The development of a post-industrial France has also coincided with the emergence of the so-called 'second' and 'third generations' of the later waves of migrants to France, who came largely from North and sub-Saharan Africa. For many of this generation, the reference to a working-class identity has disappeared, and, with it, classic forms of political mobilisation that historically had been premised on a republican conception of citizenship and civic participation.

In this chapter I will ask whether the republican concept of the citizen has to be rethought in order to accommodate a very different consciousness of Self that has emerged in contemporary France, especially among the young. This chapter will look at the challenge posed to the relationship between the individual and the Republic by a new elasticity in the construction of identity among young French North African post-migrants. This elasticity produces an individual in constant movement between the poles of 'community' and individuality, generating life choices that are dependent on the tensions between these two poles. Significantly, cultural origins or revival can, at times, be seen as a motor for subjectivity or agency, thus challenging the republican model of citizenship that conceptualises individual cultural specificities as a matter for the private sphere of civil as opposed to civic society. The debates about the 'Islamic headscarf' reveal the contemporary limits of the republican concept of citizen as culturally 'neutral', since many individuals and associations who have argued against the new law banning headscarves and other religious symbols in public sector schools define themselves as profoundly republican, *laïque* (secular) and egalitarian. More important, as will be shown below, the critics of the new law are not only the 'interested parties' but include wider feminist, anti-globalisation and left-wing movements and personalities of non-immigrant background, who are not simply defending a particular 'community' but whose action is guided, rather, by a desire for greater equality of treatment and opportunity.

In the next part of this chapter I will focus on the relationship between the Republic and its citizens by providing a brief and critical overview of the development of the republican conception of citizenship. I will question whether a universalist model of citizenship is still viable in an increasingly complex contemporary France. The following part will consider how the concepts of the Subject and subjectivity can be used to extend the republican concept of the citizen and enhance the Republic's egalitarian project, by allowing us to think through cultural specificities in terms of socio-political agency rather than in terms of political irrelevance and the fragmentation of the body politic. The last part of the chapter will concentrate on examples of how young people of North African origin draw on individual and community-oriented values in order to activate a political, social and cultural sense of citizenship. These examples will be drawn from empirical research carried out in Aubervilliers and further recent developments in the 'Islamic headscarf' and racial discrimination debates.

Rethinking republican citizenship

This section will focus on republican citizenship in terms of a universalist and homogenising project. It will therefore trace the increasingly interlinked relationship between citizenship and French nationality as being one manifestation of this project.

The revolution of 1789 and the transfer of political sovereignty from the monarchy to the people was a key defining moment in the history of citizenship. The Constitution of Year I (1793) claimed that 'Sovereignty resides within the people; it is one and indivisible . . .'[1] Article 7 proclaimed that 'the sovereign people are the universality of the French citizens', thus laying down the principle that sovereignty was to reside with the people, conceived of as a body of citizens.[2] The famous motto 'Liberté, égalité, fraternité', as well as the revolutionary principles of universalism, became the fundamental bases of French citizenship. The legacy of the revolutionary universalist ideal means that, today, the French citizen is defined as an individual, regardless of her/his cultural specificities. Indeed, it is through what sociologist Dominique Schnapper calls 'la transcendance par la politique' (transcendence through the political) that citizens can and are expected to put their cultural/linguistic/religious 'particularisms' to one side in the private domain and become active members of the political nation-state.[3]

Although today the terms 'citizenship' and 'nationality' have become almost coterminous in many different national contexts, the two concepts were not always linked in France. Political scientist Catherine Wihtol de Wenden argues that:

> The notion of citizenship that emerged during the French Revolution was a new conception based on certain philosophical values (adherence to the Revolution, acceptance of the social contract) and was quite separate from the notion of nationality. Hence, in the Constitution of year I (1793), it was possible to become a citizen without being French if the person had accomplished some civic tasks.[4]

Historian Gérard Noiriel also demonstrates that legislators showed little interest in the link between citizenship and nationality until the first law relating to 'French nationality' in 1889.[5]

Wihtol de Wenden argues that it was not until the nineteenth century that the original meaning that the revolutionaries attached to citizenship was transformed. First, there was a transfer from a more direct notion of citizenship to one based on election and representation. Second, the growing economic, military and political rivalry between France and other European powers, particularly Prussia, resulted in the implementation of many 'protectionist' measures, which meant that the question of nationality became increasingly linked with citizenship, thus allowing governments to distinguish who should benefit from citizenship rights and who should not. Noiriel notes that it is significant that, after the defeat of France in the Franco-Prussian War in 1870, a new discourse surrounding nationality developed:

> Forged at the outset to evoke a 'spiritual force', from that point onwards, the word was used to identify groups of individuals whose members shared common characteristics which were quantifiable thanks to technical means such as censuses and plebiscites. From that point onwards defining nationality involved isolating an individual and collective 'quality', selecting an aspect of people's identity (their language, their sense of belonging, etc.) in order to make it into a criteria defining the group to which they were supposed to belong.[6]

In such a climate of changing perspectives, cultural homogeneity became increasingly salient. The historical context of the rivalry with Prussia meant that the modern sense of French citizenship became a national citizenship. Noiriel shows how Ernest Renan's famous 1882 Sorbonne lecture 'Qu'est-ce qu'une nation ?' (What is a nation?), which extolled the virtues of the cult of the ancestors, meant that only those individuals who were seen to be the ancestors of the French nation should take part in the 'daily plebiscite', which defined Renan's nation. The fact that Renan's lecture developed into a general consensus meant that assimilationist concerns were attached to the concept of nationality as a result.[7] Although there was a polemic about how assimilation and homogeneity were to be achieved (the conservatives focusing on race and genealogical factors and the progressives arguing that state institutions, especially school should be central), it is more important to recognise that the idea of a certain form of national cultural homogeneity became central to the definition of French nationality.

Maxim Silverman claims that, during the Third Republic, the implementation of mass education through Jules Ferry's reforms and the cultural homogenisation this engendered can be seen as the metropole's equivalent of the 'civilising mission' which was undertaken in France's colonies. He argues that the ideals of both projects were essentially one and the same: cultural assimilation and homogenisation. He concedes that, in the colonial context, assimilation was juridical as opposed to political but the 'requirements of cultural conformity' were the same in both projects of assimilation.[8]

Thus by focusing on the increasing salience of nationality and a sense of national culture, we are able to understand more fully why the 'nation' came to offer an almost mythical vision of the French people as constituting a uniform cultural community. Finally, it is significant that in his lecture 'Qu'est-ce qu'une nation?' Renan specified that 'the essence of a nation is that all individuals have many things in common, and that they have forgotten about a good many things as well'.[9] Here, it seems, Renan was referring to the need for 'collective cultural amnesia' as a necessary partner of cultural homogenisation.

Rogers Brubaker summed up well the link between the citizen and the nation when he argued that 'Debates about citizenship in France (and Germany) are debates about what it means to belong to the nation-state. The politics of citizenship today is first and foremost a politics of nationhood.'[10] Brubaker goes on to claim that citizenship laws in France are assimilationist, since they 'automatically transform second-generation immigrants into citizens. . .'.[11] If citizenship is defined in terms of nation and assimilation then this has extremely important implications for contemporary France, which, owing to immigration in particular, is culturally very diverse. It is interesting to consider Jean Leca's claim that 'Dans le modèle dominant de l'État-nation moderne, la citoyenneté repose sur la base d'identités a-culturelles, et la politisation culturelle des intérêts est considérée comme illégitime dans un tel espace public.'[12] Leca's observation is significant because it shows how French citizenship is formulated in such a way that it cannot accommodate the public assertion of cultural difference. Furthermore, both Rainer Bauböck and Brubaker argue that the conjugation of nationality as a prerequisite for citizenship meant that citizenship in France became an instrument of 'social closure' or exclusion.[13] This can be seen as an important contradiction, since there is a disjuncture between the theory of universalist citizenship for all, as expressed in the Declaration of the Rights of Man and the Citizen (August 1789) and the reality whereby citizenship is exercised in a rather more particularist manner.

In terms of implications, although the nationality prerequisite for citizenship may seem exclusionary, especially for those residents who happen to be non-EU nationals, it is not the nationality requirement *per se* which is significant but rather what that requirement says about wider expectations of a certain form of homogeneity. Another key defining feature of the republican ideal of citizenship is the separation between the public and private spheres – the public domain being the noble and culturally 'neutral' site of the political process and the private sphere being the domain where cultural particularisms must remain. Such an understanding of citizenship is very well expressed in Dominique Schnapper's analysis: 'What underpins the principle – as well as the values – of the democratic nation is the opposition between the universalism of the citizen and the specificities of the private, individual member of civil society.'[14] Such a distinction between the individual who operates in private civil society and the citizen who operates in the public sphere of the body politic without her or his social, cultural or historical specificities is, of course, inscribed in article 1 of the Constitution of the Fifth Republic: 'La France est une République indivisible, laïque, démocratique et sociale. Elle assure l'égalité devant la loi de tous les citoyens sans distinction d'origine, de race ou de religion.'[15]

The practical and contemporary implications of such an understanding of the Republic's citizen have, today, become all too apparent. The divisive public debates over whether the 'Islamic headscarf' should be allowed in state schools is a clear example of the limits of a model which conceives of the citizen as a public *alter ego*, detached from her or his social, cultural and historical specificities. The debates about *le foulard 'islamique'* are, of course, not new. The first time the issue came to media and public attention was in 1989, when female pupils were excluded from a *collège* (lower secondary school) in Creil. The debate started again in 1994 and more recently, in 2003–04. This type of debate is not, of course, unique to France. We have seen similar debates take place in Germany and in Britain. However, the actual passing of a law in March 2004 which bans the wearing of religious symbols in schools reveals that, in France, the salience of the issue is such that national legislation has been seen to be necessary. The 2004 law bans all conspicuous religious symbols but the debate was actually sparked off by teachers' reaction to pupils wearing the 'Islamic' headscarf. The post-'Nine-eleven' context and fears about fundamentalist Islam developing amidst France's 5 million Muslims have also fed into the renewed anxieties. While defenders of the new law argue that they are preserving the fundamental principles of the Republic and that those very ideals (*laïcité*) were fought for and must therefore be protected, there is, it would seem, reluctance to explicitly acknowledge that the France of 1905, when *laïcité* was made a legal requirement in schools and public institutions through the separation of the Church and the State, was a different place from the France of the early twenty-first century. The implications of the ban on headscarves and other conspicuous religious symbols are, of course, far-reaching. While the law affects only schools, it could affect universities and the workplace. In a context where racial discrimination against populations of non-European immigrant and post-migrant origin is common, it has been argued that the recent law could aggravate the situation for certain sections of the population.

The perception of the citizen as a culturally 'neutral' political actor has also meant that the second pillar of the Republic's motto, *égalité*, or equality, has retained a formal, rather than real, sense. Some, such as Schnapper, have argued that real equality is actually a Marxist utopia.[16] Others, such as sociologist Danilo Martuccelli, have argued that real equality, or equity, is by definition in tension with liberty, since, by offering more equity, individuals can be more exposed in terms of their liberties.[17] Regardless of whether one understands equity in social or cultural terms, the underlying issue becomes one of recognition. The republican paradigm of citizenship does not recognise 'minorities' because historical, cultural, linguistic and religious specificities are matters for the private sphere of 'civil society'. However, it is possible to argue that such a politics of non-recognition has in effect hindered the egalitarian project, since many people of non-European immigrant and post-migrant origin today remain absent or invisible in positions of institutional responsibility, politics and the media. A politics of positive discrimination which would, in part, remedy this visibility issue would not involve the granting of 'cultural rights' or cultural recognition alone – something which the majority of post-migrants do not want anyway – but rather a move towards socio-historical recognition. Yet, when the issue of positive discimination or affirmative action is evoked in the French context, it has often been equated with the fragmentation the republican conception of the body politic as a universal whole.

Some argue that policies such as the *Politique de la Ville* (urban regeneratrion policy), the *Zones d'éducation prioritaire* (education action/priority zones, ZEPs), which divert extra funding and personnel to disadvantaged urban areas, often highly populated by immigrant and post-migrant populations, and the special recruitment convention passed between the elite Institut d'études politiques de Paris and certain ZEP schools can be regarded as French multicultural policies of recognition. Although these policies are specifically targeted in the pursuit of real equality or equity, they are not strictly conceived of in terms of the populations who live there. Rather, the selection criteria for such policies concern the geographical area. Indeed, Martuccelli has argued that the ZEP policies' failure in forging a new type of equity has, in part, been due to the fact that they have been socially and economically informed but are lacking in their cultural dimensions.[18] Of course, this lack of cultural conceptualisation stems from the republican framework, which does not acknowledge cultural specificity of any kind.

What then of Nicolas Sarkozy's championing of the official representation of Islam in France and the subsequent establishment and elections to the Conseil français du culte musulman (CFCM) in 2002–03? This would certainly seem to signal a cultural form of recognition with regards to France's Muslims. However, critics have shown that the CFCM is in fact a rather conservative collection of Muslim movements which do not represent the vast majority of France's practising Muslims.

It would seem, then, that when public policy engages positively with specific populations, this has either been presented as social policy or as culturo-religious recognition. It has seldom articulated both the social and the cultural in the design of policy. However, at the heart of the matter lies the question of equality and how it is to be achieved. Traditionally, equality has been conceived of within the confines of the individual–citizen paradigm. However, it would seem that this republican paradigm of citizenship is not 'delivering' in terms of equality. What then if an alternative frame was adopted, and instead of focusing on the rights and responsibilities of the culturally neutral citizen, another concept were introduced to the discussion – that of the Subject and subjectivity?

The decomposition of modernity and the re-emergence of the Subject

Intellectual and political discussions focusing on the subject emerged in France in the 1980s and 1990s in the midst of the debates around whether and how the Republic should accomodate cultural difference in a country with a high proportion of non-European immigration. As the visibilty of cultural identities increased, much of the debate focused on polarising concepts such as universalism and integration versus particularism and multiculturalism. There were two main 'camps' – the *républicains* and the *démocrates*. The *républicains* or *républicanistes* (as they were sometimes referred to) argued that any recognition of cultural difference in the public sphere would be contrary to the principles of the 'one and indivisible' Republic and would therefore have a devastating effect. Examples such as civil-war Lebanon or the war in ex-Yugoslavia were often cited as the road France could be going down if it embraced multiculturalism.[19] The opposing camp, the *démocrates*, who were less conservative about the recognition of difference, were accused by the *républicains* of being *communautaristes* (communitarians) and of wanting to harm the Republic. One of the main images throughout this debate was the United States, or, more specifically, 'American multiculturalism', which was caricatured by the *républicaniste* camp, who argued that the recognition of cultural difference would lead to the increasing 'ghettoisation' of French society.

One protagonist in the French debate who attempted to overcome the seemingly irreconcilable opposition between the Republic's universalism and the recognition of particularisms was the sociologist Alain Touraine. He argued for the combination of universalism and particularism through the introduction of the concept of the *Sujet* (Subject).[20] Touraine argues that the Subject and communication between (culturally) different Subjects should be protected at an institutional level so that a truly multicultural society is characterised by the institutionalisation of a politics of recognition and communication, rather than the fragmentation of society into bounded different communities. In *Qu'est-ce que la démocratie ?* Touraine qualifies recognition as follows: 'It is not about recognising the other in terms of her/his difference, because that often leads to segregation rather than communication, but about recognising her/him as a subject, as an individual trying to become an actor . . .'[21] So, for Touraine, the key to being able to live together as different and equal lies in the notion of the Subject as a combination of a personal identity and a particular culture with participation in the rational or civic world.

Although Touraine did not argue that the concept of the *Sujet* could be regarded as an alternative to the *citoyen*, I propose taking his argument further by applying the framework of a sociology of subjectivity to the issue of furthering the Republic's fundamentally important egalitarian project. By thinking through a sociology of the subject and subjectivity, we are able to move forward from focusing solely on the rights and responsibilities of the citizen, who is conceptualised as a culturally 'neutral' public *alter ego*, to be integrated into 'society' or the 'nation'. However, before considering the implications of adopting the subject as opposed to citizen framework, it is useful to examine how the resurgence of interest in subjectivity has developed in the social sciences.

The decline of classical sociology and the emergence of a sociology of the Subject
The sociology of the Subject should be seen as emerging out of the decline of classical sociological approaches, from the end of the 1970s onwards. In his article 'Sociologie postclassique ou déclin de la sociologie?' sociologist Michel Wieviorka argues that the dominance of Talcott Parsons's functionalist social theories in the 1940s and 1950s marked the heyday of classical sociology.[22] However, he points out that this period also marked the beginning of the 'end' of this type of approach, since the vogue for postmodernist and, later, globalisation theories reflected the disintegration of classical sociology, followed by the emergence of the notion of the Subject.

The main ideas advocated by Parsons and other earlier 'functionalists' (such as Émile Durkheim and Max Weber) were based on the notion of the existence of an integrated society which could be described as reflecting a pyramid structure (with values at the summit, then norms lower down and finally the notion of roles at the bottom). However, from the mid-1960s onwards these ideas became increasingly challenged, not least because of the growing strength of protest movements in the United States in particular, such as the anti-Vietnam War and civil rights movements. The emergence of such movements challenged the notion of an integrated society, which was supposedly reconciled with itself, and marked the end of sociology as a unitary academic discipline.

Wieviorka argues that the disintegration of the discipline accelerated during the second half of the 1970s as the idea that the 'actor' and 'the system' were becoming increasingly separated gained ground. Functionalism became increasingly challenged. The more structuralist strand of *la sociologie critique* went into decline in the 1980s, only to reappear with renewed popularity in the second half of the 1990s in the context of the general strike of 1995 in France, from which point on Bourdieu became its spokesperson. *La sociologie de la décision*, which focused on rational choice and international relations theories, has become less relevant than it was during the Cold War and consequently has increasingly restricted itself to narrower areas of enquiry.

Sociology's 'low point', according to Wieviorka, was reached at the start of the 1980s, when postmodernist theories became increasingly popular. Ideas about 'le vide social' (the social vacuum) as described by Jean-François Lyotard and Jean Baudrillard as well as the notion that modernity had 'decomposed' into identities and cultures on the one hand and the market and rationality on the other, met with great success. Two authors are cited as providing a response to the postmodernist approach, namely Jürgen Habermas and Alain Touraine. Habermas's notion of 'communicative action' and the revival of the political sphere and Touraine's notion of the *Sujet* are thus identified as possible ways out of the impasse presented by postmodernism.

Today the theme of globalisation has largely succeeded the postmodernist debate, although it emerged with some delay in France and coincided with the general strike of 1995, when, in particular, many civil servants began to feel threatened by the growth of neo-liberalism. Anti-globalisation themes have included among others, concern over the increasing polarisation of global capital and impoverished communities; concern about encroaching cultural homogenisation and new forms of cultural and social domination. It is argued that the globalisation theme is useful because it encourages observers to acknowledge the heterogeneity of cultural and social forms. However, scholars such as Peter Michael Smith or Wieviorka argue that globalisation theory can become problematic when it insists on the powerless individual or actor in the face of an abstract system of capital and economic/asocial determinism.[23]

Situating himself in the Tourainian approach, Wieviorka argues that the most appropriate manner of proceeding, once the observation that 'markets' are becoming increasingly separated from individuals and their cultures has been accepted, is to adopt a bottom-up perspective, that is, by starting with the Subject. By focusing on the Subject we can proceed from the simple observation of the separation of these two spheres to an analysis which highlights the ways in which these two realms can be articulated, or rather re-articulated. Thus a return to the notion of the Subject can be seen to renew sociological enquiry, which had hitherto been engaged in a denial of the Subject either due to the sociologie critique approach or because of functionalist or rationalist reasoning (*sociologie de la décision/sociologie politique*) which all theorise in terms of 'the system'. A return to the Subject allows the conceptualisation of human agency.

This 'return' to the Subject is visible in the work of other authors and in disciplines outside sociology. For example, the philosophers Alain Renaut and Sylvie Mesure have focused on the theme of the Subject or subjectivity in *La Guerre des dieux*.[24] Alain Renaut's *L'Ère de l'individu: contribution à une histoire de la subjectivité* also reflects this renewed interest in the notion of the Subject and subjectivity in other disciplines.[25] Transformations of modernity and the emergence of the Subject have also been a source of debate for anthropologists, such as Scott Lash and Jonathan Friedman.[26] However, this chapter will concentrate on the theories of the Subject and subjectivity as developed by Alain Touraine, since they translate quite well into a tool of analysis of the experiences of young people of immigrant and post-migrant origin.

The main lesson to be drawn from Wieviorka's tableau of the decline of classical sociological enquiry is that the concept of modernity has been seriously challenged.

Of course, this challenge to modernity is not unique to sociology and concerns many social sciences and humanities disciplines. However, for our purposes, the challenge to the modern project and all its certainties associated with rationality, progress and universalism throws light on the question of citizenship in post-migrant societies because it becomes increasingly difficult to analyse immigrant and post-migrant populations according to a dichotomous model of republican citizenship versus communitarianism. Before discussing the relevance of the theme of the subject to the experiences of young post-migrant individuals in France, it is useful to explore the issue of the decomposition of modernity further.

The 'decomposition' of modernity or the estrangement of le monde objectif *and* le monde subjectif

In *Critique de la modernité* Touraine defines modernity as: 'cette correspondance d'une culture scientifique, d'une société ordonnée et d'individus libres. . .'.[27] He argues that it was this definition of modernity, placing reason above all other principles, that has been increasingly criticised. For example, critics have pointed out that there is no necessary link between personal happiness, liberty, democracy, economic growth and the concept of reason. Touraine's own critique of modernity is that it has focused excessively on the notion of reason, science, progress and the process of rationalisation, to the detriment of the Subject. It is argued that modernity should be understood as being made up of two halves, one being reason and the other being the Subject, that is, the more 'human' face of modernity which is represented by the values of freedom and creativity. Touraine shows that, despite the efforts of certain thinkers such as Descartes and the humanists to maintain a combination of reason (*le monde objectif*) and subjectivity (*le monde subjectif*) within the modernist outlook, these two axes of modernity became increasingly separate, especially in the late nineteenth and twentieth centuries. The domination of reason, progress and science led to the eclipse of the Subject. Thus the 'triumphalist' advance of reason, progress and 'objectivity', the dominance of 'the system', the utility of 'social roles' and, in the worst cases, totalitarianism are shown to have led to the negation of the Subject. Touraine describes the resulting modern society as '[d']une société sans acteurs' (a society without actors) and he proposes that modernity be redefined through a re-articulation of its two estranged facets: reason and subjectivity.[28]

This effort to rearticulate what has been increasingly dissociated (reason and subjectivity) involves a return to the old or 'lost' idea of modernity and the Subject, which initially emerged at the same time as rationalisation. The 'end' of the pre-modern era implied the replacement of the religious with science and at the same time 'le Je du Sujet . . .' (the I of the Subject).[29] The Subject is defined by Touraine as follows:

> The Subject is the move from the Id to I, towards control over one's life, so that it has a personal sense, so that the individual becomes an actor and becomes part of social relations by transforming them, but never completely identifying with any group, with any collective. For the actor doesn't act in accordance to the place he

occupies in the social order but, rather, modifies the material and above all social environment in which s/he lives by transforming the division of labour, decision-making, situations of domination or cultural orientations.[30]

Touraine argues that the idea of the Subject is indistinguishable from that of the 'actor', since it is only through the conjunction of these two concepts that the actor is able to resist the tyrannies of the 'system', which only promotes reason and progress and prescribes certain social 'roles' to be fulfilled by the workers and citizens.

One of the most significant implications to emerge from Touraine's critique of modernity is that it is erroneous to oppose modernity and tradition, since to do so is to highlight only one facet of modernity, that is, rationalisation, and to ignore the equally important second facet, subjectivation, where all is not simply progress, reason and science but human creativity and liberty, and reference to one's *communauté d'appartenance* (community). The fact that the main aim of the process of subjectivation is the reunification of the two separated spheres (the objective and the subjective) places the idea of reconstruction at the centre of the analysis.[31] This process of reconstruction allows subjects to become 'active agents of a recomposition of a world which is tending to become increasingly divided between the centre and periphery.'[32]

The Subject is not merely a synonym for the individual. Touraine argues that the subject is distinct from the individual because the subject manages to combine both individual and community identity: 'The subject is individual and community; s/he is neither a natural nor a rational being. S/he escapes the community through reason, and the market through collective as much as personal identity.'[33]

This combination of individual and community identity is of particular signifiicance where post-migrant populations in France are concerned. The next section will focus on empirical data collected over a twelve-month period with young people whose parents or themselves were of North African origin. The fieldwork was carried out in Aubervilliers, a historically working-class and migrant town on the urban periphery of Paris. Taking the sociology of subjectivity as a conceptual framework, the section after that will show how the young people in question simultaneously draw on community-oriented and more universal elements of identity. The tensions between these two poles are generative of subjective agency. More important, the key role played by these individuals' cultural 'background' in this agency forces us to question the appropriateness of a model of Republican citizenship which is largely based on the notion of a culturally neutral universal citizen.[34]

Cultural complexity: constructing post-migrant experiences in Aubervilliers and beyond[35]

If we combine Touraine's understanding of subjectivity as the tensions between individual and community as being generative of socio-cultural agency with Michel Wieviorka's model of the 'triangle of ethnicity' or identity, then our 'reading' of the experiences of young post-migrants can be usefully interpreted. By using Wieviorka's model of the 'triangle of ethnicity' or identity as an analytical tool for the interpretation of fieldwork observations made in Aubervilliers, it becomes clear that, in terms of discourse and practice, most of the young people 'of North African origin' are in constant flux between more 'republican' and more *'communautaire'* values and norms.

Wieviorka's triangular model was useful in understanding this elasticity in identity construction because it refers to three 'poles' of identity. The first pole is the individual pole and concerns political and civic participation; demands for equality and democracy. If the individual remains on this pole of the triangle only, and effectively adopts an assimilation strategy, this may 'backfire', especially if the individual concerned is not regarded by the dominant group/s as assimilated. The second point of the triangle is the communitarian pole whereby the individual maintains a very close relationship with her or his 'community of origin' – whether this is activated in linguistic, religious or socio-economic terms. Remaining 'on' this pole alone can also be problematic if the individual is constantly subordinated to the will of the group. The third pole, which Wieviorka calls the subjectivity pole, allows us to escape from the binary opposition of the individual and the community. Subjecivity does not arise out of the simple synthesis of the individual and community poles but, rather, is born out of the circulation around the different poles of identity and the continual tensions between these different poles.[36]

As shown above, since recent sociological discussions have argued that societal norms have been seriously challenged, the notion of an integrated society becomes increasingly problematic. In relation to young post-migrants in France this is particularly significant, since in the absence of these overarching Parsonian norms, and in the face of social exclusion and racial discrimination, cultural origins become a source of resistance or socio-political agency. Such socio-cultural and political agency was significant among many of the young people interviewed in Aubervilliers.

In this sub-section I will discuss, in part, the findings of the empirical study I carried out over a twelve-month period in Aubervilliers, a town on the periphery of Paris. From 2000 to 2001 sixty-four young people aged between sixteen and thirty-one were interviewed.[37] All interviews were semi-structured, that is, a general 'interview guide' formed the basis of the vast majority of interviews.

Aubervilliers is a town which lies on the north-eastern outskirts of Paris. It has a long history as a worker and migrant town. The town's immigrants first came from Italy, Spain, Portugal, then the Maghreb, and lastly sub-Saharan Africa and the Indian subcontinent. The last census recorded 29.7 per cent of the 63,524 inhabitants as being of foreign nationality and three-quarters of these nationals are from outside the European Union. This is the second highest proportion of foreign nationals in the *département*, the highest proportion being 33 per cent. This means that many more inhabitants are, as a result, of 'foreign origin' as well, since those born in France can obtain French nationality at the age of eighteen. A large proportion (41.3 per cent) of its population live in social housing and the unemployment rate is high – 22.6 per cent compared with an average of 11.5 per cent for the Ile-de-France region. In addition, a high proportion of young people residing in the town (aged between sixteen and twenty-five) are under-qualified (33.3 per cent of the population have no qualification whatsoever). Forty-one per cent of the town's active population are described as 'workers'.[38]

The field research which was carried out focused on the younger section of the North African origin population, that is, those aged between sixteen and twenty-five, the main objective being to look at cultural and social modes of identification. In addition, a significant element of the fieldwork examined the relationship between this age group and civil society associations, since the involvement in associations could represent an 'external' form of self-realisation in the public space.[39]

Many of the interviewees demonstrated a significant degree of subjectivity and agency, which was informed by drawing on their cultural 'background'. For example, 'Myriam', a twenty-four-year-old trainee nurse and interviewee of Algerian origin, circulates within the 'triangle of identity' and reveals a capacity to reinterpret both 'community' and republican norms, thereby creating her own subjective experience. Myriam argues that she identifies more or less unproblematically with the notion of being French: 'I was born in France. I've got the French mentality . . . I regard France as my country.'[40] However, her statement does not mean that she adopts an assimilation strategy. Rather, her articulation of identity is an active individual process where she 'takes or leaves' what suits her when it comes to what she perceives as *la mentalité française*. Indeed, when alluding to the stereotypes that North African families are subjected to with regards to marriage (arranged marriages, for example) she reveals that she does not unquestioningly reproduce a celebratory discourse about liberty:

> all the prejudice that can exist about Arabs, all that annoys me a little . . . that they all have arranged marriages, that the girls aren't allowed to go out . . . when it's not true, they're not all the same, a certain amount of freedom, that's true, but, . . . freedom, freedom, afterwards, I mean, I don't know, they do some stupid things as well . . .[41]

Furthermore, despite claiming to have 'the French mentality', Myriam argues that she would like to marry a Kabyle partner, like herself, because they would be more likely to share the same 'mentality'.

Another interviewee of Tunisian origin, 'Hala', also reveals an original stance with regards to her 'origins', thereby creating her own subjective experience. This eighteen-year-old high-school pupil, who was born in France, is a committed Muslim. She claims that she considers herself as more of a Muslim than French or Arab, but that she has every intention of investing fully in her life in France, and is not concerned about marrying someone of the same 'origins':

> I was born here, my life is here, school is here, my friends are here, but the way I
> live, I speak, I also speak Arabic and I have a lifestyle which is Arab . . . it's clear that
> I obviously feel more Muslim than French or Arab . . . but I wouldn't be against, for
> example, marrying . . . a Chinese guy . . . [42]

Subjectivity and cultural agency are also at issue when 'Djamel', a thirty-one-year-old chief school supervisor of Algerian origin reflects on the importance of his cultural origins and his education in France within a republican education system:

> we have an important cultural background, which we shouldn't deny, which we
> should accept entirely, it's like religion; I think, values, we shouldn't forget our
> roots because it's important, it's the basis of our individual identity and at the same
> time one has to adapt, adapt to a milieu, to a place and environment which isn't
> the family environment . . . I think that the education system at the time that I went
> through it, in the seventies, really contributed to creating a social identity as well
> as a cultural identity [which] my parents gave me outside school, secular, republi-
> can values and friends who showed us something other than what we were cultu-
> rally, so that that helped to create a mix. [43]

Subjectivity is also relevant when 'Leila', a high-school pupil, who was born in France but whose parents are Algerian, argues that she has every intention of becoming a primary school teacher in the French public sector, despite the fact that she wears a headscarf and may subsequently face certain obstacles:

> I hope to teach but it would be silly to have to go to court to be able to teach, but if
> we're forced to we're forced to, but I'm intending on going all the way, I'm intend-
> ing on fighting, but I know that my struggle will help others after me. [44]

Such demands for cultural recognition and citizen participation in the public space are not rare and normally reveal how the notion of integration is, for most of the young post-migrants of North African 'background', inappropri-ate, unless it is qualified in socio-economic or political terms. 'Aicha', a twenty-eight-year-old care auxiliary trainee who was born in Algeria, but who was brought by her parents to France at the age of two, argues for cultural recogni-tion, equity and voting rights based on residence, not nationality:

> That they recognise us . . . in cultural terms, in terms of everyday life . . . that we
> don't talk to them about integration, that they are recognised as French citizens . . .
> and that they have the same rights. . . . We pay, we pay everything, we pay every-
> thing! Frankly, I've paid taxes and I haven't got the vote . . . I came here when I was
> two. It's, I grew up here, I . . . was educated here, I speak French perfectly . . . then
> it's 'No, you can't vote,' I haven't got the right. It's frustrating, you see, it's true that
> they don't have, you don't feel entirely, entirely integrated into the country. I'm not
> saying French but integrated fully into the country. No, because there's always that
> little something which means you're not a citizen, recognised as a French citizen. [45]

Mobilising a political sense of agency by drawing on a collective cultural *imaginaire* is prevalent in other interviewees' discourses surrounding political participation and it is linked, not with communitarian or ghettoising strategies but, rather, with claims to equity. 'Mahmoud', a nineteen-year-old high-school pupil, who was born in France to French-Algerian parents, argues that, despite being part of the so-called 'third generation', the threat of exclusion through discimination persists: 'We should vote. Why? To reduce racism. If all the Arabs voted, that would be good. . . . We should vote here. It's here that you vote. It's here that you get rid of Le Pen votes.'[46]

Other interviewees may have become politically engaged through associations. Many of these associatons were of a cultural nature and thus somehow linked with the national, regional, religious or linguistic backgrounds of the interviewees. Becoming involved in an Islamic association to provide activities for young people in run-down areas during the Aïd or teaching Arabic in one's neighbourhood are just two examples of how the interviewees' engagement with their 'cultural specificities' is actually generative of citizenship, rather than existing outside it.[47]

With the re-emergence of the 'Islamic headscarf' debate in France we have seen the establishment of a number of associations and collectives which defend the right of female pupils to wear the headscarf in public sector schools. These organisations also make a point of demonstrating their pro-republican credentials. For example, a number of Muslim associations refused to attend the highly publicised pro-headscarf demonstration on 17 January 2004 because it was initiated by the extremist Parti des musulmans de France. Instead, an alternative gathering of associations, made up of a mix of groups such as the Collectif des musulmans de France, closely linked with the controversial Tariq Ramadan, the associations Jeunesse musulmane de France and Etudiants musulmans de France (linked with the Union des organisations islamiques de France) and Participation et spiritualités musulmanes, held their own meeting and created their own collective – Collectif une école pour tous-tes. The supporters and signatories of this collective included not only Muslim associations but feminist organisations, leaders and personalities as diverse as Femmes plurielles, Femmes publiques, Collectif féministe pour l'égalité, the Parti Socialiste member and feminist Hamida Ben Sadia, the Green Party MP Noël Mamère, the feminist Christine Delphy, the sociologist Françoise Gaspard and the Confédération Paysanne's leader, José Bové. The petition which was launched by the collective argues that their movement is in fact a defence of *la laïcité* (secularism) since the laws of 1881, 1882, 1886 and 1905 guaranteed the liberty of conscience and emancipation. They argue that, as far as education was concerned, the original *laïcité* laws were intended to apply to the teachers, the school premises and the curriculum, not the pupils. The petition states, 'Notre combat est un combat démocratique, laïque, et féministe' (Our struggle is democratic, secular and feminist).[48]

On 7 February 2004 another collective of associations called the Mouvement de justice et la dignité (MJD) organised a march and were also careful to ally their defence of the headscarf in schools within a republican value framework. The march's rallying theme was *liberté, égalité, fraternité* and 'anti-Islamophobia'. In their press release of 20 January they called on 'All Frenchmen and women . . . to clearly demonstrate that the citizens of a republican France aspire to live together, peacefully, pacifically, in respect of diversities and wanting the liberty of each individual, equality for all and fraternity between human beings.'[49] The MJD defines itself not as a Muslim association but as a civic movement which defends values which are relevant to society as a whole.

The last few years have seen other movements emerge in France which point to a questioning of the traditional republican model of citizenship based on 'colour-blind' principles. The rise of the Motivé-e-s political grouping in Toulouse is an example of a politically successful movement and it won four seats in the *conseil municipal* following the 2001 municipal elections. The leader of the Motivé-e-s list was Salah Amokrane, who famously said to the France 3 cameras on election night, 'Je m'appelle Salah Amokrane et je suis français' (My name is Salah Amokrane and I'm French). The movement stood on an anti-racist, anti-sexist and participative democracy platform and three other councillors were elected to the municipality – Isabelle Rivière, Elisabeth Heysch and Michel Desmars. In a February 2002 interview with Nicolas Leblanc in the periodical *Territoires* Amokrane argued that at the outset the movement had been reticent about playing up the fact that they were from the less advantaged quartiers or of immigrant background, for fear of being accused of communitarianism. However, a year on, Amokrane points out, it is essential to ally the question of *les quartiers* more explicitly with themes linked to immigration: 'In any case, what are we talking about? When we talk about the inner-city neighbourhoods or housing estates, we're talking about French people of immigrant origin.'[50]

This type of call for frankness has also been echoed by the Convention laïque pour la l'égalité des droits et la participation des musulmans en France, a movement otherwise known as 'Clé'. This association was set up by the successful CEO of CS Communications & Systèmes, Yazid Sabeg. Sabeg, who is one of the few North African origin CEOs of France's top 'CAC 40' companies (the French stock exchange's top forty companies) wrote a report in January 2003 entitled *Les Oubliés de l'égalité des chances* in which he calls for a 'Charter on Diversity' which would advise on ethnic minority recruitment quotas for organisations and companies. Sabeg has called for CAC 40 companies in particular to sign the charter. There have been some positive reactions to Sabeg's suggestions in the business community, but further research is needed to in order to measure the impact of such a charter.

Conclusion

The examples given above of cultural complexity among the young post-migrants of North African origin in Aubervilliers and the diverse mobilisation of associations against the law governing religious symbols at school show that the goalposts of republican citizenship are being shifted. The elasticity of the experiences of young post-migrants and the role played by cultural 'origins' in individual and collective agency reveal how citizenship can be opened up through the notion of subjectivity. The subsequent blurring of the dividing line between the universal and the particular means that the republican model of citizenship and the egalitarian project may be renewed.

While we have seen government calls for *une mobilisation positive* and an annoucement by Prime Minister Jean-Pierre Raffarin in June 2004 of a 'Stratégie nationale pour l'égalité des chances', through the recuitment of French nationals 'of foreign origin' or from the overseas territories, the egalitarian project will remain limited if measures in favour of equity remain economic and social in nature. For we have seen in the previous section of this chapter how citizenship can also be cultural in nature. We have also seen how the legislation banning religious symbols, and thereby 'Islamic headscarves' at school, could run the risk of further marginalising or stigmatising a certain section of the population. Regardless of whether or not the Republic agrees with what the headscarf represents, surely preparedness to acknowledge the subjectivities of some of the young women in question could lead to increased dialogue and discouragement, rather than prohibitive legislation which could have stigmatising effects outside school. Such a scenario could thereby further enhance the original egalitarian project of French citizenship.

Notes

1 Unless otherwise indicated, all translations are mine. The original reads as follows: 'La souveraineté réside dans le peuple; elle est une et indivisible. . .'. See www.legis net.com/france/constitutions/constitution_an_I_1793_1.html, Constitution of Year I, 1793.

2 'le peuple souverain est l'universalité des citoyens français'. A. Le Pors, *Le Citoyenneté* (Paris: Presses Universitaires de France, 1999). Chapter 6 cites the Constitution of Year I.

3 D. Schnapper, *La Communauté des citoyens: sur l'idée moderne de nation* (Paris: Gallimard, 1994), p. 83.

4 C. Wihtol de Wenden, 'Immigration policy and the issue of nationality', *Ethnic and Racial Studies*, 14:3 (1991), 319–32, p. 329.

5 G. Noiriel, *État, nation et immigration : vers une histoire du pouvoir* (Paris: Belin, 2001), p. 158.

6 'Forgé au départ pour évoquer une 'force spirituelle', le mot sert désormais surtout à désigner des groupes d'individus dont les membres partagent des caractéristiques communes que l'on peut comptabiliser grâce à des moyens techniques comme les recensements ou les plébiscites. Définir la nationalité, c'est désormais isoler une « qualité » à la fois individuelle et collective, sélectionner un aspect de l'identité des personnes (leur langue, leur sentiment d'appartenance, etc.) pour en faire un critère définissant le groupe auquel ils sont censés appartenir.' *Ibid.*, p. 161.

7 Noiriel, *ibid.*, p. 162, cites E. Renan, *Qu'est-ce qu'une nation ?* (Paris: Presses Pocket, 1882 edn, 1992).

8 M. Silverman, *Deconstructing the Nation: Immigration, Racism and Citizenship in Modern France* (London: Routledge, 1992), p. 31.

9 'l'essence d'une nation est que tous les individus aient beaucoup de choses en commun, et aussi que tous aient oublié bien des choses.' E. Renan, *Qu'est-ce qu'une nation ?* in *Œuvres completes* I (Paris: Calmann-Lévy, 1947), p. 892. Anne Donadey uses the term 'collective amnesia' with regard to French attitudes to the Franco-Algerian War. See A. Donadey, *'Une certaine idée de la France:* the Algeria syndrome and struggles over "French" identity', in S. Ungar and T. Conley (eds), *French Identity Papers: Contested Nationhood in Twentieth Century France* (Minneapolis MN: University of Minnesota Press, 1996), pp. 215–32.

10 R. Brubaker, *Citizenship and Nationhood in France and Germany* (Cambridge MA: Harvard University Press, 1992), p. 182. Brubaker cites Jean Cohen, 'Strategy or identity: new theoretical paradigms and contemporary social movements', *Social Research*, 52 (1985), 663–716.

11 *Ibid.*, p. 14.

12 'Dans le modèle dominant de l'État-nation moderne, la citoyenneté repose sur la base d'identités a-culturelles, et la politisation culturelle des intérêts est considérée comme illégitime dans un tel espace public.' Interview with Jean Leca, 8 December 1986, in C. Wihtol de Wenden (ed.), *La Citoyenneté et les changements de structures sociales et nationales de la population française* (Paris: Edilig, Fondation Diderot–La Nouvelle Encyclopédie, 1988), p. 323.

13 Rainer Bauböck, *Immigration and the Boundaries of Citizenship*, Monographs in Ethnic Relations 4 (Warwick: ESRC Centre for Research in Ethnic Relations, 1992).

14 'Ce qui fonde le principe – en même temps que les valeurs – de la nation démocratique, c'est l'opposition entre l'universalisme du citoyen et les spécificités de l'homme privé, membre de la société civile.' Schnapper, *La Communauté des citoyens*, p. 92.

15 'La France est une République indivisible, laïque, démocratique et sociale. Elle assure l'égalité devant la loi de tous les citoyens sans distinction d'origine, de race ou de religion.' Constitution of 4 October 1958. See www.legifrance.gouv.fr.

16 D. Schnapper, 'Ethnic Revival and Religious Revival Welfare State Democracies'in, paper given at a conference in honour of Shmuel Noah Eisenstadt, the Hebrew University of Jerusalem, Jerusalem, 2–4 Novermber 2003.

17 D. Martuccelli, 'Les contradictions politiques du multiculturalisme', in M. Wieviorka (ed.), *Une société fragmentée? Le multiculturalisme en débat* (Paris: La Découverte, 1997), pp. 61–82, p. 77.

18 *Ibid.*

19 M. Wieviorka, 'Introduction', in M. Wieviorka, *La Différence culturelle : une reformulation des débats* (Paris: Balland, 2001).

20 A. Touraine, *Qu'est-ce que la démocratie?* (Paris: Fayard, 1994). Touraine mostly refers to the subject with the 's'in upper case as though it were a proper noun.

21 'Il ne s'agit pas de reconnaître l'autre dans sa différence, car cela conduit plus souvent à l'indifférence ou à la ségrégation qu'à la communication, mais comme sujet, comme individu cherchant à être acteur . . .' *Ibid.*, p. 212.

22 M. Wieviorka, 'Sociologie postclassique ou déclin de la sociologie?' *Cahiers internationaux de sociologie*, 108 (2000), 5–35.

23 See P. M. Smith, 'Transnationalism and the city', in R. A. Beauregard and S. Body-Gendrot (eds), *The Urban Moment: Cosmopolitan Essays on the late Twentieth Century City* (Thousand Oaks CA: Sage, 1999), pp. 119–39.

24 S. Mesure and A. Renaut, *La Guerre des dieux : essai sur la querelle des valeurs* (Paris: Grasset & Fasquelle, 1996).

25 Alain Renaut, *L'Ère de l'individu : contribution à une histoire de la subjectivité* (Paris: Gallimard, 1989).

26 See, for example, S. Lash and J. Friedman (eds), *Modernity and Identity* (Oxford: Blackwell, 1992).

27 'cette correspondance d'une culture scientifique, d'une société ordonnée et d'individus libres . . .' A. Touraine, *Critique de la modernité* (Paris: Fayard, 1992), p. 11.

28 *Ibid.*, p. 238.

29 *Ibid.*, p. 240.

30 'Le Sujet est le passage de Ça au Je, le contrôle exercé sur le vécu pour qu'il ait un sens personnel, pour que l'individu se transforme en acteur qui s'insère dans des relations sociales en les transformant, mais sans jamais s'identifier complètement à aucun groupe, à aucune collectivité. Car l'acteur n'est pas celui qui agit conformément à la place qu'il occupe dans l'organisation sociale, mais celui qui modifie l'environnement matériel et surtout social dans lequel il est placé en transformant la division du travail, les modes de décision, les rapports de domination ou les orientations culturelles.' *Ibid.*, pp. 242–3.

31 A. Touraine, 'La formation du Sujet', in F. Dubet and M. Wieviorka (eds), *Penser le Sujet : autour d'Alain Touraine* (Paris: Fayard, 1995), pp. 21–45.

32 'des agents actifs de recomposition d'un monde qui tend de plus en plus à se diviser entre le centre et la périphérie.' *Ibid.*, p. 30.

33 'Le sujet est individu et il est communauté ; il n'est ni être naturel ni être de raison. Il échappe à la communauté par la raison instrumentale et au marché par l'identité collective autant que personnelle.' *Ibid.*, p.32.

34 For some preliminary discussion of Bourdieu's sense of 'cultural capital' in transnational settings see U. H. Meinhof and A. Triandafyllidou, 'Three forms of cultural capital: displacement or cultural capital', forthcoming in K. Robins and U. H. Meinhof (eds), *Cultural Policy in a Changing Europe*.

35 Kevin Robins discusses cultural complexity in K. Robins, 'Becoming anybody: thinking against the nation and through the city', *City*, 5:1 (2001), 77–90

36 For further discussion of Wieviorka's model see M. Wieviorka, *La Démocratie à l'épreuve : nationalisme, populisme, ethnicité* (Paris: La Découverte, 1993), pp. 124–36.

37 This figure does not include the association employees and *animateurs, éducateurs,* teachers, policemen and municipally elected *Députés* who were also interviewed as part of the field research.

38 Statistics from *Recensement de la population de 1999 : les grandes tendances à Aubervilliers et des comparaisons départementales et régionales* (Observatoire de la Société Local: Mairie d'Aubervilliers, March 2001) and Anne Foussat, *Aubervilliers à la page* 5 (Observatoire de la Société Locale: Mairie d'Aubervilliers, December 1999). This study by A. Foussat contains statistics taken from the earlier 1990 census.

39 Didier Lapeyronnie uses the term *construction de soi* in Wieviorka , *Une Société fragmentée ?* pp. 251–66.

40 Author's interview with 'Myriam', 20 March 2001. The transcripts, in French, of these interviews can be found in S. N. Kiwan, 'The Construction of Identity amongst Young People of North African Origin in France: Discourses and Experiences', PhD dissertation, University of Bristol, 2003.

41 *Ibid.*
42 Author's interview with 'Hala', 18 May 2001.
43 Author's interview with 'Djamel', 15 May 2001.
44 Author's interview with 'Leila', 15 May 2001.
45 Author's interview with 'Aicha', 12 December 2000, 14 December 2000.
46 Author's interview with 'Fayçal, 'Mahmoud' and 'Razak', 13 September 2001.
47 Aïd is an Islamic celebration, following the fasting month of Ramadan, for example.
48 See Collectif Une école pour tous-tes, *Contre les lois d'exclusion : appel unitaire*, www.cedetim.org/collectifecolepourtous/appel.html.
49 'les Français de tous bords ... à démontrer clairement que les citoyens d'une France républicaine aspirent à vivre ensemble, paisiblement, pacifiquement, dans le respect des diversités en voulant la liberté de chacun, l'égalité pour tous et la fraternité entre les êtres humains.' Cited in article by Amara Bamba, 'La mobilisation pro foulard', www.saphirnet.info (2 February 2004).
50 'De toute façon, de quoi parle-t-on? Quand on parle de quartiers populaires ou de cités, on parle de français issus de l'immigration.' For both citations see '« Toulouse – Salah, Elisabeth, Michel et Isabelle : les Arabes du Capitole.» Rencontre avec Salah Amokrane, élu municipal Motivé-e-s', interview with Nicolas Leblanc in *Territoires*, 425 (2002), www.adels.org/territoires/425.htm.

Select bibliography

J-M. Helvig (ed.), *La Laïcité dévoliée : quinze années de débat en quarante 'Rebonds'* (Paris: Libération / Éditions de l'Aube, 2004).

A. Le Pors, *Le Citoyenneté* (Paris: Presses Universitaires de France, 1999).

G. Noiriel, *État, nation et immigration : vers une histoire du pouvoir* (Paris: Belin, 2001).

E. Renan, 'Qu'est-ce qu'une nation?' in *Œuvres complètes* I (Paris: Calmann-Lévy, 1947).

D. Schnapper, *La Communauté des citoyens : sur l'idée moderne de nation* (Paris: Gallimard, 1994).

D. Schnapper, *La Démocratie providentielle : essai sur l'égalité contemporaine* (Paris: Gallimard, 2002).

M. Silverman, *Deconstructing the Nation: Immigration, Racism and Citizenship in Modern France* (London: Routledge, 1992).

A. Touraine, *Qu'est-ce que la démocratie ?* (Paris: Fayard, 1994).

A. Touraine and K. Khosrokhavar, *La Recherche de soi : dialogue sur le Sujet* (Paris: Fayard, 2000).

M. Wieviorka, *La Démocratie à l'épreuve : nationalisme, populisme, ethnicité* (Paris: La Découverte, 1993).

M. Wieviorka (ed.), *Une société fragmentée ? Le multiculturalisme en débat* (Paris: La Découverte, 1997).

M. Wieviorka and J. Ohana (eds), *La Différence culturelle : une reformulation des débats* (Paris: Balland, 2001).

7

Social policy and the challenge to the 'republican model'

Jean-Paul Révauger

The connection between the 'republican compact', the celebrated *pacte républicain* which crops up in rhetoric in times of crisis, and social policy raises the questions of the definitions of the 'republican model' on the one hand and that of the much celebrated 'pact' on the other hand. The terms are highly contentious, a fact which slightly belies their mythical and nearly magical functions. 'Republic' has two meanings in France. The word is still used to refer to 'France', a nation-state with a distinct culture, history and geopolitical interests. It also refers to the particular regime that resulted from the French Revolution, and is interpreted by the French as a synonym of 'democracy'. Likewise, the 'republican compact' can be interpreted either in a national, if not nationalistic, sense – membership of a national community – or in a social and political sense – citizenship rights, including both social and political dimensions – enshrined in a set of mutual obligations for the state and individuals. The distinction between the two interpretations, however, is not always relevant, since the definition of French identity is based precisely on the confusion between political or even administrative parameters and ethnic-cultural ones. The 'republican model' may therefore prove rather fuzzy. In terms of social policy, this raises two issues. We may first of all wonder whether there is such a thing as a 'republican model', a specific French approach to social policy. On the other hand, we must also question the specific political and social contents of current social policies, and assess their significance and efficiency in terms of social cohesion.

The Republic's approach to social policy

The typology proposed by Esping Andersen[1] in the early 1990s to describe welfare systems in the developed world has been found lacking by a lot of critics.[2] However, it remains a central framework, against which all authors pit their criticisms, or buttress their own explanatory structures. It has become the equivalent of a norm, which not everybody agrees with, but to which all refer.

For Esping Andersen, welfare systems in the Western, developed world can be classified into three categories: the first one is the Continental corporatist model, epitomised by Bismarckian Germany, in which social identity and rights depend on occupation and are guaranteed by an insurance-based system jointly managed by employees and employers. The second model, typical of Scandinavian societies, is the universalist one, in which rights are derived from citizenship and nationality and the system is generously financed by taxation and managed by the state. The third one, labelled 'Anglo-Saxon liberal', is the residual one in which universal rights are confined within narrow limits, are not very generous and are replaced by private provision for most of the able-bodied working population.

France fits imperfectly within this classical typology. This does not necessarily imply that the typology, as an intellectual construction and an explanatory framework for the whole of the developed world, is faulty, but merely that the French legacy, in this respect, originated from different traditions. The French 'republican' tradition, in terms of social policy, was largely reactive: it was never based on explicitly formulated doctrines, or on master plans. Even the father of French *sécurité sociale*, Laroque, cannot be considered as an original thinker, nor can he be compared to Chancellor Bismarck or William Beveridge. Throughout the twentieth century, social policy was devised by governments of different political hues, who used it for their own ends and shaped it according to their political cultures. The mythical tale, according to which social policy results from a series of small working-class victories whose cumulated outcome is the famous *pacte républicain*, is largely unrealistic.

The Bismarckian legacy: from trench warfare to class struggle

In the late nineteenth century French republicans were very critical of Bismarck, for reasons which owed little to social policy, but which came to include it. The Chancellor was considered as the brains behind the 1870 war, whose outcome was disastrous for France, leading to national humiliation, the loss of Alsace and Lorraine, and the outbreak of a social revolution in Paris, whose violent repression cast a dark shadow over the first years of the Third Republic. Anything emanating from Bismarck, including welfare, was therefore viewed with deep suspicion. The principle of social insurance, the basis of the Bismarckian *Sozialstaat*, was criticised, in the name of the republican tradition and solidarity.[3]

In the 1920s France was influenced by the Bismarckian model, which prevailed in Alsace Lorraine under Prussian occupation until the First World War. When both provinces returned within the fold of the French Republic in 1918, national enthusiasm and nationalism prevailed over class considerations. The Bismarckian social system had been imposed and adopted in both regions and was much more advanced than anything prevailing in the French Republic. Destroying this legacy would have amounted to a scaling down of social protection, a measure which might have dampened the patriotism of the locals. It was therefore decided to maintain the Bismarckian system and to extend it, progressively, to the whole of the Republic.

Very contradictory influences were at play in 1945 when the post-war settlement was struck: 'Class' combined with the 'national issue', in the sense that the prevailing view was that the ruling class had largely failed the country and had gone much too far in collaborating with Nazism. Many working-class organisations, although not all of them, were convinced of the historical ineluctability of the dictatorship of the proletariat. They included the largest of union confederations, the Communist-led Confédération générale du travail (CGT). Unions were attracted by the notion of a welfare system which would be mostly financed by employers but directly managed by workers. *Paritarisme*, the sharing of management responsibilities within the welfare system, was out of the question at the time and was introduced by De Gaulle in the unemployment funds only in the late 1950s, once the power of organised labour had receded. The *securité sociale* funds were therefore administered by trade union representatives, until the *ordonnances de 1967* (government decrees not voted by Parliament), known in the world of trade unionists as the *ordonnances scélérates*, which clearly shows the lack of enthusiasm for power sharing on the part of unions. The self-employed middle classes, middle-ranking and managerial staff, the *cadres* and the more conservative farmers, who very naturally were not party to this anti-capitalist strategy, made sure that they did not join the *régime général* of the *sécurité sociale* but created their own health and pension funds, also on the Bismarckian model.

The post-1945 system was therefore largely Bismarckian. The support Bismarckianism enjoyed for a long time among trade unionists, and the left in general, was naturally due to the radicalism of the post-war project, whose social and political significance was exactly the opposite of the original Prussian plan. Far from emasculating the unions, it aimed at extending trade union influence over a new field, that of social welfare.

This master plan was thwarted by two developments; the Cold War and the rise to power of 'conservative modernisers' under the Fifth Republic. The Cold War split the French trade union movement and weakened the left. The major trade union, the CGT, was controlled by the Communist Party, and an anti-communist union confederation, Force ouvrière (FO), was created with the help of the American CIA. An informal but long-lasting alliance was gradually struck between FO, the employers' representatives and the agents of government, in order to deprive the majority union, the CGT, of any influence in the management of the health funds. Class allegiances and trade union solidarity came second to political considerations. The idea that social welfare could be used to gradually deprive employers and the state of any real say in the management of the already sizeable social security budgets fizzled out and was soon forgotten. The management of the funds became an opaque affair, famous for its power trading and viewed with cynicism by the public, including the 'world of labour'. Under General De Gaulle the management of the funds was modified and unions had to share power with employers on an equal basis on the management boards of the social security funds. *Paritarisme*, the joint management of funds, although in keeping with the original Prussian conservative stance, was therefore imposed on French unions in an authoritarian manner. It did not stem from any particular wish to share anything with employers.

The universalist ideal

Universalism was promoted by the Free French, who had been enthused by the Beveridge report, and chimed with the climate of republican egalitarianism and idealism which resulted from the liberation of the country in 1945. Its roots were steeped in the old republican tradition, which had opposed Bismarckianism on the grounds that rights should be equal, and should derive from citizenship, not from the occupation of the 'head of household'.

Ironically, the only area where universalism prevailed from the start, and generous provision has been maintained to this day, is family policy, which had little in common with the 'republican ideal'. In the late nineteenth century, family policy was originally conceived for demographic and nationalist purposes, as a method designed to contain trade union militancy and which fitted in the political and social strategy of the Catholic Church, with its exclusive expression of femininity through motherhood. Contrary to the situation in the United Kingdom, demography has remained a typical French obsession and Malthusianism has always been seen as somewhat obscene. The very slow increase in population throughout the twentieth century was identified as a real problem and a legitimate concern for the authorities. How the holy trinity of nationalism, Catholicism and opposition to trade unions could lead to a major social reform is one of history's great mysteries.

Apart from family policy, universalism was applied to the education sector, which is not included in 'social policy' in France, but is clearly linked with it. Education in the late nineteenth century became the focal point in the struggle between the social and political forces which identified with the Republic and those who opposed it and preferred 'the throne and the altar' to *liberté, égalité, fraternité*. No sectarian policy would be acceptable to the Republic, on any grounds, religious, ethnic or geographical. Provision was to be equal throughout the country and irrespective of parents' residence or ability to pay. Education obtained at that time preferential treatment, if not necessarily in governments' financial choices, at least in public discourses. The universalist principles of secularism, or *laïcité*, were in some ways extended very gradually and very slowly to the health sector, where nurses belonging to religious orders were encouraged not to wear their uniforms and to refrain from imposing their outlook and norms. This remained a contentious issue well into the twentieth century.

However, universalism gradually came to prevail over 'Continental corporatism' in all areas, which explains the specific mix of the current French system and its complexity. This evolution owed a lot to the modernisation of the economy, the demographic decline of farmers and small shopkeepers, and the generalisation of waged employment. The ageing of farmers and the self-employed, and the dearth of new entrants into those professions, led to a crisis in the funding of their health funds, since the needs of older people were increasing and their resources were diminishing.

In the 1970s this was also compounded by the need to provide adequate cover for people who were not protected under the Bismarckian system, such as the wives of the self-employed, and by the need to find a way of financing the system which cut through the professional barriers erected in the late 1940s. In the 1980s the universalist slant of the French system was considerably increased under the influence of two factors: the growth of exclusion and the need for new resources. France's response to the dramatic increase in the unemployment rate in the 1980s was on the one hand to increase early retirement provision, which became possible at fifty-five, and in some cases at fifty-two, and, on the other hand, to create the *Revenu minimum d'insertion* (RMI). The RMI provided assistance, on a universal basis, to all citizens who had fallen through the increasingly inadequate safety net of unemployment insurance. In other words, universalism replaced Bismarckianism, and assistance, repackaged under the grand name of 'solidarity', replaced insurance. The supposedly radical aspect of RMI, the idea of a linkage between 'social insertion' on the one hand and benefits on the other, remained largely a rhetorical exercise, since only a minority of recipients benefited from integration schemes, few schemes could lead to employment and non-compliance to an agreed training programme never implied a reduction or suspension of the benefit for claimants. The RMI fell well short of the Scandinavian active labour market policies.

In spite of the universalist, relatively egalitarian slant of the new policies, a section of the left resisted the demise of work-based Bismarckianism. To this day, the Communist Party (PCF) has refused any increase in the *contribution sociale généralisée* (CSG) – a tax invented by Socialist Prime Minister Michel Rocard. This is probably due to the fact that the Fordist, industrial culture was the matrix of Communism. The PCF has difficulty adjusting to a new world in which social domination is taking new forms. In any case, the left remained divided on this crucial issue.

The limits of universalism were reached in the late 1990s and in 2003, on the issue of pensions. The 1995 crisis was sparked by Alain Juppé's attempt at unifying pensions schemes, and, in particular, at bringing the pension schemes of railwaymen in line with others. The outcome was very disappointing. Instead of welcoming the unification of the system, public opinion interpreted it, with some justification, as an attack on the most generous of all pension schemes and supported the railwaymen. The number of working years necessary to become eligible for a full pension was eventually increased for the private sector but special cases remained for a time, including the whole of the public sector and the 'historic schemes' such as those of railwaymen, miners, etc. By 2003 the public sector came under scrutiny. The options of increasing contributions, so as to compensate for the changes in the age pyramid, or of increasing general taxation were both rejected, on the grounds that neither the labour costs of the public sector nor the tax burden in general should be allowed to increase. The only option was to toughen the rules giving access to a full pension, so as to reduce costs, as had been the case in the private sector, in the twin hopes that people might postpone their retirement or that they would resort to private pension funds and increase their savings.

The liberal streak in French social policy

Besides, France is also a liberal country, especially as far as health care is concerned, since it operates a quasi-market. Among the providers of health care are private doctors, private chemists, private clinics as well as large, state-of-the art public teaching hospitals, or establishments managed by the mutual insurance companies. Patients are free to consult the practitioner of their choice, pay their own bills and are reimbursed afterwards. Practitioners are self-regulating and settle in the areas of the country of their choice, according to market opportunities and not to central planning. This quasi-market leads to a high degree of customer and provider satisfaction but unchecked expenditure and escalating costs. This issue is a particularly sensitive one, for social and political as well as economic reasons. The political clout of the medical professions is a force to be reckoned with, particularly for right-wing parties. The existence of a large private sector in care provision and of a thriving pharmaceutical industry in France is also an important aspect. The market is naturally not really free. In a typical *colbertiste* fashion, the government makes sure to guarantee the existence of demand and the ability of 'customers' to foot the bill. For a long time this has been done regardless of cost to the *sécurité sociale* budget. This public body made sure demand was not limited by financial considerations, and the suppliers had a free hand. *Colbertisme*, which is now seen in international circles a sin against the sacrosanct principles of the market, enabled France to develop its economy and has a lot to commend it. Without it, there would probably be no French pharmaceutical industry at all.

Even more important, user satisfaction was high in the health system, and progress was made over the years, which is exactly the opposite of the situation in the United Kingdom. However, progress was uneven. There is evidence of underachievement in terms of morbidity.[4] Besides, the French hold the world record in the consumption of medicines per head, which suggests either that their health system is inefficient or that their intake of chemicals is worrying.

The French quasi-market for health can only deliver growth and lead to permanent rises in demand and resources. The professional ethos of doctors and carers leads them to apply the latest and the most efficient equipment and treatment, so as to push back the frontiers of disease. Patients and their families naturally aspire to the best available treatment. The suppliers of care are bent on maximising the delivery of equipment, care and medicines. Research laboratories have, for decades, proved capable of devising more efficient treatments and equipment. In a context where financial guidelines are still largely indicative, public authorities are torn between their wish to keep expenditure under control and the urge to encourage the system to expand and improve the quality of life.

In other areas, such as pensions, the market principle does not apply and the liberal features of the French system are therefore limited to health and, to some extent, education. Governments have, over the years, considered that the absence of pension funds in France was a problem for two reasons: pressure was exerted by French financial institutions, which watch their British counterparts with envy, on the one hand. On the other hand, governments became worried by the fact that an increasing proportion of French company shares listed on the Paris stock market were held by British and American pension funds. The figures released in the press varied from 30 per cent to 40 per cent. This is seen as problematic, since there is no reciprocity, and French investments abroad do not match foreign investments in France. Besides, the capitalist culture of English-speaking financial institutions is perceived as ruthless, blind to strategic, long-term considerations and exclusively oriented to short-term profit, irrespective of industry's needs. French pension funds, it is suggested, would invest more wisely and would be more respectful of the firms they own. Government strategies, under Socialist Dominique Strauss Kahn, mostly consisted of creating a *fonds de réserve pour les retraites*, which is a state-run fund, including part of the proceeds of privatisations under the Jospin government. Private pension funds are still very limited, since they only supplement normal pensions and do not benefit from generous tax rebates. Governments refrain from reducing tax returns below a sustainable limit, given the public debt of the country.

France therefore borrows traits from the three types of systems, the universalist, the corporatist and the market-led ones. There is no such thing as a French 'model' in terms of 'social protection', as the French call their welfare state. The 'republican model' is a hybrid, resulting from historical and social compromises, sometimes even from pure chance (such as military victory over the Kaiser) and owes its shape to national anthropological factors only to a limited extent. This is probably true of most countries, Britain being a case in point. Flexibility and adaptability are therefore much greater than is often surmised. History has proved that change is possible. The notion of a conservative, unwieldy welfare bureaucracy incapable of adjusting to new realities seems to be highly ideological.

Change and French welfare: the republican compact challenged?

The institutional interpretation

Interpretations of social policy usually fall within one, or several, of three categories. The institutional interpretation is connected with the idea of path-dependence and based on the assumption that social policy is such an unwieldy set of organisations and relationships that the existing arrangements dictate the shape of things to come. Only exceptionally strong pressures or momentous events can bring about change. The size of social policy budgets is indeed very large and reform is extremely difficult to bring about. Only consistent and irresistible pressures can bring about change. The wartime conditions in Britain, the post-war settlement in France, the forward march of European integration or of economic and ideological globalisation epitomise such pressures. It remains to be seen whether social policy change, or resistance to change in France, has really been due to institutional factors. The major long-term change since the war, the shift from corporatism to a measure of universalism, is certainly not the product of institutional factors. French institutions were Bismarckian, and government policy under De Gaulle consisted in fostering 'joint management', *paritarisme*, in an attempt at abolishing class warfare, and imposing a conservative settlement. Socialist governments since 1981 have repeatedly attempted to salvage *paritarisme* and to promote a north European model of social negotiation, based on direct social dialogue and not the mediation of conflicts by the state. It seems that, far from shaping current policy, existing institutions have been a hindrance to change but have not succeeded in preventing it, as can be seen by the momentous shift from insurance and the centrality of professional identity towards citizenship and universalism.

Is it, then, the case that France has been forced to toe the line, to adopt the commonsense sets of policies which international institutions label as 'good practice'? Have the twin pressures of globalisation and European integration at long last compelled the French to act more wisely and stop strutting about like a vain cockerel? This view, which is common in the British press, would reinforce the thesis of the primacy of 'institutional factors'. It is based on a faulty assumption, the idea that there is such a thing as an international agreement on what constitutes good practice. Such is not the case. Even the international institutions one usually associates with globalisation, such as the World Bank, are deeply divided over social policy and social spending and, as Bob Deacon has shown,[5] now have second thoughts about the social impact of economic adjustment programmes in the southern hemisphere, even though the main cause of this concern is probably their political sustainability. One of the most devastating indictments of the policies carried out by international financial agencies was written by the former director of the World Bank.[6] The degree of freedom European governments enjoy in the field of social policy is still considerable, since the summits devoted to such issues (Luxemburg and Lisbon) have consistently decided to define general targets but to leave governments to implement them by the method of their choice. The targets are, in practice, largely indicative. European policy is still a virtual reality and the amounts devoted to social issues by the European Union, even though they seem significant *in abstracto*, are negligible compared with social security budgets, which, in the case of France, largely exceed the combined total of public expenditure. Construing the debate over French social policy in terms of a conflict between a traditional 'republican model' and the forward march of 'European good practice' cannot help us make sense of the system's real significance or evolution. For one thing, the republican model is largely mythical. *Paritarisme*, the Bismarckian practice of joint decision making, is mostly the result of a historical accident. Turning administrative arrangements into principles clouds the debate and certainly provides no insight. What the French mean by the 'Republic', in terms of social policy as in other areas, would probably be referred to in other European countries as 'democracy' or 'social democracy', implying an acceptable social deal combining the advantages of a market economy with those of strong, publicly maintained public services. The minutiae of the institutional arrangements inherited from recent history are not a matter of concern. However, the net result of reforms certainly is. The drift of European discourses and policies towards a distinctly liberal approach, partly under the influence of British experts and official representatives, in whatever form it takes, is viewed as an attack on the 'republican' model. Current arrangements have not been turned into a fetish in French political discourse on social policy and there is a lot of room for flexibility and change, provided the benefits of the changes are clearly shared and not reserved for the property-owning classes. 'Institutional issues' such as the procedures used in order to finance social policy are seen as secondary, provided the burden is also spread equitably and the beneficiaries are clearly identified.

The pressures that do exist are not exerted in any direct, authoritarian way. Nor are they the result of dark satanic external forces. They are not institutional but political and ideological. There is such a thing as a body of opinion among French conservative political leaders and economic experts, which is critical of existing social policy arrangements in France and favours the expansion of the market as well as the adoption of liberal solutions, the pension system being a case in point. This is just one of the factors at play within the system, which combines and vies with other forces. Foreign examples may be invoked in support of one option or another, but that is merely a rhetorical exercise, similar to the practice of French Agriculture Ministers, who systematically claim that their policies are dictated by Brussels. The European Union does not have a policy on pensions. However, the rapid and careless import of policies which were successfully implemented abroad has often led to catastrophe; Jospin and the means-testing of the benefits for families are obvious examples.

Whether one considers path dependence and institutional factors as something that hinders change and promotes conservatism or, conversely, as the consequence of the pressures of the global market and European integration, it does not seem to provide a satisfactory explanation for the specificities of France and for the evolution of the system.

Social policy as long-term history: the cultural explanation
The second type of explanation is the cultural one, called in French *culturaliste* by its detractors. Social policy arrangements are the product of deep anthropological and cultural factors which have been embedded in religious values over

time and are sometimes also translated into political and ideological terms. The proponents of this theory, such as the anthropologist Emmanuel Todd,[7] highlight the connection between the importance of individual freedom and lack of concern for equality on the one hand, and the domination of welfare systems by market principles, as in the 'Anglo-Saxon' model, on the other. They point out that conservative cultures, such as the German one, which favour the values of authority and paternalism, have spawned the Continental corporatist system which freezes people's social status and does not promote mobility. The concern for equality and for social cohesion seems to be widely shared by Scandinavian societies, which accept high levels of social discipline and taxation; it naturally leads to the principle of universalism. For Todd, France is largely dominated by the principle of equality, which corresponds to the old culture of the *bassin parisien*. This structure draws its origin from the methods of transmitting land and property among farmers. For Todd, France became the country of equality because sons were encouraged to become independent at a tender age and property was often divided equally. Whatever the merits of this historical explanation, the existence of cultural factors and of national traits is, empirically, obvious. Maybe it is even too obvious.

However, this raises a number of problems. Counter-examples abound. Australia, New Zealand, Canada, the United States and Britain share a number of cultural features and many elements in their anthropological backgrounds are similar. Their welfare systems are nevertheless quite different. The same can be said of Hong Kong and Singapore, since those two Chinese societies have adopted widely different systems.[8]

The lack of enthusiasm among intellectuals for the 'cultural approach' is probably due to the association of anthropology with nationalism in the 1930s. From the late nineteenth century onward until the Second World War, European nations mobilised all the intellectual and symbolical resources they could muster in their bid for world power. The German *Kulturkampf* was paralleled in France by ideological constructions which often included social policy. Very serious and reliable books were published and read which described the 'English soul' or the 'French genius' in general terms which, in today's world, are considered as 'essentialist' and stereotypical. André Siegfried's *La Crise britannique au XXème siécle* (1928),[9] a *science po* textbook until the 1950s, is a case in point. The need to define neatly national identities and to eliminate borderline cases, *métissage* and indefinite identities led to oversimplification of national cultures. In today's world, dominated by the trauma of the Second World War, the reaction against narrow nationalism and the positive prospect of European integration, *Kulturkampf* is a relic of the past.

Cultural studies have, since the 1970s, displayed a concern and a respect for individual strategies as opposed to national ones. Identity is now seen as a social construct, devised by individuals alone. However, it may be the case that the 'post-everything' approach has taken us very far indeed and that the forces of nationalism and of cultural difference have remained underground, only to surge in the guise of Euro-scepticism in some countries and opposition to *mon-dialisation* in others. Just because we did not want to see them did not mean they had vanished out of existence.

If one accepts the 'cultural' explanation of social policies, a relationship must be found between ancient, anthropological features and their modern translations in institutional arrangements, policies or attitudes. Can a relationship be established between the 'republican model' and age-old reflexes and attitudes in France in the field of social policy? The situation on the French 'periphery', now considered as the European Union's 'ultra-periphery', namely the French *Départements d'Outre Mer*, is illuminating in this respect. The clash between local cultures and French policies is obvious; identity in the DOM is not structured by the work relationship, the nuclear family is not the norm and the 'deal' between the powers that be and the local population includes specific historical and geopolitical features. Today, French social policy is considered as legitimate compensation for the wrongs of the past (slavery) and for allowing France to fly its colours in the Caribbean Sea, South America or the Indian Ocean. The situation has evolved significantly from the post-war period, when *départemental-isation* was granted to local populations who clamoured for it, and when French citizenship went together with the promise of social rights and equality.

The cultural explanation of social policy raises, therefore, the issue of French identity and of the part played by the 'republican contract' in this identity. Indeed, if one was to follow strictly the 'republican approach to identity' one could dig up the historical origins of social policy in order to find its roots, but the connection would be lost very quickly. As theory has it, the 'republican model' is supposed to be 100 per cent acultural. It is not culture-specific. At the heart of the republican contract is the absolute impartiality of the public authorities, the state's refusal to take into account inherited differences and cultural features; in modern terms, the state is colour-blind and gender-blind. The emphasis on equality of outcome rather than on 'merit' and equal opportunities is naturally part of this philosophy. The culturalists contend that, to a large extent, equality and universalism were in fact quite culture-specific originally. The cultural roots of the 'republican contract' probably bear a complex relationship with the current situation. The importance of intellectual exchanges, the impact of transnational movements, such as Christianity and Communism, economic globalisation and naturally the vast number of immigrants who acquired French nationality in the twentieth century have all impacted on 'French cultural identity', and would make essentialist theoretical positions untenable.

The clash between local culture and welfare policies is obvious whenever one considers policies in the French DOM TOM, such as family policy, but this is only the tip of the iceberg. The examples of failed grafts and disastrous imports abound. To take up again familiar examples, the minimum wage for young people could not possibly be accepted by an egalitarian country where regulation by the state is the rule. Nor could the means-testing of family benefit, a move which seemed to run counter to nationalism and egalitarianism and fed the fears of the left, who expected a scaling-down of the benefit. How embedded in culture is French social policy?

The cultural explanation is also attractive because it enables us to provide explanations in a number of otherwise mysterious and puzzling cases. The current attitudes to pensions are a case in point. No doubt one can understand how early retirement became public policy and enabled the rather painless scaling down of industries such as steel-making in the 1980s. What is more difficult to account for is why early retirement was so readily accepted by decision makers, employers and employees alike. In practice, the age at which most people stop work is now well below sixty.[10] Only 41.5 per cent of males between the ages of fifty-five and sixty-four are at work, against 62.5 per cent in the United Kingdom and 70.4 per cent in Sweden.[11] The statutory retirement age is sixty and the reforms advocated by employers, which would reduce the amount paid to pensioners, were resisted on the grounds that they would not stop people from taking retirement but would reduce their income and increase poverty in old age. The split between life at work and life outside the workplace is clear-cut. There is evidence of this in the lack of enthusiasm for part-time work and flexible working hours, which are seen very negatively, partly because they blur the borderline between work and private life. This may be connected with that major tenet of French democracy, the absolute separation between public life and private life, between private morality, ethics and spiritual concerns on the one hand and citizenship on the other. This attitude may be due, historically, to political factors such as the separation between Church and State but, with time, it has become embedded in the French mentality. Put in crude terms, the work ethic applies in France only thirty-five hours a week, forty-six weeks per year and thirty-five years in a person's life. Outside this, other, more civilised concerns prevail. How the French will adapt to the reforms in pension provision limiting access to full pensions remains to be seen. If the desire to leave one's employment overrides other considerations, then people may be prepared to leave their regular employment and take up illegal work if necessary, in order to compensate for the fall in their income. Attitudes change slowly and employers still consider that older workers should be encouraged to leave and be denied promotion.

What remains to be seen is whether the importance of culture in social policy is truly exceptional in France. French culture is certainly distinctive but the impact of culture is not. Abiding by the Protestant work ethic is just as remarkable as ignoring it. The obsession with social security fraud, with control and assessment, in British administrative culture is also a cause of wonderment to all visitors.

The dynamics of a system: welfare as social regulation

The third interpretation of social policy is based on a dynamic view. Welfare can be seen as a way of regulating the relations between social groups who are represented by different political or industrial organisations and whose stance or interests are sometimes synthesised or vindicated by ideological discourses. Political scientist Bruno Jobert calls this 'the dialectic joining of social actors and institutions'[12] and 'the continuous remodelling of social systems by actors in constant conflict and co-operation, always debating and redefining common representations'.[13] In this sense, social protection enables the conduct of social negotiations even under circumstances where they seem to be impossible. Direct bargaining at shopfloor level or at national level in each professional branch often reaches a break point beyond which there appears to be no use in pursuing dialogue. In practice, social regulation takes place in different ways in European countries. France is obviously uneasy about its process of regulation, for several reasons.

Serious bargaining has always taken place at the national level. There are several reasons for this. One of them is the weakness of local trade union organisation; France has the lowest trade union membership rate in the European Union, officially 10 per cent if one includes the teaching profession and the police, much less in the private sector. Another factor is the speed at which bread-and-butter issues become political ones. This may be a consequence of weak trade union organisation or, conversely, of an intellectual ability to conceptualise issues and draw general conclusions and philosophical lessons from practical developments. Seen from another angle, it may relate to the French love of theory and be reflected in that most sacred of academic ministrations, the need for a *problématique* in every piece of research work and the contempt for mere description. As a consequence, the government is compelled to clamber out of the trench and do the dirty work itself, i.e. take decisions in the field of social regulation. Compensation for redundancies, early retirement, the minimum wage, the level of the RMI may well be welfare issues but are mostly political ones. Industrial issues just cannot be left to the so-called 'social partners', which makes life very dangerous for governments.

The specific approach to regulation in France bears a strong relation to the 'republican contract'. However, since regulation concerns mostly the relation between social groups, the interpretations of the 'republican contract' vary widely, depending on political forces' social identities. In the eyes of trade unions and left-wing political forces, what is at stake in the 'republican contract' is, on the one hand, the safeguarding of a number of arrangements and institutions which so far have guaranteed more or less satisfactory provision and, on the other hand, the maintenance of roughly equal provision for the whole of the population. While conservative political forces will accept the first goal, they insist that maintaining satisfactory standards of care, and therefore maintaining the *pacte républicain*, requires sweeping changes, including in practice significant shifts in the balance of power which put the wage-earning classes, and public employees in particular, at a clear disadvantage. Thus the very significant reforms of the pension systems were simultaneously interpreted as a breach in the 'republican contract' by the left and, by the right, as the only way of buttressing it.

Anti-poverty policies also illustrate the divide between social forces in terms of regulation. Reducing the *fracture social* is presented by the right as a major item in Jacques Chirac's policy. This is seen as evidence of the government's serious commitment to the *pacte républicain*; the horrors of living rough are openly discussed, Abbé Pierre is regularly invited to the Elysée Palace, emergency services are given a high profile and the old tradition of respectable Catholic charity has found a modern icon in Mme Chirac. In the eyes of the left, poverty is the direct consequence of changes in patterns of employment. Low employment levels, for which government policies and the new face of capitalism are blamed, therefore threaten the *pacte*. The return of Catholic charity of the most traditional kind is also seen as threatening the precarious balance between Church and State which is central to the idea of the *pacte*.

The second reason why social regulation is problematic in the English sense is that this direct intervention of the French state in social regulation is mostly seen negatively by the body politic, with the exception of the far left. Volumes could be written about the use and abuse of the term 'Jacobin' in contemporary political discourse. From Jacques Delors and Martine Aubry to Alain Minc, from Alain Madelin to Jacques Chirac, from Le Pen to the FNLC or ETA, the central theme of the contemporary *pensée unique* in France is that the role of the state is excessive. The Minc report, *La France de l'an 2000*,[14] had already criticised *la régulation par la crise* and highlighted the desire of some of the French social elites for a cultural shift towards the Continental corporatist model, which is largely seen as an ideal. The tough stance adopted by the Raffarin government in 2003 illustrates this feeling, that 'regulation through social crisis' is damaging and governments should not give in.

Ironically, a socialist public policy illustrates this concern, the thirty-five-hour week. The idea of a reduction in the working week no doubt bears some relation to the question of the sharing of time between public life and private life and meets a need which has become a strong cultural trait in contemporary France. However, the thirty-five-hour week can be seen as the ideal metaphor for the French paradox. On the one hand, it is a public policy, resulting from a political decision by the Prime Minister and the voting of a *projet de loi* by the Assemblée nationale. It is state-driven and highly political. On the other hand, the goal of the law was clearly to rejuvenate social negotiation within firms. This does not amount to saying that the reduction of unemployment was not one of the primary motivations of Martine Aubry. However, given the lack of agreement among economic experts on the impact of the reduction of the working week on the unemployment rate, there is a very strong case for suggesting that the government had at least a double agenda. Firms were given a few months during which they were expected to negotiate new working conditions, including the reduction of the working week and flexibility. Those that reached an agreement with the unions before the deadline were given strong financial incentives.[15] The thirty-five-hour week can therefore be seen as an attempt at introducing flexibility into French firms in a negotiated, socially acceptable way.[16] In fact it amounted to a cultural change, on the part of unions as well as management. The confrontational stance adopted by French employers under the Jospin governments, symbolised by the new leader of the employers' organisation (MEDEF), Baron Antoine de Seillière, and the much heralded *refondation sociale* were a direct response to the thirty-five-hour law and an attempt at wrenching back the initiative from the government and conducting negotiation on their own terms. The proclaimed aim of employers was a complete overhaul of the social protection system, including unemployment and pensions, even in the public sector, which was outside their province. This is highly ambitious as well as directly political, which suggests that the strategy of a high-profile national negotiation held in the spotlight can only result in a crisis.

This power game between government, employers and employees may have 'exceptional' traits because social regulation in France uses the channels of politics and crisis more than in other countries. However, structurally, it is no different from other nations which use different methods to solve similar problems and, in some cases, achieve similar results, in terms of flexibility, for instance.

In methodological terms, explanations can be only very modest and borrow elements from all three interpretations. The '*régulation* theory' is fairly useful because it helps account for the often illogical, messy nature of decision making in the field of social policy. The power play between social forces and the government leads to compromises, decisions or inability to take decisions, arrangements and evolutions which fly in the face of both the institutional theory and the cultural one. To take a well known example, it is just impossible to account for the role of *paritarisme* in contemporary France by relying on the cultural explanation, since France has a culture not of power-sharing but of confrontation. Likewise, the shape of *paritarisme* has changed dramatically since the 1950s and institutional conservatism or the pressure of outside forces cannot possibly explain those changes. Welfare can be seen as intrinsically linked with the continuous process of negotiation; it is indeed the privileged locus of national bargaining and regulation. It is just in a messy state because there are no such things as 'natural frontiers' in the field of industrial relations, as in that of geography. The state of social security provision reflects the battle lines between the different forces which intervene in the field. Only the passing of time, habit and a healthy fear of catastrophe grant them a aura of eternity, just like the Oder–Neisse line. Seeing social policy as regulation enables us to account for the dynamics of change and of resistance to change, which also requires some effort.

However, regulation does not take place in an intellectual vacuum. The most difficult questions always bear on the causes of events and on the roots of attitudes. The cultural approach alone can provide answers which might be tentative, impossible to demonstrate positively and to support by quantitative data, but which are the only ones on offer. Long-term trends and attitudes provide not just the backdrop for negotiations, but also the intellectual and emotional apparatus of the negotiators themselves. In the first and last instances, they play a crucial part in decision making.

Conclusion

An examination of French social policy based on the three classical models highlights the variety of sources of inspiration which have influenced the promoters, 'prime movers' and reformers of French welfare, thus belying the notion of a single, coherent 'republican model' in this respect. The three interpretative frameworks, institutional, cultural and regulationist, also show that the frequent changes in the welfare system are driven by much deeper tectonic movements in the political, social and economic landscape. Social policy in France is reactive, and was traditionally content with alleviating the collateral damage of modernisation; the term most commonly used to describe it is *protection sociale*. Barring family policy, it has rarely embarked on social engineering and stands in stark contrast to the utilitarian policies carried out in Britain in the 1830s, or the measures designed to drill the British population into employability and flexibility in the early twenty-first century. A policy such as France's is not designed to accelerate or anticipate economic and social change, but to adapt to it. The idea that France's welfare system is outdated, costly and inefficient and that the 'republican model' must give way to market-driven forces is part of the ideological pressure exerted by the 'liberal Anglo-Saxon model'. The 'republican model' in social policy is evolving, following one step (sometimes two steps) behind economic and social changes. In the field of social policy, the shape and meaning of the 'republican compact', as well as its possible survival or demise depend therefore totally on the balance of social and political forces within French society.

Notes

1 G. Esping Andersen, *Les Trois Mondes de l'État-providence* (Paris: Presses Universitaires de France, 1999).
2 J. Clasen (ed.), *Comparative Social Policy* (London: Blackwell, 1999).
3 B. Jobert *et al.*, 'Introduction', in *Comparer les systèmes de protection sociale en Europe* II (Paris: MIRE, 1996), pp. 237–41.
4 DRESS, *Données sur la situation sanitaire et sociale en France 1999*. Ministère de l'Emploi et de la solidarité (Paris: La Documentation Française, 1999)
5 B. Deacon, 'Globalisation: a threat to equitable social provision?' *University of Sussex IDS Bulletin*, 31:4 (2000).
6 J. E. Stiglitz, *Globalization and its Discontents* (New York: Norton, 2002).
7 E. Todd, *Le Destin des immigrés* (Paris: Seuil, 1996).
8 C. Aspalter (ed.), *Welfare Capitalism around the World* (Taiwan: Casa Verde, 2003).
9 A. Siegfried, *La Crise britannique au XXème siècle* (Paris: Armand Colin, 1928).
10 J-M. Charpin, *L'Avenir de nos retraites : rapport au Premier Ministre* (Paris: La Documentation Française, 1999).
11 M-T. Join-Lambert, *Politiques sociales* (Paris: Presses de Sciences Po/Dalloz, 1997).

12 Editor's translation. The original reads: 'la dialectique des acteurs sociaux et des institutions'. Jobert et al., 'Introduction', in *Comparer les systèmes de protection sociale en Europe* II.

13 Editor's translation. The original reads: 'le remodelage permanent des systèmes sociaux par des acteurs qui ne cessent de se combattre et de coopérer, de débattre et de redéfinir des répresentations communes'. *Ibid.*

14 A. Minc, *La France de l'an 2000* (Paris: Odile Jacob, 1994), pp. 166–78.

15 K. Boullier, *Maitriser la réforme des trente-cinq heures* (Paris: Editions Liaisons, 1998).

16 J-P. Révauger, 'France reduces the working week', *Social Policy Association News*, spring (1999).

Select bibliography

J. S. Ambler (ed.), *The French Welfare State* (New York: New York University Press, 1991).

C. Aspalter (ed.), *Welfare Capitalism around the World* (Taiwan: Casa Verde, 2003).

K. Boullier, *Maitriser la réforme des trente-cinq heures* (Paris: Editions Liaisons, 1998).

R. Castel, *Les Métamorphoses de la question sociale* (Paris: Fayard, 1995).

J-M. Charpin, *L'Avenir de nos retraites : rapport au Premier Ministre* (Paris: La Documentation Française, 1999).

J. Clasen (ed.), *Comparative Social Policy* (London: Blackwell, 1999).

G. Esping Andersen, *Les Trois Mondes de l'Etat-providence* (Paris: Presses Universitaires de France, 1999).

B. Friot, *Puissances du salariat : emploi et protection sociale à la française* (Paris: La Dispute, 1996).

V. George and P. Taylor Gooby, *European Welfare Policy* (London: Macmillan, 1996).

B. Jobert et al., *Comparer les systèmes de protection sociale en Europe* II (Paris: MIRE, 1996).

M-T. Join-Lambert, *Politiques sociales* (Paris: Presses de Sciences Po/Dalloz, 1997).

B. Majnoni d'Intignano, *La Protection sociale* (Paris: Editions de Fallois, 1993).

A. Minc, *La France de l'an 2000* (Paris: Odile Jacob, 1994).

S. Paugam, *L'Exclusion : l'état des savoirs* (Paris: La Découverte, 1996).

J-P. Révauger, 'France reduces the working week', *Social Policy Association News*, spring (1999).

A. Siegfried, *La Crise britannique au XXème siècle* (Paris: Armand Colin, 1928).

J. E. Stiglitz, *Globalization and its Discontents* (New York: Norton, 2002).

E. Todd, *Le Destin des immigrés* (Paris: Seuil, 1996).

M. I. Vail, 'The better part of valour: the politics of French welfare reform', *Journal of European Social Policy*, 9:4 (1999).

N. Whiteside and R. Salais, 'Comparing welfare states: social protection and industrial politics in France and Britain, 1930–60', *Journal of European Social Policy*, 8:2 (1998).

8

The interventionist state: demise or transformation?

Mairi Maclean

It is not a right of the State to help its industry. It is a duty.[1]

French state interventionism stands out as a prominent feature of the French state tradition, which may be traced back to the *ancien régime*. Economic development, republicanism and citizenship are complementary issues in France, as evinced by the success of French planning in furthering national priorities in the three decades following the Second World War. Yet global and European pressures, in particular the new dimension provided by an ever-increasing layer of European regulation that supersedes that of the Republic (theoretically at least), increasingly place a major question mark over the ability of the state to preserve and promote the national interest. This chapter focuses on state–business relations, assessing the tension between supra-national markets ostensibly governed by supranational rules and the long-standing vocation of the Republic to exercise its sovereignty in defence of French national interests: in the words of Jean-Jacques Rousseau, 'Sover-eignty, being but the exercise of the general will, cannot be alienated.'[2] The chapter begins with a brief historical overview of the role of the state in busi-ness and the economy in the post-war period, highlighting the key 'mile-stones' in its evolution. It examines the challenges which confront the state in the here-and-now, faced as it is with an enlarged European Union, where the constellation of power and interests is changing, and where the privileged status France had come to enjoy as co-leader of the Union with Germany is under threat. Under the impetus provided by liberalising EU measures, the role of the state in business has declined considerably over the years. Can the state, increasingly constrained by EU dictates and by the commercial impera-tives accompanying privatisation, still retain a guiding role in the economy to protect French national business interests, or will it ultimately be forced to become a stakeholder like any other?

Business and the state

There is a long tradition in France of state involvement in the economy, dating back to Jean-Baptiste Colbert (1619–83), Secretary of State for the royal household under Louis XIV.[3] Colbert was a tireless public administrator, and in the tradition of France's great centralisers (such as Philip the Fair, Richelieu, Mazarin and Louis XIV) he was an enlightened supporter of fledgling industries and commerce. He introduced protectionist measures, invited foreign craftsmen to France and expanded the role of the state in manufacturing industry, albeit initially for the purposes of replenishing the monarch's depleted war chests. Some of the companies he nurtured in the seventeenth century remain in existence today, including glassmaker Saint-Gobain (created in 1665 as part of Colbert's economic reflation plan), one of France's leading listed companies. Of greater importance, however, is Colbert's intellectual legacy. He lends his name to the long-standing tradition of state intervention in the economy through discriminatory fiscal and public procurement policies, designed to favour and protect public and private national champions, as well as nascent industries, in order that they might withstand foreign competition. This mindset of helping domestic companies into the driving seat survives to this day.

In the post-war period, economic management and economic sovereignty joined hands in an industrial policy whose principal objective was commercial success in the international market place through high-tech Colbertism. The state bolstered its 'national champions' (*champions nationaux*) in future industries with grants and public procurement measures designed to provide secure markets, and cushioned through subsidy its 'lame ducks' (*canards boiteux*) in sunset industries such as steel and shipbuilding. The general interest (national defence, national sovereignty and technological autonomy) has been customarily proffered as justification for what might be defined as 'offensive protectionism'.[4]

France's 'mixed economy', in which responsibility is shared by private and public actors, has not remained static during the post-war period. Following the Liberation in 1944–46, the public sector was significantly enlarged through the nationalisation of strategic financial and industrial sectors. The then Constituent Assembly adopted Acts of nationalisation first for the banks (December 1945), electricity and gas (March 1946), followed by insurance and coal (April 1946). Linked with the Resistance movement and with the vengeful atmosphere of the Liberation, nationalisation was perceived as 'democratic and patriotic retaliation against the alleged defeatist and collaborationist activities of the capitalist oligarchies'.[5] De Gaulle, as he confessed to his erstwhile Minister of Culture, novelist André Malraux, shortly before his death in 1970, perceived nationalisation above all as a means of resurrecting France.[6] In de Gaulle's mind the state was 'an institution of decision, action and ambition, expressing and serving the national interest alone'.[7] Economic planning formed a central plank of the Gaullist strategy of state-led growth. Adopted in the Fourth Republic as a means of organising and directing the process of reconstruction and economic modernisation, normally over a four to five-year period, it became one of the principal economic tools of the Gaullist era, especially during the *trente glorieuses*, the three decades of economic growth and prosperity following the Second World War.[8]

In February 1982, following the accession of the left to office for the first time in a generation, and after eight years of economic crisis, the economic recession triggered by the oil price hikes of the 1970s under President Valéry Giscard-D'Estaing, the state strengthened its hold on the economy (ostensibly at least) by taking control of another huge tranche of the financial and industrial sectors: thirty-six banks, two finance companies and twelve leading industrial conglomerates. This gave rise to proportionately the largest public sector outside the Eastern bloc, accounting for some 24 per cent of jobs, 32 per cent of sales, 30 per cent of exports and 60 per cent of investment in the industrial and energy sectors.[9] Subsequently, from the mid-1980s, the tendency has been, in France as elsewhere, to reduce the role of the state in the economy in the interests of achieving greater efficiency and effectiveness, through the implementation of deregulation and far-reaching privatisation programmes. The disengagement or withdrawal of the state was now seen as a necessary precondition for a more efficient economy.[10] Thus France went from sweeping nationalisation to sweeping privatisation in the short space of four years. The privatisation of Saint-Gobain in December 1986 proved to be the first of many.[11] Privatisation has continued since 1986 under governments from both sides of the political divide. President François Mitterrand tried, but failed, to put an end to it in 1988 with 'ni ni', his promise to the electorate that there should be no further nationalisations or privatisations, leading to privatisation by the back door in the early 1990s, termed 'la respiration du secteur public', allowing the public sector to breathe.

Privatisation is still on-going, although today it normally concerns the sale of residual government stakes in companies once fully owned by the state. In 2003 the state reduced its stake in a number of firms, including Renault-Nissan, Dassault Systèmes and Thomson. In March 2003 the National Assembly voted to reduce the state's share in Air France from 54.4 per cent to less than 20 per cent. In the event, however, privatisation was superseded by a merger with the Dutch carrier KLM in May 2004 to form Air France-KLM, Europe's largest airline. June 2003 saw the expiry of agreements freezing the core shareholdings of EADS (European Aeronautic Defence & Space Company) and the defence electronics firm Thales (previously Thomson CSF), including those of the state, opening the way to change.[12] Divestments in 2004 included SNECMA (Société nationale d'étude et de construction de moteurs d'aviation), an aircraft engine manufacturer, the government's stake in which was reduced from 97 per cent to 62 per cent, raising €1.45 billion. In May 2004 the new Finance Minister, Nicolas Sarkozy, announced an ambitious raft of sell-offs, including stakes in two firms which manage French *autoroutes*, 600 tonnes of gold belonging to the Banque de France and as much as a 100,000 m² of choice Paris office space surplus to government requirements.[13] Plans are also afoot to sell off stakes in France Télécom (in which the state has a 55 per cent holding), Aéroports de Paris, as well as Électricité de France (EdF) and Gaz de France (GdF) (though not before 2005, see below).[14] These sell-offs are driven primarily by the need to raise receipts rather than any ideological belief in private enterprise *per se*.

Unsurprisingly, perhaps, the French privatisation programmes were products of *dirigisme*, conceived of in *dirigiste* terms. In this sense, privatisation, which replenishes state coffers, reducing the budget deficit and stock of national debt, while it contributes to the downsizing of the state, is also paradoxically a tool of industrial policy. Moreover, the *noyaux durs* which were put in place during the privatisations of 1986–88 and 1993–95 (i.e. the 'hard cores' of stable investors designed to provide newly privatised firms with an anchor following their change of status) were intended to shore up company take-over defences against would-be predators, particularly foreign ones. In fact they often built on long-standing relationships, as state actors exploited existing elitist networks to ensure that controlling stakes remained in safe hands.[15] As Bauer puts it: 'The French privatisation programme did not represent any great break with the past. Quite the contrary: it fully illustrated the State's interventionist tradition and even reinforced it.'[16] Nevertheless, though the state clearly retains the reflex to intervene (in mergers, for example, granting or withholding its approval) the effect of almost two decades of privatisation has been to dilute the power of the state to dictate choices and outcomes.

Yet public service in France remains endowed with special meaning. Perhaps this goes some way to explain why France has faced such searching self-doubt in recent years regarding its particular model of state–society relations. Despite extensive privatisation, the state continues to play a pivotal role in the economy. This applies not only to basic public services such as education[17] and health care[18] but also to key economic sectors, including telecommunications, transport and energy, the gas and electricity suppliers GdF and EdF being wholly owned by the state nearly ten years after the liberalisation of European energy markets. Both sides of the political divide are now challenging the traditionally strong, interventionist role of the state. From prominent socialists such as Martine Aubry and Jacques Delors to right-wing thinkers Alain Minc and Alain Madelin, the contemporary *pensée unique* – what we might call in English 'group think', leading to the unification of outlook and policy – is that the role of the state is excessive and should be reduced.[19] President Jacques Chirac himself claims to subscribe to this view, declaring in May 1995, 'The State must be impartial. It is one of the conclusions I've come to.'[20] The proof of the pudding, however, is in the eating. Though there is now far less intervention in the appointments of the heads of leading French companies, whether public or private, than twenty years ago[21] (in 1981, for example, the incoming Socialist administration ousted as many as twenty-nine chairmen of the top thirty-six public sector companies in one fell swoop), nevertheless Chirac stands accused of putting in place an 'État-Chirac', filling key appointments with individuals loyal to himself, on an unprecedented scale. These include the heads of the National Assembly, the Senate, the Conseil d'État, the Cour des comptes, the Conseil constitutionnel, the Commission nationale de l'informatique et des libertés, the Conseil supérieur de l'audiovisuel and even public sector companies such as EdF. EdF's *président-directeur général* (PDG), François Roussely, reputed to be close to the Parti socialiste (PS), was controversially replaced in July 2004 by none other than Francis Mer, Minister of the Economy, Finance and Industry (2002–04) until the spring Cabinet reshuffle, when he was succeeded by Nicholas Sarkozy.[22]

By 2003 just twelve enterprises of any size or significance remained wholly owned by the state, including EdF and GdF; the supplier of postal services, La Poste; the national rail operator, the SNCF (Société nationale des chemins de fer); the RATP (Régie autonome de transport public) and RER (Réseau express régional), the Paris Metro and the suburban rail system; GIAT Industries, manufacturer of defence equipment munitions; and the aircraft engine manufacturer SNECMA (in which Sarkozy sold a 35 per cent stake in 2004, as mentioned). In addition, the state retained a controlling interest in companies such as Air France-KLM, France Télécom, Renault and Thales.[23] Yet the French public sector remains one of the largest in Western Europe. At the birth of the Fifth Republic in 1958 it represented just over 20 per cent of the economy (excluding agriculture), in terms of its impact on levels of investment, value added and the labour force. From a peak of 24 per cent in 1985, by the end of the twentieth century it still accounted for a sizeable 13.5 per cent of investment, 11.5 per cent of value added, and employed 10.3 per cent of the work force, representing an overall impact on the French economy of 11.8 per cent (excluding agriculture), against an EU average of 9 per cent.[24] The overall tax burden as a share of gross domestic product (GDP) remains one of the highest in the European Union, in excess of 50 per cent. How can we explain this conundrum? How is it that the marked change in policy towards state ownership since the early 1980s is apparently contradicted by a continued interventionist role played by the state in the economy?

Clearly, the needs of economic management are not necessarily compatible with the aspiration to economic sovereignty. Tension and even conflict may arise between the quest for autonomy and prestige on the one hand and the necessity of managerial efficiency on the other, between 'national distinctiveness' and 'insufficient national means of action'.[25] In the course of the past fifty years the reality of economic management has come to diverge increasingly from the goal of economic sovereignty. Once the openness of the French economy was accepted as a *sine qua non* of expansion in 1958, French economic management was likely to conflict with the aspiration for national autonomy. The latter has been compromised time and again by the need to adjust to external constraints, especially in the wake of the oil shocks of

1973–74 and 1979, which saw the price of oil increase tenfold in six years. Over the past half-century French politicians have learned from experience that the economy does not exist in a vacuum but functions as part of a complex global economy. This became all the more obvious at the beginning of the Mitterrand era. The U-turn of 1983 (from expansion to *rigueur*) marked a key turning point between the quest for economic independence, epitomised by the Socialists failed go-it-alone reflation of 1981–82, at a time when France's main economic partners were pursuing austerity programmes, and the pragmatic realisation of systemic interdependence with Europe and the wider international economy. Thereafter French economic policy has been set entirely within the parameters of European construction, a decision born not of idealism but of enlightened self-interest, realism and diplomatic necessity.[26] In short, the quest for an increasingly unachievable national independence has been superseded by the goal of constructing an economically and politically coherent Europe, in the hope that this may better serve French interests.

The French economy today

Given the key importance of long-term institutional stability to French economic success, it is useful at this point to take a closer look at current economic performance. The French economy, having performed well over the post-war period, continues to perform well by international comparative indicators. The world's fifth economy, behind only the United States, Japan, Germany and the United Kingdom, France enjoys a strong growth record. That the economy is broadly based, being especially strong in terms of the balance between sectors (agriculture, industry, services and commerce) adds to its robustness. The explanation of French economic success is also institutional, however, determined by the particular physiology, or physiognomy, of the economy. This is characterised by stable institutions as well as by long-term relations between different corporate constituencies; inter-personal, inter-corporate, between government and business, and business and politics.

Tables 8.1 and 8.2 examine the composition of French business more closely, which is compared and contrasted to that of the United Kingdom.[27] The 'top' 100 companies in France and the United Kingdom respectively in 1998 are defined here not in terms of the frequently used, but fundamentally flawed, single measure of market capitalisation but more robustly in terms of an equally weighted set of four measures: total capital employed, turnover, pre-tax profit and number of employees. What is striking in Table 8.1 is the similarity in mean scores for three of the variables: total capital employed, turnover and number of employees. Only pre-tax profit is markedly different, with UK companies outperforming their French counterparts to a significant degree. The lower profitability tolerated by French companies is reflective both of the drive for profits that characterises leading British companies,[28] but more especially of the notion of 'social interest' of the firm which traditionally infuses French

Table 8.1 *Indicators of the size of the top 100 French and UK companies in 1998*

Indicator	French companies	UK companies
Total capital employed		
Median	4,562	4,928
Mean	9,298	7,437
Standard deviation	15,783	7,416
Turnover		
Median	4,562	5,552
Mean	8,507	9,071
Standard deviation	9,465	10,403
Pre-tax profit		
Median	106	707
Mean	254	1,182
Standard deviation	480	1,308
Employees (No.)		
Median	22,572	35,706
Mean	45,065	45,945
Standard deviation	54,061	42,052

Note: Complete data series exist for UK companies, and for French companies of turnover and employees. Data are available of total capital employed for eighty-four French companies and of pre-tax profit for eighty-six French companies.
Source: EIU, *Country Report: France* (London: EIU, 2004), April, p. 37.

business. Henri Weber defines this as characterised by a belief in the common good uniting the interests of workers and employees, a belief that economic and social affairs cannot be separated, an expectation that employers should pay attention to their responsibilities as well as to their rights, and a belief that the state should intervene where necessary to correct wrongdoing.[29] The paternalism that traditionally characterised French work relations bears witness to the importance of a wider social interest. Whereas the maximisation of profit is apparently what drives British business, France has traditionally assumed a broader 'stakeholder' approach to business. These notions coalesced in the concept of *l'entreprise citoyenne* advocated by Jacques Chirac in his 1994 presidential campaign: the idea of a corporate sector exercising civic responsibility, not privileging productivity and efficiency for their own sake.[30] In short, low profitability is not necessarily in France the prelude to closure that it so often has been in the United Kingdom.

However, when reference is made to Table 8.2, which takes an industry group view of the distribution of corporate power in France and Britain, it can be seen that the business systems of the two countries are configured quite differently. The 'power' metric is based upon the four measures of corporate size presented in Table 8.1, and sharp differences can be observed in its sectoral dis-

Table 8.2 *Distribution of corporate power by industry group among the top 100 French and UK companies in 1998*

Industry group	France		UK	
	No.	% share of corporate power	No.	% share of corporate power
Construction	3	1.96	0	0.00
Financial services	2	4.87	20	25.14
Food and drink	12	4.49	9	7.90
IT and business services	6	1.45	3	1.16
Manufacturing	28	26.98	15	13.35
Media, consumer services and products	9	6.68	11	9.52
Oil and gas, mining and materials	14	13.35	9	16.37
Retailing	15	14.81	11	9.84
Transport and distribution services	5	5.51	7	4.67
Utilities and telecommunications	6	19.91	15	11.46
Total	100	100.00	100	100.00

Note: Corporate power was estimated for each company on the basis of total capital employed, turnover, pre-tax profit and employees in 1998. Industry group totals are the sum of corporate power for companies in the group expressed as a percentage of total corporate power for each country respectively.

tribution, in turn reflecting profound differences in the economic trajectories of the two countries since 1945. The most compelling differences relate to manufacturing and financial services. Whereas in France manufacturing has been preserved as pre-eminent within the corporate sector, with an extraordinary twenty-eight companies out of the top 100 engaged in manufacturing industry, testifying once more to the traditionally strong role of the state, which, through a variety of means, has helped its companies to stay in the driving seat, in Britain the historic emphasis given to the City, to banking, insurance and finance has materialised in a remarkable concentration of power in the financial sector. In 2003 industry accounted for 19.9 per cent of French GDP, the leading sectors being, in order of importance, intermediate goods, capital goods (including aircraft, dominated by Airbus), consumer goods and cars (70 per cent of production being exported abroad, the automotive sector accounting for nearly 7 per cent of annual GDP alone).[31]

A comparison of the two countries' profiles with regard to utilities and telecommunications is equally remarkable. Though France had but six of these companies in its top 100 in 1998, while the United Kingdom had more than double, these half-dozen utilities, most of them state-owned, accounted for an astonishing 20 per cent of corporate power, compared with just 11 per cent for the fifteen British-based firms. This represents an extraordinary concentration of power. French utility companies are examined more closely below, in particular the electricity supplier EdF.

One further difference between the two business systems concerns the French pursuit of glory and prestige, highlighted by a British manager at Airbus UK: 'The French don't go in for the normal rate of return. Whereas the British rate of return is profit over cost, the French rate of return is glory over cost!'[32] The maiden flight of the Airbus A-380, planned for autumn 2004, will be a cause for national celebration. This 555 seat double-decker aircraft, with wings (built in Broughton in Wales) over 36 m in length, will be the largest passenger airliner on the market. Airbus, a four-country consortium, involving the French, Germans, British and Spanish, established in December 1970, in which EADS has an 80 per cent stake, is now the world leader in the passenger airline sector, nudging ahead of its main American competitor, Boeing, in itself a cause of rejoicing.[33] The new 'super-jumbo' is due to enter commercial service in 2006.[34] Thanks to Airbus and approximately 500 local subcontractors, the conurbation of Toulouse, where Airbus aircraft are assembled, is thriving, with the population of Haute-Garonne expected to swell from its current level of 1.05 million to 1.56 million by 2030. The French government originally chose the south-west as the centre of its future aviation industry after the First World War for reasons of national security.[35]

France versus the European Commission

Nevertheless, recently the outlook for the French economy has been slightly less rosy. In the early years of the twenty-first century France, whose GDP had previously outstripped that of the United Kingdom, was overtaken by her near neighbour. Indeed, *per capita* GDP in Britain exceeded both France and Germany in 2003, behind only the United States and Japan.[36] In France real GDP growth fell from a height of 4.2 per cent in 2000 to just 0.5 per cent three years later, the lowest since 1993, and the third weakest growth performance recorded since the Second World War.[37] Unemployment, which, from a peak of 12.5 per cent of the work force in 1997 (having been in double figures since 1992), had fallen to 8.7 per cent by 2001, is again on the rise, reaching 9.7 per cent at the end of 2003, close to the symbolic threshold of 10 per cent.

Years of fiscal and monetary austerity in the run-up to Economic and Monetary Union (EMU) in 1999 clearly contributed to France's high unemployment. The 1990s were also years of prodigious engineering achievements, witnessing the extension of the TGV (*train à grande vitesse*) network northwards to Lille, Brussels and London, and southwards to the Mediterranean. Opened in 2001, the TGV Méditerrané brings the south coast within three hours of Paris. Taking more than a decade to plan, and six years to build, it illustrates what the state is capable of achieving through its centralised structure, belief in progress and willingness to back it with taxpayers' money. But all this cost much more than initially forecast. In the event, France succeeded in reducing its budget deficit and national debt levels sufficiently to meet the strict 'convergence criteria' laid down in the Treaty on European Union (the 'Maastricht Treaty'), to qualify for EMU. According to these, the general government financial deficit, or GGFD (which comprises the sum of the central government and local government balances, added to the social security balance), should not exceed 3 per cent of annual GDP, forecast or actual, while the ratio of national debt to annual GDP should not exceed 60 per cent. The French budget deficits for the years 1999 and 2000 were well within the prescribed limit, at 1.6 per cent and 1.3 per cent respectively.

However, in the new millennium, in particular since the 11 September terrorist attacks, which cast a shadow over the world economy, French government finances have been less stringent. Since 2002 France has run a budget deficit in excess of the 3 per cent of annual GDP permitted by EU rules, standing at 4.2 per cent in 2003, when the stock of national debt attained a record high of €992.1 billion, equal to 63.0 per cent of national GDP.[38] Having failed to register one budget surplus since the first oil shock of 1973–74, France failed spectacularly to capitalise on the boom years of 1999–2001, when an undervalued euro fuelled French exports in cars, pharmaceuticals, transport equipment and civil and military aircraft. From 2010 unfunded pension liabilities will drain government finances further, despite modest reform in 2003 of France's generous, state-run, pay-as-you-go pension system (according to which those who are in work pay directly for those who are retired, creating a 'pension time bomb' as the national birth rate shrinks and baby boomers reach retirement). The penalties for exceeding the maximum budget deficit, as specified in the 'excessive deficits procedure' of the Maastricht Treaty, include inviting the European Investment Bank to reconsider its lending policy towards the member state concerned, obliging the member state to make a sizeable, non-interest-bearing deposit with the European Union until the deficit has been corrected, and imposing fines of an appropriate size.[39] The excessive deficit procedure was subsequently modified in December 1996 by the Stability and Growth Pact, which specified that member states would breach the rules only if they exceeded the 3 per cent deficit limit owing to an economic contraction of 0.75 per cent or less.

Jacques Chirac's re-election campaign of 2002, however, promised sweeping tax cuts, including a massive 30 per cent cut in income tax, to be reduced by 5 per cent a year over his five-year mandate.[40] Since his re-election France's EU obligations have been subordinated to domestic promises. With unemployment climbing, it is clear that such electoral promises are likely to conflict with EU financial rules. The arrival of Sarkozy at the Finance Ministry in April 2004, however, ended Chirac's manifesto commitment to reduce income tax, on the grounds that France simply could not afford it. But he also cocked a snook at the fiscal rules governing euro zone members. Although the Raffarin government successfully introduced important (though limited) pension reform in July 2003, incurring the wrath of unions and employees,[41] the poor showing of the ruling Union pour une majorité populaire (UMP) in the regional elections of March 2004 means that future economic reform is likely to be minimal.

In April 2003 the European Commission took steps against France by invoking the excessive deficits procedure for its failure to keep within the prescribed 3 per cent deficit limit in 2002. Two months later, EU Finance Ministers agreed with the Commission that France had breached the budgetary rules in 2002, and was likely to do so again in 2003, requiring the French government to remedy the situation by October. The then Finance Minister, Francis Mer, attempted to pre-empt matters, however, by presenting a draft budget proposal in September, one month before the deadline, which nevertheless did not satisfy EU Finance Ministers' demands. In mid-September, at a meeting of the Commission and Finance Ministers in Stresa, while M. Mer announced some minor budgetary concessions (amounting to just 0.07 per cent), it was agreed that France would in all likelihood fail to meet the 3 per cent budgetary limit in again 2004, and that this persistent flouting of EU law should incur the necessary penalties.

However, that is not in fact what happened. At a meeting of EU Finance Ministers convened on 25 November 2003, rather than enforce the excessive deficits procedure by fining one of the Union's founding and most influential member states, it was decided on the contrary to 'temporarily suspend' the rules themselves, denounced as 'stupid' by the Commission's president, Romano Prodi, and widely viewed as inflexible. Germany, which had come under pressure from the Commission to get its finances in order, had belatedly come to the aid of its partner. Although member states such as Spain, Austria, Finland and the Netherlands supported the Commission, when confronted with a common Franco-German position the political will to stick to the procedure evaporated. Dismayed, the Commission threatened to take the matter to the European Court of Justice (ECJ), while the European Central Bank spoke of the 'grave dangers' of the European Union dismissing its own financial rules. The upshot is that French finances are likely to remain weaker for longer. But the event leaves an indelible impression that, to quote George Orwell, 'some animals are more equal than others', that France and Germany are not in fact subject to the same EU rules as other member states.[42] While it would seem that France is happy to cede some sovereignty to Europe, in the hope that this may better serve French interests, France is less willing to subscribe to EU rules when they do not overtly serve the national interest. In other words, where European rules fail to satisfy French national interests they are apparently to be resisted or even ignored, seemingly without risk of incurring the normal reprisals which other member states might expect to incur for flagrant disobedience of EU legislation. When push comes to shove, it seems, the reflex of sovereignty still applies.[43]

French state aid to industry has been a further thorn in the Commission's side, responsible as it is for ensuring fair competition throughout the European Union. Three cases have vexed the Commission in particular, namely those of the ailing engineering giant Alstom, a specialist in energy and transport infrastructure, including trains and cruise liners; the French computer manufacturer Bull; and electricity supplier EdF.

In December 2000 a new EU regulation suppressed all government subsidies for shipbuilding. According to the new ruling, no further subsidies were to be permitted for any orders for vessels deliverable after 31 December 2003. This added to Alstom's existing woes, dominated by a tumbling share price due partly to Nine-eleven and partly to an extraordinary run of bad luck: the purchase of overpriced defective gas turbines; problems with the new, post-deregulation risk environment of the UK regional rail network, for which it was contracted to build 119 trains; and the bankruptcy of one of its main cruise ship customers in September 2001, to which Alstom had delivered eight cruise liners, and for which it had assumed the financial risk through a 'vendor financing' agreement.[44] Faced with this concatenation of circumstances, the Alstom share price collapsed, free falling from €36.00 in January 2001 to €12.85 in October 2001 to just €0.97 in March 2003.[45] By September 2003 the company was on the brink of bankruptcy, with estimated debts of €5 billion. The French government was only too keen to put together a rescue package which involved a capital injection of €3.4 billion, and which would have seen it emerge with 31 per cent of the company's shares. The European Commission, however, vetoed the restructuring package, on the grounds that it breached EU rules on state aid, and another rescue plan was produced in its stead. According to the new, renegotiated deal, Alstom's thirty creditor banks accepted a €3.2 billion rescue plan, while the French government ploughed €1.2 billion in short-term aid into the company, designed to cover short-term liquidity needs, exchanging a direct stake in the company for a twenty-year €300 million eurobond, subsequently convertible into Alstom shares.[46] Yet whether the rescue package involved an infusion of equity, a subsidy or a direct stake in the company is a matter of detail and ultimately, perhaps, immaterial. As Charkham points out, 'The point is the investment, not its classification.'[47] Alstom was safe for the time being, and its thousands of employees in France at least breathed a sigh of relief.[48]

The fact that Alstom had been bailed out by the French state without the prior approval of the European Commission prompted a year-long EU investigation into the terms of the Alstom rescue package. Nicolas Sarkozy, however, remained committed to saving the engineering giant, stating in May 2004 that he would do everything in his power to prevent its break-up.[49] In May 2004 he succeeded in negotiating a four-year deadline for Alstom to enter into a partnership with a firm from the private sector, proving that heroic capitalism is not dead after all. While the Commission favours the German Siemens, the French government has its sights on a partnership with the French nuclear group Areva, the company formed by the merger of Cogema, Framatome and CE Industrie in 2002.[50]

The case of Bull involves a €450 million loan to the computer manufacturer by the French government. The European Commission had originally approved the loan, and even its subsequent extension, on condition that it should be repaid by June 2003. In November 2003, however, the government took the decision to 'forgive' 90 per cent of the loan as part of a broader refinancing plan. The case has since been referred to the ECJ. Originally conceived as a would-be 'national champion', with the potential perhaps to become a European champion, Bull has received a total of €2.7 billion in state aid over the past decade. The company is currently seeking a capital injection of €44 million from the private sector, though this may now be in jeopardy should the ECJ refuse to give the plan its support.[51]

The final case of EdF is the most complex, but also, perhaps, the most interesting. EdF is currently the second largest electricity producer in the world, possessing the greatest export capacity of any EU electricity generator. Since the 1996 EU electricity directive on market liberalisation it has embarked on a strategy of international expansion, acquiring assets (power stations and physical interconnectors) in the European Union as well as customers (supply businesses). Its primary European export markets include Germany, Italy, Spain, Belgium, Switzerland, Andorra and Britain.[52] Farther afield it supplies a growing customer base in Asia, Africa and South America. Altogether, in 2003, it supplied 49.9 million customers at home and abroad, 18 million of them outside the Hexagon.[53]

Eight years after the 1996 electricity directive, however, the French market remains the least open in the European Union.[54] While other EU member states have broken up their electricity industries, EdF remains integrated and monolithic, handling almost all generation, transmission, distribution and supply.[55] For all its international expansion, it remains a public sector monopoly.[56] As such it continues to benefit from the tutelage of the state, including financial support and a state credit guarantee which provides the company with a triple A credit rating, allowing it to raise capital far more cost-effectively than its main rivals. The cost-of-capital advantage derived by EdF from state ownership should not be underestimated. EdF is able to raise money for acquisitions at a rate of interest lower than government bond rates (approximately 4 per cent), while its private-sector European competitors, such as struggling British Energy, can do no better than central bank base rates (about 8 per cent). In short, EdF is using government finance terms to acquire assets abroad, engaging in this way in a strategy of international expansion that is state-funded. EdF's assets include, in the United Kingdom, London Electricity, Sweb and Seeboard, as well as generation assets such as Sutton Bridge power station. It has purchased the right to control the flows of electricity throughout continental Europe, buying up the interconnectors that link France to the United Kingdom, France to Spain, and so on.[57] It has also acquired the interconnectors that join continental Europe to external electricity systems such as Eastern Europe and the Nordic countries.

In short, EdF is operating in the commercial spheres but not on commercial terms. It has no shareholders to satisfy, nor any stock price sensitivity. Its expansion abroad is supported by protection at home, coupled with unrivalled access to low-cost capital. It is a formidable combination and a unique source of competitive advantage. As the company becomes increasingly international, however, questions of its ownership are beginning to loom large. State subsidy is permissible under EU rules where it meets a social objective, or alternatively to enable a state-owned company to restructure or privatise in preparation for entering the market economy, neither of which applies in this case. Justification for non-competitive behaviour comes instead from a variety of sources and amounts to little more than a smokescreen. In this case, union entitlement to a percentage of EdF income (for pension funds) is the reason commonly cited for the alleged difficulties concerning privatisation, restructuring or market access in France.[58] EdF's fellow state monopoly, GdF, has followed a similar path, capturing international markets through export and acquisition while benefiting from state ownership coupled with closed, *de facto* monopolistic markets at home. This protected position has allowed both companies to take full advantage of market liberalisation elsewhere in the European Union with relative impunity, to the bitter resentment of energy producers in neighbouring EU member states, such as Germany, Spain and the United Kingdom.[59]

Successive French governments since 1996 have used the special meaning with which public service is endowed in France opportunistically as a convenient shield to market opening. In this they have been backed by powerful public sector unions, keen to avoid competition in energy and rail services. There is no doubt that the French have used their considerable influence in Brussels effectively to counter obvious complaints from fellow member states that have opened their markets already. Regular bilateral Franco-German summits and ministerial meetings, dubbed 'Sauerkraut diplomacy', enable France and Germany to reach prior agreement on contentious issues in advance of EU summits. Despite presenting itself as one of the more pro-European member states, France lags behind in terms of implementing EU single-market legislation.[60] Ignoring the obvious contradictions of the pan-European aspirations of its public utilities with a concomitant desire for market protection, the French government treads an increasingly lonely (but highly profitable) path in Europe. However, French attachment to protectionism within such sectors stands in flagrant contradiction to its professed aspirations for European construction. As Alain Vernholes observes, 'It is incoherent to rejoice that a firm such as EdF should control a large part of electricity distribution in London while refusing – or deferring – reciprocity on national territory on the pretext of protecting the general interest which depends on a public monopoly'.[61]

Though the French are seriously (and successfully) playing the long game with regard to the market opening, the French energy market nevertheless has gone some way along the path to greater openness. In December 1998 the Jospin government approved the draft Bill transposing the EU electricity directive into French law. In February 1999 it was passed to the National Assembly for consideration, and in February 2000 the directive finally appeared on the statute book, one year behind the European Union's official deadline.[62] In August 2002 the incoming right-of-centre government headed by Jean-Pierre Raffarin confirmed that the partial privatisation of EdF and GdF, presented as a 'non-negotiable political choice', would commence in 2004. In June 2004 Nicolas Sarkozy presented a legislative Bill to the National Assembly to change the status of EdF and GdF from that of *établissement public à caractère industriel et commercial* (EPIC) to *société anonyme* (SA) or limited company. The Bill includes a provision to tackle the two companies' pension liabilities. Their privatisation, however, is unlikely before late 2005 at the earliest.[63]

The European Commission concluded a fourteen-month investigation into EdF's affairs in December 2003, prompted by the anger of energy producers in neighbouring EU member states, who made allegations of illegal state aid. The Commission found that EdF should repay the French government a record sum of £1 billion, in return for tax breaks enjoyed during the period 1986–97 for the construction of high-voltage electricity networks. It demanded that the state's credit guarantee should be abolished, and further that it should terminate the arrangement according to which other energy companies contribute to the retirement provision of EdF's 144,000 pensioners.[64] EdF itself is now labouring under the debt accumulated since 1996.[65] Flush with cash from domestic customers, who, never having benefited from competition at home, continued to pay high tariffs for their electricity, EdF regularly paid over the odds for its acquisitions, systematically outbidding its rivals. As one commentator put it, 'EdF can go after targets rather like Real Madrid goes after footballers – value for money is not a concern.'[66] Denied a rise in domestic tariffs (of 2.35 per cent) by Prime Minister Raffarin in July 2003, in the wake of strong protest from unions and consumer groups, EdF is more in need of divesting unwanted purchases than it is of further investment. The privatisation of EdF and GdF is now actively desired by the companies themselves, as a means of raising further finance to pursue their expansionist strategies. But the French government's policy of a belated and minimal implementation of EU rules, where they do not suit French interests, is likely to continue to bear fruit. Many of EdF's competitors have already gone to the wall. (Of the fourteen electricity suppliers created in the United Kingdom after privatisation, for example, only two survive.) Notably, the privatisation of EdF and GdF, when it finally materialises, will be only partial: the state will retain a majority stake, and the companies will remain in the public sector.

The above example is not an isolated incidence of behaviour on the part of a French utility. The SNCF, for example, restructured in 1997, transferred the management of its track to Réseau ferré de France (RFF). Jean-Claude Gayssot, then Transport Minister, rejected EU attempts to dent the monopoly which SNCF enjoyed by refusing to consider EU proposals to open up the French railway network to foreign freight operators. He did so despite the fact that two French operators, SNCF and Vivendi-Connex, had already exploited the opening up of Deutsche Bahn's lines by launching ultra-modern trains in

Germany, while Vivendi-Connex operated a franchise in southern England. In a stark case of 'what's mine is mine, what's yours is negotiable', this exemplifies the furthering of French interests in Europe while deferring reciprocity.[67]

French economic interests in the enlarged European Union

In the European Union France has attempted to build an economically strong and politically coherent counterpoint to US hegemony. But the constellation of power and interests in the Union is currently changing. May 2004 saw the admission of ten new member states, mainly from Eastern Europe, generally pro-Atlanticist in orientation, with a further two countries preparing to join in 2007. As the European Union's centre of gravity shifts eastwards the Franco-German axis is becoming less pivotal. The danger for France is that the relation is seen increasingly by other member states for what it is: a mechanism for protecting Franco-German interests rather than an engine of EU integration. Chirac was noticeably lukewarm about enlargement, while his opposition to the US-led coalition's military action in Iraq in 2003 led to his making disparaging remarks about Central and Eastern European countries which few new member states are likely to forget quickly.[68]

It has not been easy for France to come to terms with a larger Germany, run by a younger generation of politicians, eager to engage in new relations with new partners. Enlargement provides Germany with a huge adjacent market but offers the French nothing. Chancellor Schröder is clearly no longer prepared, as his predecessors were, to subordinate German interests to French interests. The Franco-German relationship has been at low ebb since 1995, with Germany seeking to reduce its net contribution to the EU budget, much of which goes to benefit French farmers. Enlargement has almost doubled the European Union's agricultural labour force and increased its agricultural area by 50 per cent. Against the odds, France has managed, so far at least, to hold on to most of the benefits it enjoys from the Common Agricultural Policy (CAP), while the continued existence of the British rebate, by contrast, is far from guaranteed.

But this may now be set to change. On 31 July 2004 negotiators representing 147 countries at the World Trade Organisation (WTO) trade talks in Geneva, begun in Doha, Qatar, in 2001, reached a compromise that went some way towards meeting the demands of developing nations for a cut in agricultural subsidies. The agriculture proposals aim to improve competition by eliminating export subsidies and elements of other export support that distort trade while driving down tariffs to improve market access. The Geneva compromise was reached when France withdrew its opposition to a cut in farm subsidies. President Chirac had resisted the deal but, realising that France was isolated, lacking the support of any other EU member state, he instructed Agricultural Minister Hervé Gaymard to withdraw his objections – an indication, perhaps, that French influence in the European Union may not be all that it once was.[69]

That said, October 2004 saw the appointment of former Labour MP Peter Mandelson, a long-standing critic of the CAP, to the role of EU Trade Commissioner. The CAP costs £30 billion every year, pushing down world crop prices and undermining the income of poor farmers in developing countries. Having announced that his objective was to free up trade for the good of Europe and the wider world, Mr Mandelson then appeared to 'go native' in Brussels. Asked by a Belgian MEP whether he would be advocating further CAP reform (which would be to the detriment of French farmers), Mr Mandleson replied that he would not, a 'radical reform package' having already been agreed.[70]

Conclusion

It would be a mistake to toll the knell of the CAP too soon. France has a long track record of protecting its interests in Europe – French benefits from the CAP have been under attack before, and survived. The French government has displayed marked reluctance in recent years to be constrained by EU rules, subordinating EU obligations to the domestic electoral agenda. There is not doubt that the state is being pared back – the ambitious Nicolas Sarkozy has promised to replace only one in every two retiring *fonctionnaires*.[71] But at the same time, paradoxically, in asserting itself and challenging the supremacy of EU dictates the French state continues to play a pivotal role in Europe. In a triumph of the nation-state over supranational regulations, and irrespective of whether or not it is in the interests of Europe, France's repeated flouting of the excessive deficit procedure led, as we have seen, to the 'temporary suspension' of the rules themselves rather than to any punishment for the offending nation. The strength of France's manufacturing base testifies to continued political will to support manufacturing industry in the general interest, where necessary through state aid, even if it leads to controversy. While the British tend to follow the rules to the letter, the French behave in a much more flexible manner, demonstrating that old-style *dirigisme* is alive and kicking, down but clearly not out.[72] In agreeing a four-year deadline to find a private sector partner for Alstom, Sarkozy's hope is clearly that the lie of the land will have changed by 2008, and that a more flexible EU Competition Commissioner will be in post. French utilities have similarly furthered their own interests in Europe, exploiting EU market liberalisation to expand internationally while deferring reciprocity, on the assumption that when domestic markets are finally prised open their position will be unassailable. Though it cannot be denied that state interventionism in France has declined significantly since its heyday of the early 1980s, following successive privatisation programmes, *dirigisme* survives, albeit in attenuated form. Skilful economic management in the defence and promotion of French national economic and business interests, which rest on the continuing reflex of national sovereignty, has served France well in the past. It will doubtless continue to do so in the future.

Notes

1 Nicolas Sarkozy, cited in A. Sage, 'French Minister pledges state sell-offs', *The Times*, 5 May 2004.
2 J-J. Rousseau, *Du Contrat social* (Paris: Garnier Flammarion, 1966), p. 63.
3 This section draws on material contained in my recent book, M. Maclean, *Economic Management and French Business from de Gaulle to Chirac* (Basingstoke: Palgrave Macmillan, 2002).
4 E. Cohen, 'France: national champions in search of a mission', in J. Hayward (ed.), *Industrial Enterprise and European Integration: From National to International Champions in Western Europe* (Oxford: Oxford University Press, 1995), pp. 30–1.
5 R. F. Kuisel, *Capitalism and the State in Modern France: Renovation and Economic Management in the Twentieth Century* (Cambridge: Cambridge University Press, 1981), p. 202.
6 A. Malraux, *Les Chênes qu'on abat* (Paris: Gallimard, 1971), p. 29.
7 C. de Gaulle, *Salvation 1944–1946*, trans. R. Howard (London: Weidenfeld & Nicolson, 1960), p. 100.
8 See J. Monnet, *Mémoires* (Paris: Fayard, 1976); Commissariat Général du Plan, *Cinquante ans de planification à la française* (Paris: Commissariat Général du Plan, 1998).
9 P. A. Hall, *Governing the Economy: The Politics of State Intervention in Britain and France* (Cambridge: Polity Press, 1986), p. 204.
10 J. Hayward, '*Moins d'état* or *mieux d'état:* the French response to the neo-liberal challenge', in M. Maclean (ed.), *The Mitterrand Years: Legacy and Evaluation* (Basingstoke: Macmillan, 1998), pp. 23–35.
11 See, for example, M. Maclean, 'Privatisation, *dirigisme* and the global economy: an end to French exceptionalism?' *Modern and Contemporary France*, 5:2 (1997), 215–18.
12 Economist Intelligence Unit (EIU), *Country Report: France* (London: EIU, 2004), p. 38.
13 Sage, 'French Minister pledges state sell-offs'.
14 EIU, *Country Report: France* (London: EIU, 2004), p. 18.
15 See M. Loriaux, 'France: a new capitalism of voice?' in L. Weiss (ed.), *States in the Global Economy* (Cambridge: Cambridge University Press, 2003), pp. 101–20 (p. 113); B. Clift, 'The French model of capitalism: exceptionalism under threat?', paper presented at Political Studies Association, University of Lincoln, April 2004.
16 M. Bauer, 'The politics of state-directed privatisation: the case of France', *West European Politics*, 11:4 (1988), 57. Edouard Balladur, former Minister of the Economy (1986–88) and Prime Minister (1993–95), explained the *dirigiste* nature of privatisation in France as follows: this concentration of power in the hands of one individual (Balladur himself) saved much unnecessary discussion and time! E. Balladur, *Je crois en l'homme plus qu'en l'État* (Paris: Flammarion, 1987), p. 96.
17 Prior to the demise of Communism in Eastern Europe it was a standing joke that *l'éducation nationale* employed more people than the Red Army! There are currently 800,000 schoolteachers in France.
18 France, which has 1.7 million health employees, of whom 180,000 are doctors, spends as much as £111 billion annually on health care, equal to a *per capita* spend

of £1,815. This dwarfs the amount spent in England (excluding Scotland, Wales and Northern Ireland), £69 billion. Figures cited in *The Daily Telegraph*, 31 July 2004.

19 See A. Minc, *www.capitalisme.fr* (Paris: Grasset, 2000).

20 'L'Etat doit être impartial. C'est une des conclusions auxquelles je suis arrivé'. Televised debate with Lionel Jospin, 2 May 1995.

21 Personal interview with Mr Pierre Bilger, former PDG of Alstom, Paris, 3 January 2003.

22 H. Gattegno and P. Le Cœur, 'L'État-Chirac' : impose les siens au sommet du pouvoir', *Le Monde*, 13 July 2004; F. Lemaître, 'Les proches du chef de l'État trustent les postes-clés dans le secteur public et les medias', *Le Monde*, 13 July 2004.

23 EIU, *Country Profile 2004: France* (London: EIU, 2004), p. 32.

24 Centre européen des entreprises à participation publique (CEEP), *L'Importance et l'évolution des entreprises à participation publique et des entreprises d'intérêt économique général dans l'économie française depuis 1996* (Paris: CEEP, 2000).

25 S. Hoffmann, 'France and Europe: the dichotomy of autonomy and co-operation', in J. Howorth and G. Ross (eds), *Contemporary France* I (London: Frances Pinter, 1987), p. 49.

26 D. R. Cameron, 'From Barre to Balladur: economic policy in the eras of the EMS', in G. Flynn (ed.), *Remaking the Hexagon: The New France in the New Europe* (Oxford: Westview Press, 1996), pp. 117–57.

27 This section draws on material from my study funded by the Leverhulme Trust into business elites and corporate governance in France and the United Kingdom.

28 Such that the most profitable European company in 2004 is the British-based bank HSBC, or such that £750 million annual profit achieved by Marks & Spencer in 2003 was seen as 'poor'. J. Waples and L. Armistead, 'HSCB crowned Europe's most profitable company', *The Sunday Times*, 1 August 2004.

29 H. Weber, *Le Parti des patrons : le CNPF 1946–1986* (Paris: Seuil, 1986), pp. 113–15.

30 J. Chirac, *Une Nouvelle France : réflexions* I (Paris: Nil Editions, 1994), p. 24; J. Chirac, *La France pour tous* (Paris: Nil Editions, 1994), p. 92.

31 EIU, *Country Report: France* (London: EIU, 2004), April, p. 37.

32 Personal interview, Airbus UK, Filton, Bristol, 10 July 2004.

33 See D. Gallois and F. Lemaître, 'Le patron d'EADS veut « doubler Boeing » d'ici dix ans', *Le Monde*, 13 July 2004.

34 Personal interview with Iain Gray, Managing Director and General Manager, Airbus UK, Filton, Bristol, 4 February 2003.

35 Airbus, *The Airbus Way* (Blagnac: Airbus, 2002); Datamonitor Report, EADS, March 2003; EIU, *Country Report: France* (London: EIU, 2004), April, p. 37.

36 In 2003 GDP amounted to US$1,795 billion in the United Kingdom and US$1,764 billion in France, while *per capita* income was US$29,759 in the United Kingdom and US$29,294 in France. EIU, *Country Profile 2004: United Kingdom* (London: EIU, 2004), p. 32.

37 EIU, *Country Report: France* (London: EIU, 2004), July, p. 5.

38 *Ibid.*, p. 16.

39 See 'Protocol on the excessive deficit procedure' annexed to the Maastricht Treaty, Articles 1–3. See also Article 104c of the Maastricht Treaty.

40 In June 2002 income tax was cut by 5 per cent as part of a three-year programme

of income tax cuts announced in August 2000. This followed a reduction in value added tax (VAT) from 20.6 per cent to 19.6 per cent in April 2000.

41 'Retraites : la grande manifestation', *Le Monde*, 25–26 May 2003. Guéland, 'Controverses sur les effets possibles du plan Fillon', *Le Monde*, 25–26 May 2003. French *salariés* will now have to work longer than before to achieve a full pension.

42 See EIU, *Country Report: France* (London: EIU, 2004), January, pp. 16–18.

43 G. Raymond, 'The End of Sovereignty?', paper presented to the conference of the South Wales and West of England Regional Centre for Contemporary French Studies, University of Bristol, May 2001.

44 Alstom Annual Report, 2003; Alstom Annual Report, 2001–02.

45 See Datamonitor Report, Alstom, 2003, p. 199; Alstom, Annual Report, 2001–02.

46 See A. Sage, 'Europe set to approve €3 bn rescue for Alstom', *The Times*, 22 September 2003; 'Alstom rescue approval', *The Times*, 23 September 2003.

47 J. Charkham, *Keeping Good Company: A Study of Corporate Governance in Five Countries* (Oxford: Clarendon Press, 1994), p. 120.

48 Alstom's work force numbered almost 110,000 in seventy countries in 2003, down from 118,000 in 2002.

49 A. Sage, 'French Minister pledges state sell-offs'.

50 EIU, *Country Report: France* (London: EIU, 2004), July, p. 19.

51 *Ibid.*, January, p. 18.

52 EdF has been so competitive that French imports have come to be seen as a permanent feature of Britain's baseload supply. S. Cooke, 'Iniquities of the French connection', *Management Today*, March 1993, p. 38.

53 Datamonitor Report, EdF, March 2003, pp. 5, 11.

54 See Maclean, *Economic Management and French Business from de Gaulle to Chirac*, pp. 195–8.

55 L. Nardoni, *The European Electricity Markets*, Reuters Business Insight Report, June 2000.

56 P-E. Tizier and N. Mauchamp, *EdF–GdF : une entreprise publique en mutation* (Paris, La Découverte, 2000).

57 Access to the British market is provided through the interconnector that lies on the sea bed, equivalent to having a large power station in Sussex.

58 I owe this information to David Love, Head of Regulation, British Energy.

59 David Love, British Energy, personal interview with the author, 11 May 2001.

60 D. Lister, 'EU attacks Britain on directives backlog', *The Times*, 29 May 2001.

61 A. Vernholes, 'La France n'accepte pas de payer le prix de ses ambitions', *Modern and Contemporary France*, 9:3 (August 2001), 291.

62 A. Evans, *Energy: customer retention and acquisition*, Reuters Business Insight Report, 2000, p. 13.

63 Datamonitor Report, EdF, March 2003, pp. 21–2; EIU, *Country Report: France*, July, p. 20.

64 EIU, *Country Report: France*, January, p. 19.

65 Mr Sarkozy's legislative Bill proposes to transfer some of existing EdF pension liabilities to the social security *régime général* in return for a one-off payment to the company pension scheme.

66 Cited in Datamonitor Report, EdF, March 2003, p. 31.

67 Vernholes, 'La France n'accepte pas de payer le prix de ses ambitions'; EIU, *Country Profile: France* (London: EIU, 2000), pp. 19–20.

68 See EIU, *Country Report: France*, April, p. 7.
69 A. Sage, 'Rich and poor unite to rescue trade talks', *The Times*, 2 August 2004.
70 BBC News, 4 October 2004.
71 A. Sage, 'French Minister pledges state sell-offs'.
72 Interview with Mr Per Staehr, Chairman and Chief Country Representative of Bombardier Transportation rail companies in the United Kingdom, Milton Keynes, 28 April 2003.

Select bibliography

Airbus, *The Airbus Way* (Blagnac: Airbus, 2002).

Alstom Annual Reports 2001–02, 2003.

M. Bauer, 'The politics of state-directed privatisation: the case of France', *West European Politics*, 11:4 (1988).

D. R. Cameron, 'From Barre to Balladur: economic policy in the eras of the EMS', in G. Flynn (ed.), *Remaking the Hexagon: The New France in the New Europe* (Oxford: Westview Press, 1996).

Centre européen des entreprises à participation publique (CEEP), *L'Importance et l'évolution des entreprises à participation publique et des entreprises d'intérêt économique général dans l'économie française depuis 1996* (Paris: CEEP, 2000).

J. Charkham, *Keeping Good Company: A Study of Corporate Governance in Five Countries* (Oxford: Clarendon Press, 1994).

J. Chirac, *Une Nouvelle France : réflexions* I (Paris: Nil Editions, 1994).

J. Chirac, *La France pour tous* (Paris: Nil Editions, 1994).

A. Cole, *Franco-German Relations* (Harlow: Pearson, 2001).

Commissariat général du plan, *Cinquante ans de planification à la française* (Paris: Commissariat général du plan, 1998).

C. De Gaulle, *Salvation, 1944–1946*, trans. R. Howard (London: Weidenfeld & Nicolson, 1960).

Economist Intelligence Unit (EIU), *Country Profile 2004: France* (London: EIU, 2004).

EIU, *Country Profile 2004: United Kingdom* (London: EIU, 2004).

EIU, *Country Report: France* (London: EIU, 2004), January.

EIU, *Country Report: France* (London: EIU, 2004), April.

EIU, *Country Report: France* (London: EIU, 2004), July.

A. Evans, *Energy: Customer retention and acquisition*, Reuters Business Insight Report, 2000.

A. Guyomarch, H. Machin and E. Ritchie, *France in the European Union* (Basingstoke: Macmillan, 1998).

P. A. Hall, *Governing the Economy: The Politics of State Intervention in Britain and France* (Cambridge: Polity Press, 1986).

R. F. Kuisel, *Capitalism and the State in Modern France: Renovation and Economic Management in the Twentieth Century* (Cambridge: Cambridge University Press, 1981).

M. Maclean, *Economic Management and French Business from de Gaulle to Chirac* (Basingstoke: Palgrave Macmillan, 2002).

M. Maclean and J-M. Trouille (eds), *France, Germany and Britain: Partners in a Changing World* (Basingstoke: Palgrave Macmillan, 2001).

A. Malraux, *Les Chênes qu'on abat* (Paris: Gallimard, 1971).

A. Minc, *www.capitalisme.fr* (Paris: Grasset, 2000).

J. Monnet, *Mémoires* (Paris: Fayard, 1976).

J-J. Rousseau, *Du Contrat social* (Paris: Garnier Flammarion, 1966).

A. Stevens with H. Stevens, *Brussels Bureaucrats? The Administration of the European Union* (Basingstoke: Palgrave, 2001).

P-E. Tizier and N. Mauchamp, *EdF–GdF : une entreprise publique en mutation* (Paris: La Découverte, 2000).

H. Weber, *Le Parti des patrons : le CNPF 1946–1986* (Paris: Seuil, 1986).

Acknowledgements

I wish to thank the Leverhulme Trust for funding a Leverhulme Research Fellowship ('Corporate Governance and Business Elites' in France and the United Kingdom), which has informed the present chapter. I would like to thank the following business leaders for kindly agreeing to be interviewed, in particular Mr Xavier Barrière, Director, L'Air liquide; Mr Pierre Bilger, former PDG of Alstom; Mr Jean-Claude Le Grand, Director, L'Oréal; Mr Iain Gray, Managing Director, Airbus UK; Mr Rémi Lallement, *Commissariat Général du Plan*; Mrs Agnès Lépigny, Director, *Mouvement des entreprises de France* (MEDEF); Mr David Love, British Energy; Senator Philippe Marini; Mr Per Staehr, Director, Bombardier; and Mr Jean-François Théodore, CEO of Euronext. I am grateful to Charles Harvey and Jon Press for their invaluable assistance. I also wish to thank Holly Combe for her research assistance.

9

Exporting the republican model? A critique of France's historic mission in Africa

Gordon Cumming

Between the sixteenth century and the twentieth, France established colonial rule over a vast empire which included territories in North America, South East Asia, the Caribbean and Africa. The realities of empire were, of course, hard to reconcile with French republican ideals such as freedom, equality and fraternity. Yet Paris was largely successful in 'justifying' the colonial enterprise by portraying it as part of a *mission civilisatrice*, that is, a civilising project to assimilate (mainly African) colonial subjects and 'elevate' them to the rank of French citizenship.

This chapter will begin by examining how this civilising mission in Africa served to bolster the French republican paradigm during the colonial and early post-colonial eras. It will then focus on the domestic, European and global pressures which France is facing in her quest to maintain her unique African vocation. It will argue that, while French governments have had to make changes, they have nonetheless managed to preserve the basic thrust of their 'universal' republican message. Finally, it will assess the future threats and opportunities facing Paris's African mission.

France's historic mission

Paris had, from the time of the Revolution, proclaimed the unique and moral nature of her civilising mission. France was, of course, not the only colonial power to claim to be motivated by ethical values. Britain, for its part, spoke of the 'white man's burden', while all European colonisers shared the belief that Africa was 'irreducibly "other"' and in need of exposure to their superior cultures and languages.[1]

Paris's claims to uniqueness were not, however, entirely without substance. For a start, France was a republic with radically different political ideals from those of the other European colonising powers, which were, for the most part, conservative monarchies. While there was never any real attempt to replicate French republican traditions systematically in Africa, colonial governors (the equivalent of French *préfets*) did adopt a system of 'direct rule', designed to rid the colonies of the last vestiges of feudal 'aristocracy' by undermining the authority of hereditary chiefs and promoting francophile elites, the so-called *évolués*, to positions of some (limited) power.[2] They did, moreover, act decisively to put an end to 'uncivilised' practices, which were deemed abhorrent to the French Republic, not least cannibalism, slave trading, witchcraft and human sacrifice.

Second, France distinguished itself from other colonisers by claiming that it was affording access to a culture and language which were uniquely suited to conveying the 'universal' values associated with the Revolution. This claim was based on the supposed clarity and linearity of French syntax and on the belief that French, as the language of the Enlightenment, was also the successor to the ancient universal language, Latin.

Finally, Paris argued that, unlike other imperial powers, who saw themselves as trustees of territories which would one day become independent, it was working to integrate its colonies into a Greater French Republic. This *République de cent millions de Français* was to be achieved through a process known as assimilation, whereby colonial subjects would gradually be integrated culturally and politically into the French way of life. Assimilation was usually understood in abstract terms but it was not an empty concept. In fact Paris took its first step towards assimilating colonial peoples in 1794, when the leaders of the Revolution abolished slavery and declared that 'all men, without distinction as to colour, who are residents of the colonies, are French citizens'.[3] The year after, the French constitution affirmed that the colonies were 'integral parts of the Republic . . . subject to the same constitutional laws'.[4] While these provisions were subsequently annulled by Napoléon Bonaparte in 1802, they were not the last gesture in the direction of republicanism. Thus, after the 1848 revolution, the French Second Republic turned Algeria into an outlying 'district' of France and conferred French citizenship on the inhabitants of the 'old colonies' (Martinique, Guadeloupe, Guyane, Réunion and the four communes of Senegal). Although these rights were subsequently eroded under France's authoritarian Second Empire, further decrees were passed such as the Crémieux declaration of 1870, which allowed the naturalisation of the Jewish population in Algeria; the *loi* Diagne of 1916, which enabled inhabitants of the Four Communes to remain French citizens without giving up their religious customs; and the Jonnart reforms of 1919, which granted French citizenship to Algerians who agreed to 'live like Frenchmen'.

The rhetoric and the reality

It would, however, be naive to take France's claims to be on a unique, moral mission at face value. Thus, while republican state structures were mirrored, to some extent, in the colonies, the fact remains that French law applied only to 'white', European settlers. As for indigenous populations, they were forced to accept a form of colonial rule that had nothing to do with the Declaration of the Rights of Man. They did not enjoy democratic freedoms but were ruled by decree and given virtually no say in colonial affairs. They did not benefit from equality before the law but were subject to forced labour, taxation, compulsory military service and the *indigénat* (a legal code which allowed French administrators to impose summary penalties on 'troublesome natives').

Furthermore, despite France's promises to 'raise up the native, educate him and guarantee his existence',[5] there was never any serious attempt to educate the wider African population in the French language and culture. The likely cost of a mass education programme, coupled with the fact that colonial administration was paid for out of African head taxes, ensured that only a small percentage of Africans gained access to any form of education and fewer still went on to study at prestigious African *grandes écoles*. In fact, as late as 1950, French colonial areas had illiteracy rates ranging from 95 per cent to 99 per cent.[6]

Finally, it would be wrong to overstate Paris's willingness to grant citizenship to African subjects. As mainstream republicanism in France moved away from its revolutionary idealism from the 1880s onwards it moved away too from the idea that French citizenship could be obtained simply through an act of will and began introducing more stringent conditions by which access to citizenship was restricted.[7] In the end, citizens' rights were only ever accorded to a small number of subjects, mainly concentrated in the 'old colonies'. And, even here, they were under constant threat from white settlers like the *pieds noirs* (who blocked legislation in the late 1930s to extend the vote to more Algerian Muslims) and from authoritarian figures like Marshal Pétain (who quashed freedoms and introduced racial discrimination in France's Vichy-occupied colonies in the early 1940s).

Despite the obvious discrepancy between republican ideals and colonial practice, Paris's civilising mission did not come in for any sustained criticism until the end of the Second World War. Protest within France came primarily from left-leaning intellectuals like Jean-Paul Sartre, from African socialist politicians living in Paris in the post-war period (e.g. Léopold Sédar Senghor) and from the French Communist and Socialist Parties.[8] As a whole, the French left had lost faith in the concept of assimilation and had come to recognise that the extension of liberty and equality to non-European people could not be accomplished by simply treating them as notional French citizens. They should be equal in all rights, but they might also be different. They should be able to choose to adopt a French identity, but free to accept or reject French civilisation, or to accept parts of it and reject others.[9]

On the international scene, France's continuing colonial mission was criticised by the Soviet Union (the arch-opponent of capitalist imperialism), the United Nations (the mouthpiece of newly independent states like India) and above all the United States. Conscious of its own colonial past and of the minority coloured population in its midst, the United States drew up the Atlantic

Charter of 1941, insisting on the right of all people to self-determination, and subsequently pressed France into holding, in Brazzaville in 1944, a major colonial conference at which steps were taken towards granting African colonies some limited autonomy.

The greatest threats to the *mission civilisatrice* came, however, from within the French empire. As France's richest and most populous colonial possessions, with their own languages, cultures and religious identities, Indo-China and Algeria were prepared to fight to ensure that their people were not submerged in a uniform, secular French Republic. More than any other overseas events, France's wars with Indo-China and Algeria (1946–54 and 1954–62) brought about the moral and political collapse of the Fourth Republic. They exposed a whole generation of Frenchmen to the brutality of war and to the sight of torture and summary executions. They also dealt a near fatal blow to France's image of itself as a republican country and resulted in the founding of a new (Fifth) Republic under Charles de Gaulle.

While relations with these former colonies were strained for the next three decades, France did have greater success in carrying through its assimilationist project in other parts of the empire. Thus in 1946 Paris was able to integrate its 'old colonies' (the so-called Départements et Territoires d'Outre-Mer or DOM TOM) into the French Republic. Perhaps even more surprisingly, France was also able to carry on its historic mission in the newly independent states of francophone Africa. There were a number of reasons why this was possible. For a start, these nascent states were led by Africans who were already well versed in French republican virtues and some of whom (e.g. Félix Houphouët-Boigny) had even served as French government Ministers during the Fourth Republic. Other factors included France's political will to 'stay on' after decolonisation and, as the analysis below will demontrate, its readiness to adapt the *mission civilisatrice.*

New Republic, same old mission?

With the advent of the Fifth Republic in 1958 and the decolonisation of most of francophone Africa two years later, France quickly recognised the need to take account of the sensibilities of newly independent states and to make changes in its original mission. For a start, Paris moved swiftly away from the idea that Africans would one day become French citizens. France also stopped referring to its *mission civilisatrice* or its desire to create *la plus grande France* and talked instead of her *besoin de rayonnement* (that is, her need to excel culturally and intellectually) and her wish to be at the heart of a Franco-African 'family'. In so doing, the French political classes were able to retain key features of France's republican mission, not least a long-standing emphasis on centralised states as the key to societal progress and an emphasis on the French language as the ideal vehicle for conveying Paris's universal values.

159

To begin with the emphasis on Jacobin states, this became a marked feature of French African policy from the time of decolonisation, when the French bequeathed to their former colonies a hastily prepared form of republican government which mirrored, albeit imperfectly, France's highly centralised political system. Over the next three decades, Paris proceeded to channel most of its development, budgetary and military assistance to African central governments. By contrast, France provided only scant support to sub-state and non-state actors, which were deemed to be representative of sectional interests rather than the general will. To illustrate, France provided one of the lowest percentages of official development assistance in the Western world to French non-governmental organisations (NGOs) and did nothing to encourage the transfers of technical and financial support which French local authorities (*régions*, *départements* and *communes*) had been making to African local governments since the end of the Second World War.

France's state-centric focus was also apparent from its encouragement of *dirigiste* developmental planning by African governments and from its reluctance to promote free market policies south of the Sahara. In this latter context, France encouraged over a dozen francophone and other African states to join, or remain, within the franc zone, a protectionist monetary bloc, whose currency, the Communauté Financière Africaine (CFA) franc, was pegged to the French franc at a fixed rate and shielded from currency fluctuations. Paris was, at the same time, instrumental in ensuring that the European Community's aid and trade programme, known as the Yaoundé and later the Lomé Convention, included preferential tariffs and mechanisms such as Stabex and Sysmin, which protected the value of African exports and minerals against sharp falls in market prices.

As to France's emphasis on its language and culture, this was clearly reflected in the thousands of scholarships given to African students to attend French universities and in the phenomenal number of French teachers being sent to Africa: some 11,000 in 1985, with around 3,000 in Côte d'Ivoire alone.[10] This focus on the French language was expected to serve many purposes: it was to be a means of reducing African ethnic and linguistic divisions; a mechanism of creating unitary states, whose official languages included French; and a vehicle for the dissemination of French revolutionary values.

French governments did not, of course, confine themselves to promoting African *liberté*, *égalité* and *fraternité* by linguistic means alone. While France did little to promote 'liberty' or political freedom during the Cold War, it did provide sufficient aid and trade incentives to keep African countries out of the arms of the more repressive Soviet bloc. Paris, did, moreover, affirm its attachment to 'equality' by loudly backing African demands for a New International Economic Order, that is, a more equitable and redistributive international economic system. Finally, France gave substance to the revolutionary ideal of 'fraternity' or 'solidarity' by establishing itself as the largest single bilateral donor to Africa; by creating, in 1960, a Development or 'Co-operation' Ministry, which was almost exclusively reserved for Africa; and by intervening militarily to protect African states from external aggression and other threats.

Needless to say, Paris's claims to have a universal republican message which could 'illuminate the progress of humanity'[11] did not go unchallenged over the first three decades of the Fifth Republic. The authors of numerous parliamentary reports, disaffected Socialist politicians like the former Development Minister, Jean-Pierre Cot, and a handful of actors from French civil society, all accused France of focusing excessively on its former African colonies and of using the veil of republicanism to conceal concerns over *Realpolitik* and the pursuit of private gain.[12] They cited in support of these allegations occasional scandals involving former French Ministers like Christian Nucci (embroiled in the 1984 Carrefour au Développement affair) and the former President Giscard d'Estaing (accused of accepting a gift of diamonds from the Central African Republic's despotic leader Jean-Bedel Bokassa).[13]

Other criticisms came from the European Community, whose new members, notably Great Britain (1973), Spain and Portugal (1986), called for European aid and trade preferences to be extended beyond Africa to the poorest countries of Asia as well as the commercially more attractive states of North Africa and Latin America. American-led international organisations like the World Bank and the IMF were also critical of France's advocacy of state-centred, *dirigiste* economic planning and pressed Paris to endorse their neo-liberal development programmes. Finally, occasional voices of dissent were even heard in Africa, where leftist leaders like Guinea's Sékou Touré condemned France's African mission as an exercise in neo-imperialism.

As a rule, however, domestic criticism was too sporadic and low-key to impact seriously on public opinion or force French Presidents to make radical changes in French African policy. As for European pressures, these were easily deflected, thanks to France's preponderant influence within European institutions like the Directorate General of development (DG VIII). Protests from US-led international organisations were equally muted at the time, given America's perception that Paris was playing a vital role in the Cold War by keeping large swathes of Africa in the Western orbit. Finally, pressures from Africa were limited, given the continent's economic and military dependence on France and given the readiness of most disgruntled African regimes to re-enter the francophone fold once enough had been offered in the way of financial incentives.[14]

It follows that the above criticisms did not undermine French claims to have a special vocation in Africa. Nor did they undercut France's republican paradigm at home, which was, if anything bolstered by the readiness of African countries to buy into France's 'universal' message, by the apparent success of initial French efforts at integrating African immigrants in the 1960s,[15] and by the strong performance of France's *dirigiste* economic policies in the first three decades after the Second World War (the so-called *trente glorieuses*).

Yet, in the post-Cold War context, France has come under much more intense pressure to revise, or even abandon, its unique mission in Africa. These pressures have come both from domestic and international sources.

Domestic pressures

Galvanised above all by France's shameful activities in Rwanda in the early 1990s,[16] domestic critics have become more vociferous in their demands for reform of French African policy. Pressure groups like Agir ici and Survie have published damning reports while leading NGOs such as Médecins du Monde and the Comité Catholique Contre la Faim et pour le Développement (CCFD) have developed policy advocacy departments to help them lobby more effectively.[17] At the same time, France's normally cautious quality press and even some reformist government Ministers have joined in these calls for reforms of African policy.[18]

While domestic critics have, as a rule, continued to accept the legitimacy of French claims to have a 'universal' mission, they have been much more rigorous than in the past in exposing the rift between France's rhetorical attachment to republican ideals and its actual practice south of the Sahara. They have shown how, rather than promoting liberty, Paris has colluded with francophile African dictators like Zaire's Mobutu Sese Seko, Gabon's Omar Bongo, and even Rwanda's Juvénal Habyarimana, whose Hutu regime carried out one of the worst genocides of the twentieth century. They have also questioned France's commitment to the ideal of 'equality', given how little of the French aid programme is geared to promoting basic health care, primary education or poverty eradication.[19] They have even challenged Paris's claims to 'solidarity', pointing out that a great deal of its aid is either squandered on showcase projects or used to subsidise the products of uncompetitive French exporters.[20]

At the same time, these critics have gone further than in the past by pointing out that such abuses are not merely isolated incidents by rogue actors. They are, in fact, symptomatic of a wider problem which is inherent in the nature of the Fifth Republic, with its emphasis on strong executive authority and limited parliamentary scrutiny. They have protested that African policy, since the time of Charles de Gaulle, has become the sole preserve (*domaine réservé*) of the President, his unelected unit of advisers in the Africa cell and a number of networks, or *réseaux*, of semi-official actors operating in Africa. They have also complained that these *réseaux* (with the connivence of the Elysée, senior civil servants and French secret service agencies) have exploited or corrupted other key republican institutions. These networks are said to have tapped into the aid budgets of the French Co-operation and Finance Ministries and then used the monies as bribes to secure lucrative arms and oil contracts.[21] They have also been linked with scandals involving formerly state-owned oil companies like Elf and closely associated with the efforts of French political parties to secure 'donations' from African leaders for their election campaigns.[22]

International pressures

International pressures have arguably been more serious insofar as they have challenged the appropriateness and validity of the French republican project, not only as it is exported overseas but also as it is applied at home. These pressures have come, as the analysis below will suggest, from the European Union, international organisations and African leaders.

Pressures from the European Union

It is, of course, beyond the scope of this chapter to explore the many ways in which European pressures have challenged the French republican paradigm at home.[23] Suffice it to say that European integration, particularly since the 1992 Maastricht Treaty, has led to a hollowing out of the French state as sovereignty has gradually been transferred to Brussels in areas such as monetary policy, home affairs and justice. It has, in the process, made it problematic for France to continue promoting Jacobin, unitary republics south of the Sahara while itself moving closer towards the European federal model.

The 'Europeanisation' process has, at the same time, had a more direct impact on France's African mission. For a start, the budgetary constraints imposed by European Monetary Union have forced French governments to cut back on aid to Africa and to be more receptive to the views of other European member states, many of whom have called for reductions in the cost of the Cotonou Accord (the successor to Lomé); expressed concern at the pegging of the CFA franc to the euro; and refused to back French calls for European military intervention in troublespots like Zaire–Congo (1996).

European integration has, moreover, accelerated moves towards a Common Foreign and Security Policy (CFSP).[24] This has, in turn, reduced France's scope for independent action in Africa and induced it to sign up to 'joint action' such as European supervision of the 1994 South African elections and 'common decisions' such as the EU-wide suspension of aid to Togo's authoritarian regime in 2002. It has also encouraged Paris to subscribe to the idea of an EU emergency aid policy, co-ordinated by the European Commission's Humanitarian Office (created in 1992), and a common security policy, supported by a 60,000-strong European Rapid Reaction Force (established in May 2003).

Forces for globalisation

A related set of pressures have been exerted by international organisations such as the World Bank, the IMF and the World Trade Organisation (WTO). These US-led pressures, together with the strengthening of EU competition laws and the liberalisation of international capital markets, have encouraged successive French governments to move away from *dirigiste* economic planning and to undertake the privatisation of key sectors of the economy. They have, at the same time, encouraged France to tone down both its support for state-led *dirigiste* policies south of the Sahara and its objections to World Bank-led neo-liberal strategies such as structural adjustment, public–private partnerships and regional free-trade zones.

African concerns

Turning finally to African pressures, these have also called into question the French republican paradigm. In the French domestic context, protests have been voiced primarily by North African and, to a lesser extent, black African immigrants,[25] who have refused to allow their 'otherness' to be dissolved into France's indivisible, 'egalitarian' and secular state system. These concerns over Paris's integrationist model have, moreover, been echoed in African states, particularly those led by the so-called 'new generation' of African Presidents. These (mainly anglophone) leaders have deemed France's assimilationist practices to be unworkable in a region where widespread conflict and porous state borders lead to frequent and massive movements of refugee populations. They have instead embraced the idea of separate communities within a single state, and have, more generally, emphasised the need for 'African solutions to African problems'. Their views have been shared by francophone opposition parties and counter-elites, which have challenged France's constitutional claims to be a *terre d'asile*, or refuge, and protested at its increasingly restrictive visa policies. These disaffected elements within African society have engaged in anti-French demonstrations and, in many cases, departed for scholarships in the United States, whose republican model of individual freedom and communautarianism (the so-called 'melting pot') is more appealing.[26]

Time to abort the mission?

Faced with the above pressures, France has been forced to water down some elements of its 'republican' mission, not least its advocacy of strong central government and its emphasis on the unique nature of its African vocation. French ruling elites have come to recognise that Jacobin states may not be the solution, and may in fact be part of the problem, in an African context where public resources are regularly hi-jacked by small factions and single ethnic groups. They have, as such, begun to support international efforts to make African nation-states more accountable to supranational institutions like the World Bank in the governance of their economies and the United Nations in the treatment of their civilian populations. They have, at the same time, started to encourage African central governments to be more responsive to sub-state and non-state actors. In this context, French policy makers have begun to co-finance the international development efforts of French local authorities engaged in projects to bolster the institutional capacity of African local government. They have also, under a system of *contrats de désendettement* (C2D) or debt-reducing contracts, started to link substantial flows of debt relief with a commitment on the part of African governments to consult indigenous NGOs and pressure groups on public spending priorities.

Following a similar logic, France has also begun to move away from promoting *dirigiste*, state-led development strategies and towards accepting the need for more market-based solutions to Africa's chronic problems. This is clearly illustrated by France's adoption, in September 1993, of the Balladur Doctrine, by which French bilateral aid has been made conditional upon the signature by African states of World Bank and IMF neo-liberal recovery programmes. It is equally apparent from France's decision, in 1994, to allow the CFA franc to be devalued and brought closer into line with its market value.

Turning to France's claims regarding the uniqueness of its African vocation, these, too, have had to be watered down, as French African policy has undergone a process of 'multilateralisation' and 'normalisation'. The multilateralisation process is clearly reflected in Paris's growing propensity to intervene militarily in Africa under the auspices of the United Nations (e.g., Somalia, 1992; Rwanda, 1994) and the European Union (e.g. Operation Artémis in the Democratic Republic of Congo, 2003). It is also apparent from France's collaboration with Britain and the United States on inter-African peacekeeping initiatives[27] and from its increasing tendency to use the G-7 as a forum to lobby for international debt relief.

That France's African policy has undergone a degree of normalisation should be clear from a cursory glance at its economic, military and cultural assistance policies. Over the course of the 1990s France brought its economic assistance budget into line with (much lower) international donor norms; extended its privileged aid fold well beyond francophone Africa;[28] and linked its African assistance with the pursuit of a form of 'electoral democracy' that is closer to the English-speaking model of individual choice and communautarism than to the republican paradigm. Paris also closed military bases in the Central African Republic, diverted African elites to regional (rather than 'metropolitan') military schools, and reduced the number of French soldiers stationed in Africa by well over a third, to 5,300 personnel, between 1998 and 2002.[29] Finally, Paris even began to encourage the use of indigenous languages at lower levels of education and slashed the number of technical assistants, many of whom take part in cultural activities, from 7,669 in 1988 to 2,919 ten years later.[30]

The Republic strikes back?

It might be assumed from the above that France has given up its pretensions to a universal republican mission. Such an assumption would, however, underestimate the level of attachment felt by the French political classes to their African vocation. These supporters of France's republican project, who include government Ministers, officials and large sections of the business community and media, have contended that the French Republic has ultimately stayed true to its historic mission, punishing those who fall short of republican standards, adapting French institutions to reflect the will of the people better, and preserving the basic thrust of France's universal message.[31]

In support of the first claim, namely that the Republic has brought to book those who betray France's revolutionary ideals, it can be noted that Paris has indeed taken a much tougher line than in the past towards those embroiled in financial or other scandals in Africa. A case in point was the successful conviction, on bribery or corruption charges, of over thirty employees of the French state-owned oil company Elf, as well as the sentencing of a former French Foreign Minister, Roland Dumas, and his ex-mistress, Christine Deviers-Joncour, on related charges.[32] Investigations have also been carried out in connection with the financial dealings of two former Interior Ministers (Charles Pasqua and Michel Roussin) and an ex-presidential adviser on African affairs (Jean-Christophe Mitterrand) accused of trafficking arms to Angola. Whilst most wrongdoers have no doubt continued to go unpunished, the fact that action has been taken against such senior figures is seen by some as proof that the 'standards by which politicians are judged (and increasingly found wanting) are still defined by republican parameters. In other words, public expectations as to what politics should be about continue to be informed by republican ideals'.[33]

As to the second contention, namely that the French Republic has adapted its institutions in reponse to public concern about France's African policy, this is at least partly supported by recent reforms. The institutional innovation known as *cohabitation*, whereby Presidents and Prime Ministers of different parties have shared power periodically since 1986, has led to the *domaine réservé* becoming a *domaine partagé* as Prime Ministers have sought to make African policy more accountable to the French Parliament. The creation of an Haut Conseil de la Coopération Internationale (HCCI) in November 1999, as a non-governmental unit of advisers reporting to Parliament on African development issues, and the holding of parliamentary missions of inquiry into France's role in Rwanda (1998) and in the African oil sector (1999) have involved further intrusions into an area of public policy normally reserved for presidential prerogatives. Significantly, too, the downgrading of the Co-operation Ministry, the various restrictions on fund raising for election campaigns, the privatisation of Elf in 1994 and the reduction in the presidential mandate from seven to five years (discussed earlier in this volume) have all served to limit the financial and political capacity of the Elysée to pursue its own, often extravagant, African agenda.[34] They have also helped to bring the Fifth Republic closer into line with the 'classic republican paradigm', whereby the executive is held rigorously to account by the legislature and the people.

The third contention is that France has retained the basic thrust of its universal message. This claim has already been partly contested by our earlier analysis but it is not without substance. For a start, Paris has continued to see centralised governments, however imperfectly elected, as the only actors with the authority and institutional capacity needed to collect taxes, set national spending priorities and maintain stability in a part of the world which is marred by ethnic conflict and civil disorder. France has, as such, continued to allocate most of her bilateral aid to African central governments and has given a comparatively tiny proportion of her development budget to sub-state and non-state actors like French and African local authorities and NGOs.[35] Paris has, moreover, persisted in sheltering African governments from the rigours of market forces, bailing out African regimes which fail to respect World Bank economic austerity programmes or privatisation schedules,[36] and adapting the legal and commercial environment of the franc zone in ways which should encourage investment by French companies.[37]

At the same time, France's *politique africaine* has continued to be marked by a degree of exceptionalism. Thus, while Franco-African relations have undergone a process of multilateralisation, they have nonetheless continued to operate essentially at a personal and bilateral level, through regular state visits and through the activities of French embassies, some forty-five of which are in Africa.[38] Furthermore, in so far as multilateralisation has taken place, it has done so within forums where Paris exerts decisive influence, most notably the European Union. To illustrate, France is now the leading contributor to the Cotonou Agreement and, in 2002, channelled 64 per cent of its multilateral aid through the European Union.[39] Paris has, moreover, assumed a leadership role in EU-wide military operations and contributed two-thirds of the troops sent to the Democratic Republic of Congo in 2003.[40]

As to the much heralded normalisation of French African policy, this too has to be qualified. Thus, despite recent cutbacks, France's aid programe is still the largest in the G-7, as a percentage of GNP, and it is scheduled to reach the UN target of 0.7 per cent of GNP by 2010 .[41] Paris has, moreover, continued to direct almost two-thirds of its bilateral assistance to sub-Saharan Africa[42] and has remained reluctant to cut off support to African regimes which refuse to undertake democratic reforms. At the same time, Paris has been the only external power to maintain a significant military presence and to engage in open-ended unilateral military missions south of the Sahara.[43] Finally, France has also hung on to and, in many ways, reinforced the distinctive cultural focus of its African policy. In this context, France has, for example, continued to provide scholarships to over 36,000 African students;[44] to allocate almost 20 per cent of its development assistance budget to cultural activities;[45] and to fund some thirty-five cultural institutes and centres in francophone Africa alone.[46] Paris has, moreover, managed to get French recognised as the second language in schools in Africa's most populous country, Nigeria,[47] and as a working language in the eleven, mainly anglophone, states of the Southern African Development Community.[48] Significantly, too, French policy makers have come to see the defence of the French language and culture in Africa as part of a much wider struggle against the spread of English and English-speaking values. This battle has been waged above all through *la francophonie*, which has backed French efforts to exclude francophone cultural products from multilateral free-trade agreements.[49]

Conclusion

This chapter began by showing how, during the colonial and early post-colonial eras, the French political establishment was able to portray its policies south of the Sahara in terms of an enlightened mission to expose Africa to the benefits of French culture and civilisation. It then demonstrated how, in the last decade or so, Paris has been forced to make changes but has managed to preserve the basic thrust of its universal republican message.

The above survey has found that France's 'civilising mission' has survived, albeit in a modified form, from the time of colonisation to the present day. While this is, in itself, an interesting conclusion, it does leave a number of questions unanswered. For a start, why has France remained so attached to its African vocation? How has Paris managed to perpetuate its republican mission in a hostile post-Cold War climate? And for how much longer can it hope to do so? Each of these questions will be addressed briefly below.

In response to the first question, Paris's attachment to its mission is often explained away by 'realists' who claim that talk of a *vocation spéciale*[50] has simply provided a useful cover to enable France to shore up its sphere of influence in Africa (a major claim to world power status), to better exploit African raw materials, and to secure up to fifty-three African votes in the UN General Assembly. There is certainly truth in these allegations, and there can be little doubt that France's republican rhetoric has helped Paris to pursue a conspicuously interventionist African policy without facing too many allegations of neo-colonialism.

However, this 'realist' reading fails to take account of France's very real conviction that it has a duty to disseminate its universal republican model. This point is made quite cogently by Michel Guillou in a policy document he wrote for the French centre-right party, the Rassemblement pour la République. Guillou claims that 'Our traditional republican regard for the rights of man obliges us, more than others, to adopt a generous attitude and by itself identifies our profile in the wider world'.[51] He goes on to explain that it was only through idealism, the *rayonnement* of French culture and the quality of its message that France was able to aspire to great-power status and influence overseas which were far superior to her economic or demographic weight in the world. With so much at stake, it is hardly surprising that successive French governments have been so keen to ensure that the republican experiment is seen to work, not only in France but also in drastically different conditions in sub-Saharan Africa and, for that matter, the DOM TOMs. For, if the republican project fails, or is rejected by France's former colonies, that could undermine the whole basis of French claims to have a 'universal' message and could, in the process, inflict a telling blow on the republican paradigm at home.

Our second question asks how Paris has managed to preserve its republican mission in a less than favourable post-Cold War context. The answer would appear to lie in France's skilful use of discourse and symbolism; its political will to remain involved in African affairs; and its readiness to adapt the model of republicanism it is exporting overseas.

To begin with French discourse, this has been used successfully by France's ruling elites to imply that their African policy is still exceptionally generous, even where their practice may suggest the opposite. To illustrate, French government spokesmen have loudly affirmed Paris's commitment to African democratisation and poverty reduction. This message has struck a chord with the French public but has borne little relation to reality, given that France's record on each of these issues has been one of the least impressive in the Western world. As for symbolic gestures, these have been used by France to suggest that it still has a 'special relationship' with Africa. A case in point was the high-profile visit of French President Mitterrand to South Africa in July 1994. By ensuring that he was the first Western leader to speak to the newly elected Parliament of South Africa, Mitterrand was able to imply that France had been (true to its revolutionary credentials) an unflinching opponent of the racist apartheid regime and a friend of black Africans everywhere. The reality was, of course, that France's policy towards South Africa had always been ambivalent and had even, at times, been condemned by the United Nations.[52]

French discourse and symbolism have not, of course, been entirely without substance, as Paris's continuing readiness to devote vast resources to Africa amply demonstrates. France's political will to remain engaged is clear from its eagerness to continue pushing Africa to the top of the European foreign policy agenda; from its willingness to resist WTO demands for an immediate end to African trade preferences under the Cotonou Accord; and from its refusal to lapse into the kind of Afro-pessimism which has afflicted other leading donors like the United States.

Finally, France's ruling elites have taken the view that republicanism is 'not a rigid ideological construct'[53] and have been quite prepared to adapt the 'universal' message, which they are exporting to Africa. They have, for example, been willing to jettison key republican ideals such as state education for all and a single official language (French), which would either be unworkable in the African context or would require a level of investment that is beyond the means of the French state. French policy makers have, at the same time, been more than happy to exploit the ambiguities and contradictions inherent in France's revolutionary message. They have, for example, claimed that Paris's indulgence towards African regimes which refuse to democratise should be viewed as a gesture of 'fraternity' or 'solidarity' rather than as evidence of France's failure to adhere to its republican ideal of 'liberty' for all citizens. They have similarly contended that Paris's extensive support for African farmers, many of whom are among the poorest people in African society, should be taken as proof that France is committed to promoting 'equality' south of the Sahara. In so doing they have cleverly disguised the fact that France's subsidies to European farmers and its opposition to WTO-led efforts to liberalise agricultural exports have actually made it harder for African smallholders to sell their produce in local and global markets.

Whither?

Turning finally to the future of France's republican mission, this is of course hard to predict. It does, however, seem likely that it will come in for tighter scrutiny, as domestic critics liaise ever more closely with English-speaking NGOs and journalists, who have a longer tradition of challenging government policy. France's universal message may also begin to look increasingly anachronistic as the international political economy comes to be dominated by free-market forces, 'small' states and a vehicular form of the English language. Ultimately, it may even be rejected by francophone African leaders, a growing number of whom 'no longer feel close to France'.[54]

Perhaps, however, the most serious threat to the future of France's African vocation will come from Europe. Two developments are likely to pose particular problems, namely the drafting of a new constitution and the enlargement of the European Union eastward. The new constitution, if it ever comes into force, could undermine France's capacity to act independently in Africa by increasing the power of the European Parliament over the EU aid budget and by creating a new 'twin-hatted' post of European Foreign Minister, which rolls into one the current roles of External Affairs Commissioner and 'High Representative' for Foreign Policy. It is widely feared that this latter innovation, which places European security and emergency relief policies under the control of a single office, could lead to a diversion of resources away from humanitarian disaster zones like Africa and towards strategically vital areas like the Middle East.[55]

As regards the enlargement of the European Union to include ten new states, essentially from Central and Eastern Europe, this evolution is likely to make it harder for France to continue pursuing her African vocation through Europe. For a start, most of these countries of what US Defense Secretary Donald Rumsfeld has called the 'new Europe' are devoid of any historical connection with Africa and have strong interests in their immediate region. As Atlanticists and free-marketers they are, moreover, unlikely to be impressed by France's state-centred, protectionist recipes for African development.

Paradoxically, however, the European Union could also provide the key to ensuring the long-term survival of France's republican project. As the largest aid donor in the world, a major force in WTO-led free trade negotiations and an actor with its own instruments for military intervention the EU could provide 'the extra scale, strength and resources which would allow French values, ambitions and assertiveness to be . . . preserved and imparted to others'.[56] For this to happen, however, Europe's ever growing membership would have to agree that its common foreign and security policy should be inspired by France's 'universal' republican mission. This is not inconceivable, given that French African priorities are already deeply embedded in today's EU African policy and given that French revolutionary ideals are already widely shared by most European powers. Such a scenario will, however, come about only if France is prepared to stretch its republican ideology even further and recognise, not only that the success of the socio-democratic model depends as much on market forces as it does on the state, but also that the French language can at best aspire to some kind of 'universal status' among the policy elites of Europe and Africa.[57] It will, moreover, be possible only if France's ruling elites are willing to set an example and adhere much more rigorously to their own republican ideals in the conduct of their African policy. If they do, they may come closer to disseminating the true values of the French Revolution than they ever have in the past. They may even, in the process, help to revive confidence in the republican paradigm at home.

Notes

1 A. Conklin, 'Colonialism and human rights: a contradiction in terms?' *American Historical Review*, 103:2 (1998), 419–42.
2 France could not actually do without the support of African chiefs, and its colonial practice was often not that different from the lower-cost system of 'indirect rule' operated by other colonial powers.
3 Cited in D. B. Marshall, *The French Colonial Myth* (New Haven CT: Yale University Press, 1973), p. 20.
4 *Ibid.*
5 Editor's translation. The original reads as follows: 'relever l'indigène, l'instruire, assurer son existence'. J. Ferry, cited in C-R. Ageron, *France coloniale ou parti colonial?* (Paris: Presses Universitaires de France, 1978), p. 66.
6 C. Quigley, 'Education in overseas France', *Current History*, 35 (1958), 100–12.
7 Colonial subjects were, for example, required to live according to the French civil code, to be well educated in French and to have served three years in the French public service or military.
8 See, for example, Sartre's now famous preface to Senghor's 1948 *Anthology of New Black Poetry*. A founder of the *négritude* movement, Senghor argued that assimilation should be a two-way process and should lead to a form of *métissage* ('hybridity'), whereby 'Black' and 'European' identities would create a new 'mixed' culture.
9 E. Mortimer, *France and the Africans, 1944–1960* (London: 1969), p. 80.
10 J. Adda and M-C. Smouts, *La France face au Sud : le miroir brisé* (Paris: Karthala, 1989), p. 46.
11 'éclairer la marche de l'humanité'. F. Mitterand, investiture speech, Paris, www.archive.premier-ministre.gouv.fr, 21 May 1981.
12 See, for example, J-P. Cot, *A l'épreuve du pouvoir : le tiersmondisme, pour quoi faire ?* (Paris: Seuil, 1984); P. Péan, *Affaires africaines* (Paris: Fayard, 1983).
13 For details see G. Penne, *Mémoires d'Afrique* (Paris: Fayard, 1999), pp. 123–49; C. Wauthier, *Quartre présidents et l'Afrique* (Paris: Seuil, 1995), pp. 301–24.
14 Guinea and Benin were among the left-leaning regimes reintegrated into the francophone family in the 1980s.
15 P. Ireland, '*Vive le jacobinisme: les étrangers* and the durability of the assimilationist model in France', *French Politics and Society*, 14:2 (1996), 33–46.
16 G. Prunier, *The Rwanda Crisis: History of a Genocide, 1959–1994* (London: Hurst, 1995).
17 See, for example, Agir Ici / Survie (1996) and Verschave (1998).

18 Examples include Stephen Smith's articles in *Libération* and Patrick de Saint-Exupéry's in *Figaro*. Reformist Prime Ministers include Edouard Balladur, Alain Juppé and Lionel Jospin.

19 In 2001 and 2002 France allocated only 4 per cent of its total aid (US$152 million) to primary education and only 1 per cent to basic health care (US$50 million). See Development Assistance Committee (DAC), *Peer Review: France* (Paris: OECD, 2004), p. 81.

20 S. Brunel, *Le Gaspillage de l'aide publique* (Paris: Seuil, 1993), pp. 55–69.

21 S. Smith and A. Glaser, *Ces Messieurs Afrique* (Paris: Calmann-Lévy, 1992); S. Smith and A. Glaser, *Ces Messieurs Afrique 2* (Paris: Calmann-Lévy, 1997).

22 Agir ici / Survie, *Dossiers noirs de la politique africaine* (Paris: Harmattan, 1996).

23 See, in this context, A. Cole and H. Drake, 'The europeanisation of the French polity: continuity, change and adaptation', *Journal of European Public Policy*, 7:1 (2000), 26–43; R. Ladrech, 'Europeanisation of domestic politics and institutions: the case of France', *Journal of Common Market Studies*, 32:1 (1994), 69–88.

24 For details of earlier attempts to create a common foreign policy see P. H. Gordon, 'Europe's uncommon foreign policy', *International Security*, 22:3 (1997), 74–100.

25 J. Barou, *L'Immigration en France des ressortissants des pays d'Afrique noire* (Paris: Secrétariat général à l'intégration, 1992).

26 M. Sot (ed.), *Étudiants africains en France 1951–2001* (Paris: Karthala, 2002).

27 P. Marchesin, 'Politique africaine de la France en transition', *Politique africaine*, 71:3 (1998), 91–106.

28 France's priority aid fold (the Zone de solidarité prioritaire) now includes anglophone African states (e.g. Zimbabwe, Nigeria) and other recipients with no historical connection with Paris (e.g. Cuba, Surinam).

29 www.défense.gouv.fr/actualités/dossier.

30 P. Marchesin, 'Politique africaine de la France en transition', *Politique africaine*, 71:3 (1998), 97.

31 See, in this context, the writings of former Development Ministers, M. Roussin, *Afrique majeure* (Paris: France-Empire, 1997) and J. Godfrain, *L'Afrique, notre avenir* (Paris: Michel Lafon, 1998).

32 For a personal account of these scandals see C. Deviers-Joncour, *La Putain de la république* (Paris: Calmann-Lévy, 1999).

33 S.Hazareesingh, *Political Traditions in Modern France* (Oxford: Oxford University Press, 1994).

34 Extravagant gestures have included gifts of private jets to African leaders, paid for out of the Co-operation Ministry budget. See Brunel, *Le Gaspillage de l'aide publique*, p. 48.

35 This amounted to only €33.5 million, or 0.57 per cent of French aid, in 2003. See A. Canonne, 'Effets d'annonce ou réelle inflexion?' in Observatoire français de la coopération internationale, *Rapport 2002–2003* (Paris: Karthala, 2003), pp. 21–36.

36 France has breached its own rules, as set out in the Doctrine Balladur, in the case of Côte d'Ivoire. *Le Monde*, 28 November 2000. Paris has also slowed down World Bank progress on privatising the cotton sector in Benin.

37 See, in this context, DAC, *Peer review: France*, pp. 79–81.

38 J-P. Pondi, *Revue internationale et stratégique*, 45 (2002), 127–37.

39 DAC, *Peer review: France*, p. 36.

40 www.defense.gouv.fr/ema/index.htm, 30 April 2004.
41 Canonne, 'Effets d'annonce ou réelle inflexion?'
42 DAC, *Peer review: France*, p. 79.
43 France's intervention in Côte d'Ivoire, a large and populous state, is on a different scale from Britain's short-term operation in the small, impoverished state of Sierra Leone; see R. Utley, 'Franco-African military relations: meeting the challenges of globalisation?' *Modern and Contemporary France*, 13:1 (forthcoming).
44 DAC, *Peer review: France*, p. 35.
45 *Ibid.*, p. 92.
46 D. E. Ager 'French cultural, languages and telecommunications policy towards sub-Saharan Africa', *Modern and Contemporary France*, 13:1 (forthcoming).
47 *Le Monde*, 3 January 1997.
48 D. E. Ager 'French cultural, languages and telecommunications policy towards Sub-Saharan Africa'.
49 For details of France's defence of the *exception culturelle* and *unité dans la diversité* see M. Majumdar, 'The francophone world moves into the twenty-first century', in K. Salhi (ed.), *Francophone Post-colonial Cultures: Critical Essays* (Lanham MD: Lexington Books, 2003).
50 Adda and Smouts, *La France face au Sud : le miroir brisé*, p. 7.
51 M. Guillou, *Pour un dialogue Nord–Sud* (Paris: Albatros, 1984), p. 25.
52 G. Martin, 'The historical, economic and military bases of France's African policy', *Journal of Modern African Studies*, 23:2 (1985), 189–208.
53 Hazareesingh, *Political Traditions in Modern France*, p. 66.
54 A. Bourgi, 'On peut bien se passer de Paris', *Jeune Afrique l'intelligent*, 2098 (2000), 28. In Côte d'Ivoire, President Gbagbo promotes Ivoirien nationalism with talk of a 'second decolonisation' from France (*Le Monde diplomatique*, April 2003) while in Senegal the government of Abdoulaye Wade was not, for the most part, educated in France; see T. Chafer, 'France and Senegal : the end of the affair?' *SAIS Review*, 23:2 (2003), 165–6.
55 The European Parliament wants to 'budgetise' all EU aid, including pluri-annual credits allocated under Cotonou. While this would make development policy more transparent, it would also mean that unused budgets would be clawed back at the end of the financial year. See S. Grimm, 'International Development and Foreign Policy', briefing paper (London: Overseas Development Institute, 2004).
56 J. Hayward, 'Ideological change: the exhaustion of the revolutionary impulse', in P. Hall *et al.*, *Developments in French Politics*, rev. edn (London: Macmillan, 1994), p. 28.
57 French is one of the three working languages of the European Commission and is fast becoming the second language of thousands of officials from new member states, thanks to the efforts of the Centre européen de langue française in Brussels. See C. Haignère, speech by Minister of State for European Affairs, *Figaro*, 17 June 2004.

Select bibliography

J. Adda and M-C. Smouts, *La France face au Sud : le miroir brisé* (Paris: Karthala, 1989).
C-R. Ageron, *France coloniale ou parti colonial ?* (Paris: Presses Universitaires de France, 1978).
Agir Ici/ Survie, *Dossiers noirs de la politique africaine* (Paris: Harmattan, 1996).

J. Barou, *L'Immigration en France des ressortissants des pays d'Afrique noire* (Paris: Secrétariat général à l'intégration, 1992).

S. Brunel, *Le Gaspillage de l'aide publique* (Paris: Seuil, 1993).

A. Conklin, 'Colonialism and human rights: a contradiction in terms?' *American Historical Review*, 103:2 (1998), 419–42.

J-P. Cot, *A l'épreuve du pouvoir : le tiersmondisme, pour quoi faire ?* (Paris: Seuil, 1984).

Development Assistance Committee (DAC), *Coopération pour le développement : France* (Paris: OECD, 2000).

C. Deviers-Joncour, *La Putain de la république* (Paris: Poches, 1999).

J. Godfrain, *L'Afrique, notre avenir* (Paris: Michel Lafon, 1998).

M. Guillou, *Pour un dialogue Nord–Sud* (Paris: Albatros, 1984).

S. Hazareesingh, *Political Traditions in Modern France* (Oxford: Oxford University Press, 1994).

D. B. Marshall, *The French Colonial Myth* (New Haven CT: Yale University Press, 1973)

E. Mortimer, *France and the Africans, 1944–1960* (London: Faber, 1969).

P. Péan, *Affaires africaines* (Paris: Fayard, 1983).

G. Penne, *Mémoires d'Afrique 1981–1998* (Paris: Fayard, 1999).

G. Prunier, *The Rwanda Crisis: History of a Genocide, 1959–1994* (London: Hurst, 1995).

M. Roussin, *Afrique majeure* (Paris: France-Empire, 1997).

S. Smith and A. Glaser, *Ces Messieurs Afrique* (Paris: Calmann-Lévy, 1992).

S. Smith and A. Glaser, *Ces Messieurs Afrique 2* (Paris: Calmann-Lévy, 1997).

M. Sot (ed.), *Etudiants africains en France 1951–2001* (Paris: Karthala, 2002).

F-X. Verschave, *La Françafrique : le plus long scandale de la République* (Paris: Stock, 1998).

C. Wauthier, *Quatre présidents et l'Afrique* (Paris: Seuil, 1995).

Acknowledgement

The author would like to thank the Leverhulme Trust for its support with the research.

Index

Lightning Source UK Ltd.
Milton Keynes UK
16 May 2010

154229UK00003B/16/P